The Psychology of Cybersecurity

This book takes a fresh look at the underappreciated role of human psychology in cybersecurity and information technology management. It discusses the latest insights from practice and scholarly work on the role of cognitive bias and human factors in critical decisions that could affect the lives of many people.

Written by an experienced chief information security officer (CISO) and an academic with over two decades of lived experience dealing with cybersecurity risks, this book considers the psychological drivers and pitfalls of the four key personas in cybersecurity – from hackers and defenders, to targeted individuals and organisational leaders. It bridges state-of-the-art research findings with real-world examples and case studies to show how understanding the psychological factors in cybersecurity can help people protect themselves and their organisations better.

Full of advice on security best practices that consider the human element of cybersecurity, this book will be of great interest to professionals and managers in the cybersecurity domain, information technology, and governance and risk management. It will also be relevant to students and those aspiring to grow in this field.

Tarnveer Singh is an award-winning Chief Information Security Officer with decades of security experience across a wide range of sectors. He is Director (Security and Compliance) at Cyber Wisdom Ltd, an Information Security and Compliance Consultancy, helping clients to address security threats affecting their business. He is also a Fellow of the Chartered Institute of Information Security and a Chartered IT Professional with the British Computer Society.

Sarah Y. Zheng, PhD, is a neuropsychologist investigating emerging crime and security risks from technological advances. Through her research, she helps organisations become more resilient to phishing attacks and improve people's awareness of new (cyber)security threats. Before returning to academia, she developed AI applications and worked in data science for financial, retail, and government institutes. With her unique understanding of both people and technology, her mission is to protect the human element in technology.

Current Issues in Cyberpsychology

Current Issues in Cyberpsychology brings together books that explore the psychology behind human interaction with digital technology, and the impact of the internet on individuals and society as a whole.

It showcases books that will be relevant to both an academic and professional market, bringing together the work of established and emerging authors. The series spans a range of topics relating to cyberpsychology; including the influence of technology on behaviour and attitudes, the effects of social media, human factors in cybersecurity, and digital identities. Ideas for new books are welcome.

For more information about the series, please visit: https://www.routledge.com/our-products/book-series/CIIC

The Psychology of Cybersecurity
Hacking and the Human Mind
Tarnveer Singh and Sarah Y. Zheng

The Psychology of Cybersecurity

Hacking and the Human Mind

Tarnveer Singh and Sarah Y. Zheng

Routledge
Taylor & Francis Group

LONDON AND NEW YORK

Designed cover image: Getty © Pobytov

First published 2026
by Routledge
4 Park Square, Milton Park, Abingdon, Oxon OX14 4RN

and by Routledge
605 Third Avenue, New York, NY 10158

Routledge is an imprint of the Taylor & Francis Group, an informa business

© 2026 Tarnveer Singh and Sarah Y. Zheng

British Library Cataloguing-in-Publication Data
A catalogue record for this book is available from the British Library

ISBN: 9781041005711 (hbk)
ISBN: 9781041005704 (pbk)
ISBN: 9781003610533 (ebk)

DOI: 10.4324/9781003610533

Typeset in Times New Roman
by codeMantra

Contents

PART 2
Inside the line of defence   71

PART 3
The target's perspective   115

Foreword

In 2023, Microsoft customers around the globe received over 600 million cyber-attacks each day [1]. It is no surprise, then, hardly a week goes by without a security breach somewhere. Just in the UK, over 700,000 businesses reported having experienced a cybersecurity breach or attack in 2023, where a breach cost an average of £10,830 to medium and large businesses [2]. These incidents undermine people's trust in organisations, institutions, and governments. Thus, with the continuous developments in engineering and computing technology, the world is set for the cybersecurity field to take centre stage – or, at least, be the essential backbone thereof.

Cybersecurity is the practice of protecting computer systems, networks, and sensitive information from unauthorised access, theft, or damage. It ensures the safety and integrity of our digital world. As two experts in this field, we are closely observing how the cybersecurity landscape is evolving. One of us has been implementing cybersecurity in various organisations as a CISO for over 20 years. The other has been researching human behaviour for over a decade and has a doctorate degree on (not *in!*) social engineering attacks. Digital technologies are increasingly permeating every area of modern life indeed, with emerging technologies such as artificial intelligence (AI) and the Internet of Things (IoT) creating new vulnerabilities that cybercriminals can exploit. And while innovation is exciting in its own right, at the end of the day, cybersecurity is about people protecting people. They are the only stable factor in this otherwise whack-a-mole field. We therefore must understand the psychology behind cyber-attacks and how it affects lines of defence, to allow people to develop better strategies to protect themselves from these threats.

In a way, it does not matter if criminals are breaking into buildings or breaking into computer systems. We named the former burglary, the latter hacking. The tools to execute either have changed, but the objectives remain the same. Offenders will be out there to intercept things of value, from jewellery to intellectual property and personal data, and wreak havoc. Our job as cybersecurity professionals is to prevent cyber offenders from achieving such goals. This has typically been done through deep technical expertise about computer systems, which led to numerous risk and compliance policies, security frameworks, and certification programmes like OWASP, CISSP, and SSCP.

What we are seeing now, especially with the rise of sophisticated AI technologies, is that focusing on technical expertise is no longer enough. Hackers are becoming more apt at using psychological tactics in their attacks, exploiting new vulnerabilities with AI and the IoT. As cybersecurity professionals, we therefore must study the psychological factors in cyber-attacks to develop effective countermeasures, and improve people's overall safety and security. Similarly, organisations need to leverage psychological strategies to enhance their cyber defences. This involves understanding what motivates cybercriminals and how they think, why people are often called the "weakest link" in the security chain, the contextual effects of cybersecurity on operational decision-making and methods to effectively encourage individuals to embrace secure practices.

People play a significant role in cybersecurity, because a significant proportion of cybersecurity incidents is caused by human error – when we overlooked something or wrongly discarded a possible explanation for an event. Even with the most sophisticated security technology and protocols, individuals who are not educated or trained inadequately can still (unknowingly) compromise their own or their organisation's security. For example, cyber-attackers often use social engineering tactics, such as phishing e-mails and phone scams, to trick people into revealing sensitive information or performing other insecure actions. If people are not aware of these tactics and do not know how to identify or avoid them, they can inadvertently expose themselves or their organisations to further attacks. Moreover, people may unwittingly give away sensitive information on social media, (re)use weak passwords and unintentionally download untrustworthy software.

At the same time, if security protocols are too complicated or difficult to use, employees will try to circumvent them. Or, if they are too easy to use, they may not provide adequate protection. Similarly, security awareness training that is not engaging may not properly prepare employees to identify and respond to cyber threats. We therefore turn to the field of cyberpsychology to examine how technology affects human behaviour. In other words, how people interact with information technology systems, and how this impacts our thoughts, feelings, and actions.

As we all interact more and more through computer technologies in our day-to-day lives, we have to keep the human *in the loop* to improve cybersecurity. Indeed, as technology continues to advance, the field of cyberpsychology will become increasingly important in the fight against hacking attempts. A technically elegant cyber defence system simply becomes moot if people are not given usable tools, training and cybersecurity programmes to keep their organisations secure. Various elements influence how securely people behave, such as their awareness and risk perception, the significance of the data and assets being safeguarded, and the time and resource investments required for implementing security measures. CISOs are uniquely positioned in this landscape, as they need to address human errors in cybersecurity, develop strategies for mitigating human fallacies, advocate the need for a human-centred approach, and provide training and education to reduce human error. This includes addressing the under-researched cognitive biases in system administrators, software developers and cybersecurity domain experts. Thus, just as attackers take advantage of human psychology, the cybersecurity industry must also understand human behaviour when developing security systems and training, and how to communicate with general computer users.

Equipped with numerous case studies of real-world security breaches, and state-of-the-art crime and cybersecurity research, this book will take you on a journey through the minds of those conceiving cyber-attacks, people working to defend their organisations, attack targets and the CISO. We structured this book into four corresponding parts that will give you a solid, foundational understanding of the psychological factors that make the key personas in cybersecurity. We will use this knowledge to provide practical advice, and show how cybersecurity could be made more usable and therewith more effective. Through this journey, we will see that cybersecurity is, indeed, a sociotechnical field, where "people knowledge" can often be more important than technological expertise. With this, we aim to inspire you to incorporate human-in-the-loop thinking in your own cybersecurity approach and make this world a safer place.

References

1 Microsoft, "Microsoft digital defense report 2024," 2024. Available: https://www.microsoft.com/en-us/security/security-insider/intelligence-reports/microsoft-digital-defense-report-2024

2 Department of Science, Innovation & Technology, "Cyber security breaches survey 2024," 2024. Available: https://www.gov.uk/government/statistics/cyber-security-breaches-survey-2024/cyber-security-breaches-survey-2024#summary

Part 1

Enter the world of cybercrime

1 Most cybercriminals are made, not born

Most crime, including cybercrime, does not happen by accident [1]. It consists of carefully deliberated manoeuvres aimed at serving a personal desire. Seeing cyber-attacks as crime allows us to apply the knowledge gathered over many years from criminology and crime science on understanding why and how people commit criminal offences. It lets us think like an attacker and see what factors facilitate or hamper the execution of an attack. Ultimately, this will help us create better deterrents and response mechanisms to improve cybersecurity.

In this chapter, we will introduce a fundamental crime science theory to explain what makes someone *choose* to commit (cyber)crime. *Chapter 2: Hackers: the good, the bad and the ugly* will detail what drives different types of hackers and how their lives may evolve, using real-life examples. *Chapter 3: How an attack is devised* then describes how they carry out various attack types. Lastly, in *Chapter 4: Special cases,* we describe cybersecurity threats from special case offenders – whistle-blowers, insider threats, and third parties.

Let us first define what we mean by cybercrime and see how cyber-attacks fit with that definition. The European Commission (EC) defines three broad types of cybercrime: (1) Internet-specific crimes, such as phishing attacks, (2) Online fraud and forgery, such as identity theft and selling fake products, and (3) Illegal online content, such as child sexual abuse material (CSAM), and incitement or glorification of hatred and terrorism, for example, via social media and on the dark web [2]. The EC's definitions roughly correspond with "Cyber-Dependent Crimes", "Economic Related Cybercrime", and "Cyber-Enabled Crime", respectively, as defined in the UK's Crown Prosecution Service guidance on prosecuting cybercrime [3]. Although people often associate cybersecurity with preventing cyber-attacks (i.e., internet-specific or cyber-dependent crime), it is worth briefly reflecting on cybersecurity in the broader sense. Fundamental cybersecurity measures such as authentication and identification are implied in all cybercrime – to find out who is behind creating and uploading scams, fake ads, fake LinkedIn profiles, CSAM, fake news, or disseminating extremist sentiments. However, for the purpose of this book, we will focus on cybersecurity in relation to internet-specific crimes.

An activity typically becomes a crime when it intentionally causes significant harm to others, either directly (e.g., in the case of violence and abuse) or by undermining systems (e.g., in the case of corruption and money laundering).

DOI: 10.4324/9781003610533-2

Launching cyber-attacks to break (into) computer systems (i.e., hacking) can have devastating impacts on people and systems – and, naturally, is illegal when done for nefarious purposes [3]. Even seemingly inconsequential cyber-attacks can levy tremendous damage by traumatising individuals, undermining societal cohesion, and exacerbating pre-existing cycles of violence. They can cause significant psychological harm, equal even to that caused by conventional political violence and terrorism. In fact, malicious hacks into national critical infrastructure and obtaining large-scale volumes of sensitive data could be regarded as cyber terrorism and thus warrant heavy-handed counterterrorism measures against hacking [4].

Now you might wonder, why would anyone turn into a criminal hacker? What motivates them? There is no single answer to this question, as hackers are also people motivated by different things – but it is clear someone needs to have a reason to commit a crime [5]. Although most hackers may primarily be motivated by financial gain, others may mostly be motivated by the challenge of breaking into a system, as we will see in the following chapters. Some may be motivated by a desire to expose vulnerabilities in a system, and yet others use it to protest against a particular company or political ideology.

Regardless of their underlying motivation, cyber-attacks all serve the same goal: to access information systems not meant for them, which they can then exploit for financial and/or political reasons. This can include personal information like credit card details, social security numbers, or medical records, as well as sensitive government information and intellectual property that could be used for blackmail, extortion, or espionage.

To really understand what makes a cybercriminal, we need to consider both the psychological and situational factors that facilitate crime. Traditional crime research has shown that crime cannot be explained (solely) by people's personal dispositions, such as their morality and risk appetite. For a criminal act to happen, there needs to be an opportunity at a specific time and place, where a motivated individual can interact with a suitable target [6]. This theory is commonly depicted as the "crime triangle", shown on the left in Figure 1.1. In short, if the circumstances are right for crime, it will happen – as the wonderful Dutch saying "de gelegenheid maakt de dief" goes.

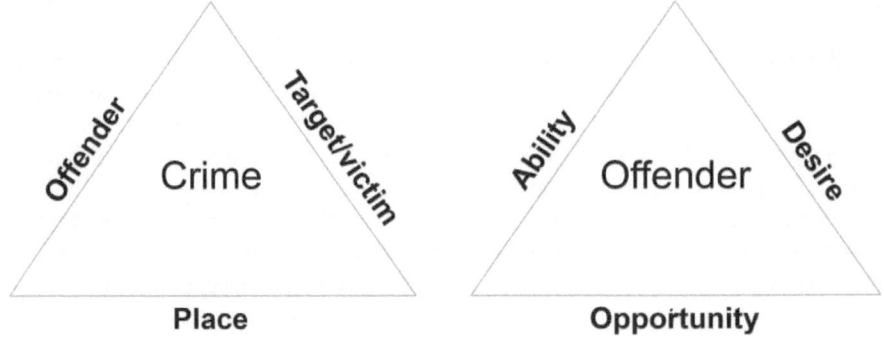

Figure 1.1 Crime triangles.

The right triangle in Figure 1.1 shows three psychological elements that further drive someone to become an offender: (1) desire, (2) opportunity, and (3) ability [7]. Someone needs to feel strongly about reaching a specific goal, *perceive* an opportunity to act on that desire *and* have the right skills to capitalise on that opportunity. Popular crime series often use similar terms such as "means, motive and opportunity" to help public jurors and viewers judge whether a suspect could indeed be guilty. It may only work in one direction, however. That is, if a person has the desire, opportunity, and ability to commit a crime, it does not automatically make them guilty. What it means is that they will generally be more likely than average to commit an offence that is opportune in their environment.

Together, these theories imply that crime can be prevented or at least reduced by blocking just one of the three elements of either triangle. That is, if you take away either someone's desire, ability or opportunity to commit an offence, or make potential targets and locations much harder to reach, crime will happen less. For example, thwarting opportunities for theft and burglary by introducing better controls in places known to be prone to these crimes, such as placing surveillance cameras in and around expensive shops [8]. We will elaborate on these situational crime prevention measures in *Chapter 9: Improving organisational cybersecurity*.

When it comes to cyber-attacks, offenders are often called hackers who target specific computer systems and/or individuals (i.e., the "target/victim" in the crime triangle) through the internet (i.e., the "place"). As the internet is not a heavily regulated "place", and widely available and accessible across the world, hackers and targets could be anywhere and act at any time. In other words, the internet is rife with opportunities for cyber-attacks. The alarming rise in cybercrime over recent years should thus come as no surprise [9]. In fact, some people argue that for this reason, we should require people to authenticate themselves with an internationally recognised identity to use the internet, so to render anonymous internet use impossible. It is not a technical question whether this is possible. In many ways, big tech companies such as Google, Microsoft, and Weixin are already capable of identifying unique users without necessarily knowing their true, physical identities. The issue is that even if there were geopolitical will to implement such a system, reaching international agreements on the specific terms and conditions thereof would pose an even bigger challenge in itself – apart from the possibility that in this scenario, unlawful anonymous internets may still be set up and maintained. An alternative future concept of the internet is the setup of an artificial intelligence (AI) adjudicator that switches users between regional AI-driven internets that follow local regulations and political values [10]. Still, it is highly questionable whether any of these systems would completely stop hackers and state-sponsored criminals from committing attacks.

There are many types of offenders, depending on their ability, desire, and circumstances. They may be lone actors, part of hacktivist groups, nation-state-sponsored, or even coerced into such role. Certain organised crime groups in Southeast Asia, for example, are known to recruit people for "better economic opportunities" abroad. In reality, they take innocent recruits hostage and force them to commit cybercrime, such as online fraud and social engineering attacks [11]. In those cases, not complying with the organisation's requests typically results in abuse. The only differentiator between these coerced offenders and voluntary cybercriminals then is the desire to stay alive versus a sole desire to get rich quickly, respectively.

At the same time, obscure regional technology and intelligence companies may be "legitimately" sponsored by corporations and governments to carry out cyber-attacks for espionage and meddle with adversarial politics. Examples include Russian state-sponsored disinformation campaigns disseminated to American social media users [12], the role of Cambridge Analytica in such practices [13], and Israeli intelligence companies skilled at developing spyware [14]. People who work there may have been tempted by attractive salaries and a desire to act on their own political ideology (i.e., "desire"), and secure jobs at renowned, stable organisations (i.e., "opportunity") that suit their skills set (i.e., "ability"). They carry out or facilitate cyber-attacks as "legitimate" parts of their job, and can be especially dangerous and difficult to prosecute, as they are protected by their local governments with secure material and financial resources. Then there is a group of lone actors who may work in different (anonymous) constellations for each new "project" (i.e., every next cyber-attack) that most people probably think of when they hear the word "hacker".

This is a good moment to delve deeper into the circumstances that shape the lives of different types of offenders, starting with the various types of hackers there are today.

References

1 G. Laycock, *Crime, Science and Policing*, 1st ed. London: Routledge, 2023.
2 European Commission, "Cybercrime," European Commission, Brussels, 2024.
3 Crown Prosecution Service, "Cybercrime - prosecution guidance," Crown Prosecution Service, London, 2024.
4 N. K. H. O. Ryan Shandler, "Public opinion and cyberterrorism," *Public Opinion Quarterly*, vol. 87, no. 1, pp. 92–119, 2023.
5 C. H. Burt and R. L. Simons, "Self-control, thrill seeking, and crime: Motivation matters," *Criminal Justice and Behaviour*, vol. 40, no. 11, pp. 1326–1348, 2013.
6 R. V. Clarke, "Situational crime prevention: Theory and practice," *British Journal of Criminology*, vol. 20, no. 2, pp. 136–147, 1980; R. V. C. Marcus Felson, "Opportunity makes the thief: Practical theory for crime prevention," *Police Research Series*, vol. Paper No 98, pp. 1–36, 1998.
7 K. H. Vellani, "Crime analysis for problem solving security professionals in 25 small steps," Houston, TX: Karim H. Vellani, 2010. Available: https://www.popcenter.org/library/reading/pdfs/crimeanalysis25steps.pdf
8 D. L. W. John Eck, "Crime places in crime theory," *Crime and Place: Crime Prevention Studies*, vol. 4, pp. 1–33, 2015.
9 N. Kshetri, "Positive externality, increasing returns, and the rise in cybercrimes," *Communications of the ACM*, vol. 52, no. 12, pp. 141–144, 2009; Interpol, "Cybercrime: COVID-19 impact," Interpol, Lyon, 2020.
10 Schmidt, Eric, Henry A. Kissinger, and Craig Mundie. *Genesis: Artificial Intelligence, Hope, and the Human Spirit*. Hachette UK, 2024.

11 H. L. A. W. Bryan Tzu Wei Luk, "The thrive of Chinese transnational organized crimes in southeast Asia under OBORization and the COVID-19 pandemic: The case of Cambodia and K. K. Park Criminal Hub in Myanmar," SSRN, 2023.

12 D. Freelon and T. Lokot, "Russian Twitter disinformation campaigns reach across the American political spectrum," *Harvard Kennedy School Misinformation Review*, vol. 1, no. 1, pp. 12–23, 2020. https://doi.org/10.37016/mr-2020-003; F. Hjorth and R. Adler-Nissen, "Ideological asymmetry in the reach of pro-Russian digital disinformation to United States audiences," *Journal of Communication*, vol. 69, pp. 168–192, 2019.

13 H. Berghel, "Malice domestic: The Cambridge analytica dystopia," *Computer*, vol. 51, no. 5, pp. 84–89, 2018.

14 H. Shezaf and J. Jacobson, "Revealed: Israel's cyber-spy industry helps world dictators hunt dissidents and gays," *Haaretz Daily Newspaper*, 2018. https://www.haaretz.com/israel-news/2018-10-20/ty-article-magazine/.premium/israels-cyber-spy-industry-aids-dictators-hunt-dissidents-and-gays/0000017f-e9a9-dc91-a17f-fdadde240000; War on Want, "Israeli spyware is threatening our rights and freedoms," 2023. Available: https://waronwant.org/resources/israeli-spyware-threatening-our-rights-and-freedoms; S. Woodhams, *Spyware: An Unregulated and Escalating Threat to Independent Media*. Center for International Media Assistance, 2021; E. Zureik, "Settler colonialism, neoliberalism and cyber surveillance: the case of Israel," *Middle East Critique*, vol. 29, no. 2, pp. 219–235, 2020.

2　Hackers

The good, the bad, and the ugly

When you hear the term "hacker", perhaps you picture a nerdy boy in a black hoodie at his laptop in a dimly lit room. He is surfing the dark web, procuring the tools he needs to launch his next cyber-attack. Although this stereotype may not be far from the reality of many hackers [1], it is only part of the story of people who call themselves hackers.

It is important to understand that not all hackers have criminal intentions. In fact, when the terms "hacker" and "hacking" were used among MIT students back in the 1950s to refer mostly to practical jokes, it did not have the same commanding connotation we may attach to the term now [2]. Generally, we can distinguish three types of hackers that each have their own motivational drivers:

- **"White hat" or ethical ("good") hackers**: They use their skills to help organisations identify and fix vulnerabilities in their systems, before they can be exploited by malicious actors. They are often hired to help improve cybersecurity through penetration testing and red teaming exercises to see how far they can hack into an organisation's system. Organisations may also organise hackathons to invite people who do not normally work as ethical hackers to try to break a system.
- **"Grey hat" (arguably, "the bad") hackers**: These hackers are somewhere in between white and black hat hackers. They may break into a system without permission, but they do not necessarily have malicious intent. They may expose vulnerabilities in a system and then inform the company or organisation so that they can fix the problem. Grey hat hacking is a controversial topic in the cybersecurity community. Some argue that grey hat hacking is unethical, because it involves the exploitation of vulnerabilities in a system for personal gain. Others argue it can be ethical if done for the greater good.
- **"Black hat" ("the ugly") hackers**: These are the people that most people will think of when they hear the term "hacker". They commit cybercrime for a living by breaking into systems with malicious intent, often to gain money by stealing sensitive information and causing damage to systems.

In general, hackers often target organisations with valuable data, such as financial institutions and government agencies. In addition, hackers may target organisations

DOI: 10.4324/9781003610533-3

with less potential value to gain from to challenge and test their skills. The consequences for organisations can be immense, ranging from major financial losses due to fraud, lawsuits, paying ransoms, and espionage, to theft of sensitive information and reputational damage. Significant attacks may attract negative media coverage and lead to erosion of customer trust. Non-ethical hacking is strictly illegal, and individuals or organisations caught doing so can face severe legal consequences, including imprisonment.

Ethical hacking, on the other hand, is an increasingly important aspect of cybersecurity that is growing into a lucrative profession. Ethical hackers can expect to earn salaries ranging from $50,000 to $150,000 per annum. They are in high demand, because they can help prevent cyber-attacks and improve security with their knowledge of programming, networking, and cybersecurity. They need to follow best practices to ensure that vulnerabilities are identified and disclosed responsibly. Good practices for ethical hacking include obtaining permission beforehand to test a system, documenting all testing activities, reporting vulnerabilities to system developers, and avoiding black hat hacking.

As professionals working in cybersecurity, we have always been fascinated by the psychology of hackers. It is not just about technical skills and tools, but also about how they think and can manipulate people during a hack. Many cybersecurity professionals probably have themselves hacked before in their lifetime [3] and there is a kind of appreciation for the skills it takes to perform a successful hack. Similar to how major criminals such as mafia bosses and illegal drug lords can be revered and romanticised for their deviant characters and ability to evade law enforcers for as long as they can, black hat hackers may seek to establish themselves as the most redoubtable kingpin of the online underground.

To understand hackers, we need to understand their motivations – the "desire" part of our offender triangle. Hackers are not a monolithic group. As mentioned before, many hackers are primarily motivated by money. Yet, a potentially growing number of hackers is also motivated by political or ideological reasons (whom may call themselves "hacktivists"), and still others mainly seek the thrill of breaking into a system – where financial gain may only be of secondary, practical interest to sustain hacking as a profession. At the same time, hackers also share a set of common drivers, as described by Tim Jordan and Paul Taylor (1998): a computer addiction, curiosity, the thrill of an illicit online life in contrast with hackers' boring offline lives, gaining power of computer systems, peer recognition from other hackers, and serving society by identifying computer vulnerabilities [3].

An obsession over how computer systems and networks work strongly drove notorious hackers like Kevin Mitnick [4], whose life we will highlight later on in this chapter. Reminiscent of Feynman's famous line "what I cannot create, I do not understand", hackers might say "what I cannot break, I do not understand". Elite hackers especially may have a strong intellectual curiosity to understand computer systems, and will use creative problem-solving skills to think outside the box and come up with innovative approaches to hacking. This is the "ability" part of the offender triangle. They see them as puzzles solve, adventures to go on, and enjoy the challenge of finding vulnerabilities and exploiting them. The thrill many hackers report from hacking indeed can make them feel addicted to it [3], as may well be the case for other types of criminals such as illegal drug dealers, and fills the void they may experience in their offline life.

Although hackers may tend to be self-motivated, feel a strong sense of autonomy, and a desire for freedom and independence, they are not operating from solitary confinements. It may look like it from the outside, but the internet has allowed for many online communities to form and flourish, including online black hat hacker and cybercrime groups. Hackers may identify as individual "positive deviants" from mainstream society [5], but find contentment in knowing there are likeminded individuals out there with similar motivations and challenges whom they can connect with anonymously through the internet. Although some people may wonder how anyone could possibly want to commit terrible cyber-attacks unless they are mentally ill, there is no reliable evidence to indicate whether hackers suffer more from psychopathologies than any other person. In fact, the more compelling possibility seems that with the worldwide availability of computers and the internet, the (criminal) opportunity to engage in hacking is a stronger cause for people to do so rather than any specific mental condition.

Hacktivism

Through our combined lifetime experience in cybersecurity, we have come across various types of cyber-attacks, ranging from phishing scams to ransomware attacks. One of the most interesting types of cyber-attacks comes from hacktivism: the use of hacking techniques to promote a social or political cause.

Unlike "conventional" hackers driven by financial gain, hacktivism is driven by ideology. Hacktivists are usually members of a group who use their hacking skills to promote social, political, or environmental goals. In some cases, hacktivists use their skills to expose corruption or illegal activities. Sometimes, individuals or groups may choose to present themselves as hacktivists rather than cybercriminals or cyberterrorists, to be more socially accepted [6]. Interestingly, although very few women are generally known to be hackers compared to an overwhelming majority of male hackers, a few studies suggest that women hackers tend to be hacktivists that act on political ideologies [1,7].

Like all cyber-attacks, hacktivism can cause significant damage to the target's reputation and financial stability. The first recorded instance of hacktivism was in 1989 when a group of hackers that called themselves the "Chaos Computer Club" hacked into the computer systems of the US Air Force. Since then, hacktivism has evolved. Today, there are numerous hacktivist groups operating around the world, each with their own agenda. One of the most well-known hacktivist groups is called Anonymous. They have carried out numerous high-profile attacks, including the sweeping attack on HBGary to not only make the point that Anonymous could not be penetrated by HBGary, but also exposed various unsecure practices such as password reuse within the cybersecurity company. The attack caused the company's website to go down and the CEO at the time to resign. Another well-known hacktivist group is LulzSec, which was responsible for a series of attacks on high-profile targets, including the CIA, Sony, and the UK's Serious Organised Crime Agency.

Hacktivism has thus had a significant impact on cybersecurity in recent years. In 2016, a hacktivist group calling itself "The Shadow Brokers" released a trove of the US' National Security Agency (NSA)hacking tools, including zero-day exploits. The release of these tools allowed cybercriminals to carry out attacks using previously unknown vulnerabilities. Another example of hacktivism is the 2017 Equifax data breach, which exposed the personal information of millions of people. It carried out by a hacktivist group that called itself "The Protectors" and claimed that the attack was carried out to highlight the vulnerability of Equifax's system.

Protecting against hacktivist attacks could be especially challenging for organisations strongly associated with certain ideologies or activities. Naturally, these are government agencies, but also fossil fuel and tobacco companies. There are basic steps, however, that organisations can take to reduce their risk [8]. At a fundamental level, it is important to implement strong security measures, such as firewalls, intrusion detection systems and antivirus software. Organisations should also conduct regular security assessments to identify vulnerabilities in their systems. This can help them patch vulnerabilities before they can be exploited by hackers. Then, one of the most effective ways to protect against hacktivism is through greater vigilance and understanding potential threat actors. Improving threat intelligence is important in identifying threat actors, so that the risk associated with these can be mitigated. Understanding what (mis)information regarding your organisation is being discussed online and on the dark web can be fed back into threat identification.

Once a hacker, always a hacker?

Because the barrier to engage in hacking and hackerspaces is practically nonexistent for anyone with stable internet connectivity, curious minds may easily learn basic hacking tactics online. But whether they build a professional career out of it, do it part-time or occasionally as a hobby depends on their ability and desire (remember Figure 1.1: Crime triangles). Some hackers have previously said that until they "find a girlfriend to suck up their time" [3] – which would change both desire and opportunity, they probably will continue. Given the open and anonymous nature of hacking communities, it is also easy to move away from it. But what happens if one gets caught in the act?

In some nation states, proficient hackers may be recruited by national intelligence agencies to carry out further cyber-attacks as a "legitimate" career. It is difficult to prevent and prosecute such actors, as the true identities of nation state(-sponsored) hackers are typically protected by their state. Moreover, it is rare for nations to sue other nation-state actors for fear of retaliation. If a hacker decides to make a living off of hacking independently and become a fulltime cybercriminal, they will have to bear the stresses of knowing they are engaging in illegal behaviour. Alternatively, they may decide it is better to work as a white hat hacker, that is, for a legitimate organisation.

Since a remarkable number of hackers starts in their teenage years [9,10], breaking the law at a young age can have detrimental effects on their lives. Sometimes people, especially youngsters, can be attracted to hacking to prove a point, to demonstrate their skills or just for fun. In these cases, just punishing them for their illegal activity will not prevent them from recidivism. In fact, dragging young, sometimes vulnerable, people through the criminal justice system can set them up for a lifetime of trouble. Rehabilitation thus plays a very important role. We should not just focus on legal punishments, but also aim to redirect their energy through an educational approach that could benefit everyone.

We can offer hackers the chance to attend camps to educate them on forensic analysis skills, help them continue their passion in a safe environment, carry out hacking games, and help them learn about bug bounty programmes where large organisations pay people to find vulnerabilities in their systems. In the UK, the National Crime Agency has a hacker "rehab" programme directed specifically at young people who have been guilty of unethical hacking. There, they receive guidance to become white hat hackers and collaborate on real-world organisation applications where they can be a force for good. Similarly, the Dutch police started testing a programme for young hackers in collaboration with multiple companies to help them use their skills towards legitimate ends [11].

Although the long-term effectiveness of these new programmes remains to be tested, these are excellent examples of how hackers' valuable skills can in fact be honed further to protect people better. We would greatly applaud more and further development of these approaches where we truly try to better understand both perpetrators and victims, and offer better support for both – which could help reduce cybercrime and improve society at large.

Notorious hackers

To see how the theories we described earlier translate in real life, we will explore the backgrounds of three famous hackers and their motivations.

Kevin Mitnick

Kevin Mitnick is perhaps one of the most well-known individual hackers. He was active in the 1980s and 1990s and was known for his ability to bypass security measures and gain access to sensitive information. He was eventually caught and spent five years in prison [4].

Mitnick's motivations were primarily financial. He would break into corporate systems and steal sensitive information, which he would then sell for a profit. He was also motivated by the challenge of breaking into secure systems and seeing what he could find.

After his release from prison, Mitnick became a security consultant and then worked to help companies improve their cybersecurity [12].

He was a renowned hacker who gained notoriety in the 1980s and 1990s for his hacking activities. Mitnick was born on 6 August 1963, in Los Angeles, California.

He was a curious child and loved to tinker with electronics. However, his curiosity soon turned into an obsession with hacking.

Mitnick's hacking career started in his teenage years when he hacked into the Pacific Bell telephone network. He was caught and sentenced to probation. However, this did not deter him from continuing his hacking activities. He continued to hack into various computer networks, stealing information and causing chaos.

Mitnick's reputation as a hacker grew, and he became known as one of the most dangerous hackers in the world. He was able to hack into some of the most secure computer networks in the world, including the Pentagon and the FBI.

Mitnick's hacking activities were not limited to stealing information. He was also involved in identity theft and wire fraud. One of his most notable hacks was the theft of Motorola's source code for their mobile phone technology. This hack cost Motorola millions of dollars in lost revenue.

Mitnick was also involved in a high-profile hack of the computer systems at the *Los Angeles Times*. He was able to gain access to their computer systems and change the headlines of their articles. This hack caused chaos and confusion, and Mitnick was soon caught.

Mitnick's hacking activities eventually caught up with him, and he was caught by the FBI in 1995. He was charged with wire fraud, computer fraud, and other cybercrimes. Mitnick went on the run and became one of the most wanted men in America.

After a two and a half-year manhunt, Mitnick was finally captured in North Carolina. He was sentenced to five years in prison, with four and a half of those years spent in solitary confinement.

During his time in prison, Mitnick had a transformation. He realised the error of his ways and decided to use his skills for good. Mitnick started to study computer security and became an expert in the field. After his release from prison, Mitnick started his own security consulting company. He used his knowledge and expertise to help companies and organisations improve their cybersecurity practices. Mitnick has also become a public speaker, sharing his story and knowledge with others. He has written several books on cybersecurity and is a recognised expert in the field.

The case study of Kevin Mitnick provides several important lessons. One of the most important lessons is the importance of cybersecurity. Mitnick was able to hack into some of the most secure computer networks in the world, highlighting the need for strong cybersecurity practices. Another lesson is the importance of rehabilitation. Mitnick's transformation shows that even the most notorious hackers can change their ways and use their skills for good.

The case of Kevin Mitnick had a significant impact on cybersecurity policies and practices. Mitnick's hacks exposed weaknesses in computer systems and led to improvements in cybersecurity practices.

The case also highlighted the need for stronger laws and regulations to prevent cybercrimes. Mitnick's case led to the development of new laws and regulations that have helped to improve cybersecurity practices.

The impact of Mitnick's case on cybersecurity policies and practices cannot be overstated, and we can all learn from his story.

Adrian Lamo

Adrian Lamo was an American computer hacker and threat analyst. Born on 20 February 1981, in Boston, Massachusetts, Lamo gained notoriety in the early 2000s for his high-profile hacks of major corporations such as *The New York Times*, Microsoft, and Yahoo!. Lamo was known for his unconventional approach to hacking, which often involved exploiting vulnerabilities in large organisations' security systems, gaining access to sensitive information, and then disclosing those vulnerabilities to the companies themselves [13].

Lamo's motivations were a bit different than Mitnick's. He was motivated by a desire to expose vulnerabilities in systems and to show companies that their systems were not as secure as they thought. Lamo was eventually caught and sentenced to six months of house arrest, followed by two years of probation. He passed away in 2018 at the age of 37.

Lamo's interest in technology began at an early age. As a child, he was fascinated by the workings of computers and other electronic devices. He taught himself how to code and was soon contributing to open-source software projects online. However, his interest in hacking began to take a darker turn when he was a teenager. Lamo became involved in the hacking community and started to explore the limits of what he could do with his skills.

Lamo's hacking activities began to escalate in the early 2000s. One of his most high-profile hacks was the intrusion into the internal computer network of *The New York Times*. Lamo gained access to the personal information of thousands of the newspaper's employees, including their Social Security numbers and birth dates. He also accessed the paper's internal database and added himself to the list of expert contributors. *The New York Times* eventually discovered the breach and reported it to the authorities, leading to Lamo's arrest.

Another notable hack that Lamo was involved in was the breach of Yahoo!'s internal network. Lamo used a combination of social engineering tactics and technical exploits to gain access to the company's servers. Once inside, he was able to access sensitive user data, including e-mail addresses and passwords. Lamo then notified Yahoo! of the breach, which led to the company improving its security measures.

Lamo's hacking activities eventually caught up with him, and he was arrested in 2003. He was charged with computer fraud and sentenced to six months of home confinement and two years of probation. Lamo was also ordered to pay $65,000 in restitution to *The New York Times*.

After his arrest, Lamo became something of a celebrity in the hacking community. Many hackers admired him for his technical skills and his willingness to challenge established companies' security systems. However, others criticised him for his actions, arguing that they had put innocent people's personal information at risk.

Lamo's legacy in the hacking community is complex. On the one hand, he is remembered as a skilled and daring hacker who was unafraid to challenge the status quo. On the other hand, his actions had real-world consequences, and many people were affected by the data breaches that he was involved in. Some in the hacking community argue that Lamo's actions helped to highlight the importance of cyber-security and the need for companies to take their security measures seriously.

The impact of Lamo's actions on cybersecurity is still being felt today. The breaches that he was involved in helped to raise awareness of the need for improved security measures and the importance of regular security audits. Companies and organisations around the world have been forced to take a more proactive approach to cybersecurity in response to the growing threat of cybercrime.

As we continue to navigate the ever-changing landscape of cybersecurity, it is essential to remember the lessons that can be learned from the actions of people like Adrian Lamo.

Gary McKinnon

Gary McKinnon is a British hacker who gained notoriety in the early 2000s for breaking into the systems of the U.S. government. He was able to gain access to sensitive information about the military and NASA.

Born in Glasgow, Scotland, in 1966, McKinnon grew up in the UK and developed an interest in computers at a young age. He was diagnosed with Asperger's syndrome in his mid-20s, which may have contributed to his obsessive interest in hacking [14].

McKinnon's other motivations were primarily political. He was looking for evidence of a government cover-up of the existence of extra-terrestrial life. He was eventually caught and faced extradition to the United States, but the extradition was blocked by the British government due to McKinnon's mental health.

In 2001 and 2002, McKinnon hacked into several US government computer systems, including those of NASA and the Department of Defence. He claimed that he was looking for evidence of unidentified flying objects (UFOs) and other extra-terrestrial activity, but in the process, he caused damage to the systems he accessed and deleted important files.

The US government launched an investigation into the hacking incident, and in 2002, McKinnon was arrested in the UK. He was indicted by a US grand jury in 2005 on charges of computer fraud, conspiracy, and other offenses.

McKinnon fought extradition to the United States for several years, arguing that he would not receive a fair trial there and that he would face harsh treatment in US prisons. His case became a cause célèbre for many in the UK, who saw him as a victim of US overreach.

In 2012, after a lengthy legal battle, the UK government blocked McKinnon's extradition on the grounds that his mental health would be at risk if he were sent to the United States for trial. He was allowed to remain in the UK, where he faced no charges for his hacking activities.

The McKinnon case sparked a heated public debate about the ethics of hacking and the appropriate response to cybercrime. Some saw McKinnon as a heroic whistleblower who was exposing government secrets, while others saw him as a dangerous criminal who had compromised national security.

The case also raised questions about the relationship between the UK and the United States and the extent to which the United States could exert its legal authority over UK citizens.

The McKinnon case had significant implications for cybersecurity and national security. It highlighted the vulnerability of government computer systems to hacking and underscored the need for stronger security measures to protect sensitive data.

The case also spurred increased cooperation between the UK and the United States on cybersecurity issues, as both countries recognised the importance of working together to prevent future hacking incidents.

Throughout the legal battle, McKinnon maintained that he was not a malicious hacker and that he had not intended to cause harm. He argued that he was motivated by a desire to expose government secrets and to reveal the truth about UFOs and other phenomena.

McKinnon's case also shed light on the challenges faced by individuals with Asperger's and other conditions that make them more vulnerable to the criminal justice system. His supporters argued that he should be treated with compassion and understanding, rather than punished harshly for his actions.

In the end, the McKinnon case was resolved in a way that satisfied few. McKinnon was allowed to remain in the UK, but he was not exonerated for his hacking activities. He faced no charges in the UK, but he also did not receive the recognition he sought for his claims about UFOs and other phenomena.

Some saw the resolution of the McKinnon case as a victory for justice and human rights, while others saw it as a missed opportunity to hold a hacker accountable for his actions.

The McKinnon case offers several important lessons for policymakers, law enforcement officials, and the public. First, it underscores the need for strong cybersecurity measures to protect sensitive government data. Second, it highlights the importance of treating individuals with mental health conditions fairly and compassionately in the criminal justice system. Finally, it reminds us of the complex ethical and legal questions surrounding hacking and cybercrime.

Gary McKinnon's legacy is a complicated one. Some see him as a hero who exposed government secrets and challenged the power of the state. Others see him as a criminal who put national security at risk and caused significant damage to government computer systems.

Regardless of one's views, his case remains a powerful reminder of the importance of cybersecurity and the need to balance security concerns with individual rights and freedoms. It is a case that will be studied and debated for years to come.

This case is a fascinating and complex case study in hacking, cybersecurity, and the criminal justice system. It raises important questions about the ethics of hacking, the limits of state power, and the challenges faced by individuals with mental health conditions in the criminal justice system.

As we continue to grapple with the challenges posed by cybercrime and cybersecurity, the lessons of the McKinnon case will remain relevant and important. It is a case that reminds us of the need to balance security concerns with individual rights and freedoms, and to treat all individuals fairly and compassionately in the criminal justice system.

Lessons we can learn

All three hackers were driven by a deep curiosity and a desire to explore and understand systems. Kevin Mitnick was fascinated by the idea of "hacking" as a form of magic. This innate curiosity often leads hackers to push boundaries and seek out new challenges. He later acknowledged he felt bad about violating other people's rights and wished at the time he could have controlled his behaviour [15].

Kevin Mitnick popularised the concept of social engineering, exploiting human psychology rather than technical vulnerabilities to gain access to systems. This highlights the importance of understanding human behaviour and the need for robust training to mitigate such risks.

Adrian Lamo's actions, such as reporting Chelsea Manning to authorities, demonstrate the complex ethical dilemmas hackers navigate. Lamo's decision to report Manning sparked debate about loyalty, whistleblowing, and the ethical responsibilities among hackers [16].

Gary McKinnon's case shows how personal circumstances, such as his diagnosis of Asperger's syndrome at the time (now on the spectrum of autism disorder), could influence hacking behaviour. His hacking was driven by a desire to uncover information about UFOs and free energy suppression, reflecting how personal beliefs and mental health can shape actions. The UK's National Autistic Society argued that people with Asperger's syndrome are often much more vulnerable than appearances would suggest and can be highly susceptible to additional mental health problems [17].

The legal battles faced by these hackers underscore the serious consequences of hacking activities. Mitnick, Lamo, and McKinnon all faced significant legal repercussions, highlighting the importance of greater awareness of the potential outcomes of such actions, but also how this was not enough of a deterrent.

Kevin Mitnick's journey from hacker to security consultant illustrates the potential for better rehabilitation, redemption, and adaptation. After serving his time, Mitnick used his skills to help organisations improve their security, showing that it is possible to turn a negative past into a positive future.

There are several ways in which we can advance rehabilitation programmes for unethical hackers, starting with offering training and certifications in ethical hacking and cybersecurity. Such curricula should include courses on cybersecurity laws, ethical hacking principles and the potential consequences of illegal activities. This can help them transition from illegal activities to legitimate careers in cybersecurity. The second element should aim to connect these "graduates" to jobs in reputable organisations. As in the pilot programmes we described earlier, we can do so by offering networking opportunities and work placements and internships through partnerships with government agencies, cybersecurity firms and educational institutes. Mentoring programmes can help hackers benefit from someone who has been in their shoes before can guide them through the process of rehabilitation and help them navigate the challenges of reintegration. They can provide valuable advice, support and networking opportunities. Reformed hackers can be engaged in community outreach programmes where they can share their experiences and knowledge with others. This can help raise awareness about cybersecurity and discourage others from engaging in illegal activities.

We also need to provide better access to mental health services to address any underlying issues that may have contributed to the illicit hacking behaviour. Counselling and therapy can help individuals develop healthier coping mechanisms and build resilience. Lastly, restorative justice programmes can help hackers to make amends for their actions. This can involve community service, educational workshops, or contributions to cybersecurity awareness initiatives. We should celebrate the positive contributions of reformed hackers like Kevin Mitnick to the cybersecurity community. Public acknowledgment can help rebuild their reputation and reinforce their commitment to ethical behaviour.

Interviews with real-life cybercriminals

We interviewed three cybercriminals who earn their living by hacking into computer systems around the globe, of whom one is a reformed hacker that now works for a legitimate organisation. These interviews came about as we have spent decades in the cybersecurity industry operating at a senior level and witnessed all forms of cybercrime and hacking. We saw how the investigations of these cybercriminals and legal ramifications played out and gained a really good understanding of the impact – not only on their victims, but on their own lives as well. The interviews were agreed through mutual connections, and clear assurances were provided over anonymity, as in many cases there remained the potential of further legal repercussions. Our experience and understanding of their work allowed us to build trust and rapport more quickly, navigating their sensitivities whilst probing deeper into their mindset. These interviews help delve into the intruiging minds of cybercriminals and hackers, unravel the complexities of their behaviours and the underlying psychological factors driving their actions. We personally found these conversations eye-opening, as they gave us a first-hand insight into how cybercriminals justify their actions, as well as the desires, abilities or opportunities that shaped their decisions.

Interview with a cybercriminal

What follows is a transcript from a broader interview conducted between one of the authors and a cybercriminal. It was enlightening to see how self-aware they were, how well they understood the impact this line of work had on their psychology and the choices they deliberately made.

Author: Thank you for agreeing to this interview. Let's start with the basics. How did you get into cybercrime?

Cybercriminal:	It started out of curiosity, really. I was always fascinated by computers and how they work. Over time, I realised how vulnerable many systems are and saw an opportunity to exploit those weaknesses for financial gain.
Author:	That's quite a leap from curiosity to criminal activity. What was your first major scam?
Cybercriminal:	My first big hit was a phishing scam targeting a mid-sized company. I created a fake website that looked identical to their login page and sent out e-mails to employees. Once they entered their credentials, I had access to their internal systems.
Author:	How do you choose your targets?
Cybercriminal:	I look for companies with weak security protocols. Smaller companies often don't have the resources to invest in robust cybersecurity, making them easier targets. I also keep an eye on industries that handle sensitive data, like finance and healthcare.
Author:	What tools and techniques do you use?
Cybercriminal:	Phishing is a big one, but I also use malware, ransomware, and social engineering. It's all about finding the right tool for the job. Sometimes, it's as simple as exploiting a known vulnerability that hasn't been patched.
Author:	Do you ever feel remorse for the damage you cause?
Cybercriminal:	Not really. To me, it's a game of cat and mouse. Companies should be better prepared. If I can get in, so can others. It's their responsibility to protect their data.
Author:	What do you do with the data or money you steal?
Cybercriminal:	I sell the data on the dark web or use it to blackmail companies. The money is usually laundered through various channels to make it untraceable. It's a complex process, but it pays off.
Author:	Have you ever been close to getting caught?
Cybercriminal:	A few times. It's a risk that comes with the territory. But I'm always learning and adapting to stay ahead of law enforcement.
Author:	What advice would you give to companies to protect themselves?
Cybercriminal:	Invest in good cybersecurity measures. Regularly update and patch your systems. Educate your employees about phishing and other common scams. And always have a backup plan in case of a breach.
Author:	Let's delve deeper into your mindset. What drives you to continue engaging in cybercrime?
Cybercriminal:	It's a combination of factors. The thrill of outsmarting security systems, the financial rewards, and the challenge itself.

There's a certain satisfaction in knowing I can bypass defences that others rely on.

Author: Do you see yourself as a villain or a hero in your own story?

Cybercriminal: Neither, really. I see myself as a problem solver. I'm exploiting weaknesses that already exist. If it wasn't me, it would be someone else. I don't think in terms of good or evil—just opportunity and execution.

Author: How do you justify your actions to yourself?

Cybercriminal: I rationalize it by thinking about the flaws in the system. Companies and individuals need to be more vigilant. If they fall for my tricks, it's a lesson for them to improve their security. In a way, I'm pushing them to be better.

Author: Do you ever worry about the consequences of your actions on the victims?

Cybercriminal: Not really. I focus on the task at hand. Thinking about the victims would only distract me. It's a harsh reality, but in this line of work, you have to detach yourself emotionally.

Author: Have you ever considered using your skills for positive purposes, like cybersecurity?

Cybercriminal: I've thought about it. The skills are transferable, and there's a growing demand for cybersecurity experts. But the allure of the underground world is strong. The freedom and the potential for high rewards are hard to give up.

Author: What do you think about the future of cybercrime?

Cybercriminal: It's only going to get more sophisticated. As technology evolves, so do the methods of attack. AI and machine learning are already being used to automate and enhance cyberattacks. The landscape is constantly changing, and those who adapt will thrive.

Author: Do you have any regrets about the path you've chosen?

Cybercriminal: Not really. Every choice has its consequences, and I've accepted mine. The skills I've gained and the experiences I've had are invaluable. It's a unique path, and I wouldn't trade it for anything else.

Author: Given the serious risks involved, what keeps you motivated to continue in this line of work?

Cybercriminal: The risks are definitely high, but so are the rewards. The financial gain is a significant motivator. The money I make from a successful operation can be substantial, and it's often more than what I could earn through legitimate means.

Author: Is it just about the money, or is there more to it?

Cybercriminal: It's not just about the money. There's also the thrill of the chase. Outsmarting security systems and staying one step ahead of law enforcement is exhilarating. It's like a high-stakes game, and I thrive on that adrenaline rush.

Author:	How do you handle the constant pressure and fear of getting caught?
Cybercriminal:	It can be stressful, but I've learned to manage it. I stay updated on the latest security trends and law enforcement tactics. Being well-prepared and having contingency plans helps mitigate the fear. Plus, the excitement often outweighs the anxiety.
Author:	Do you ever think about the long-term consequences, like potential jail time?
Cybercriminal:	Of course, it's always in the back of my mind. But I try to minimize the risk by being meticulous and cautious. I use various techniques to cover my tracks and avoid detection. It's a calculated risk, and so far, it's paid off.
Author:	What would make you consider leaving this life behind?
Cybercriminal:	If the risks started to outweigh the rewards significantly, or if I found a legitimate opportunity that offered the same level of challenge and excitement. But for now, the balance is still in favour of continuing.
Author:	Do you ever feel isolated because of your activities?
Cybercriminal:	Sometimes. It's not something you can openly talk about with friends or family. But there's a community of like-minded individuals online, and that helps. We share tips, techniques, and support each other.
Author:	What advice would you give to someone considering entering the world of cybercrime?
Cybercriminal:	I'd tell them to think long and hard about the consequences. It's not a decision to be taken lightly. The risks are real, and the stakes are high. If they're looking for a challenge, there are legitimate ways to use their skills. But if they do choose this path, they need to be prepared for the potential fallout.
Author:	Let's talk about the increasing risks. What drives you to take bigger risks despite knowing the potential consequences?
Cybercriminal:	It's a combination of factors. As I gain more experience and confidence, I naturally push the boundaries to see what else I can achieve. The bigger the risk, the bigger the reward. It's about testing my limits and seeing how far I can go.
Author:	Does the thrill of taking bigger risks play a significant role?
Cybercriminal:	Absolutely. There's a certain rush that comes with high-stakes operations. The adrenaline, the challenge, and the sense of accomplishment when you succeed—it's addictive. Each successful operation pushes me to aim higher.
Author:	How do you balance the thrill with the fear of getting caught?
Cybercriminal:	It's a delicate balance. I stay informed about the latest security measures and law enforcement tactics. I also invest in tools and techniques to cover my tracks. The key is to stay

	one step ahead and never get complacent. The fear is always there, but it keeps me sharp.
Author:	Have you ever faced a situation where you felt the risk was too great?
Cybercriminal:	A few times. There have been moments where I had to pull back because the risk outweighed the potential reward. It's important to know when to walk away. But those situations are rare. Most of the time, careful planning and execution mitigate the risks.
Author:	What do you think drives others in your field to take similar risks?
Cybercriminal:	It's similar motivations—money, thrill, and the challenge. Some are driven by a desire to prove themselves, while others might be in it for the financial gain. The reasons vary, but the underlying drive is often the same.
Author:	Do you ever think about the long-term sustainability of this lifestyle?
Cybercriminal:	It's something I consider. The landscape is always changing, and staying ahead requires constant learning and adaptation. There might come a time when the risks become too great or the rewards diminish. But for now, the balance is still in favour of continuing.
Author:	What would you say to someone who is considering taking bigger risks in cybercrime?
Cybercriminal:	I'd advise them to weigh the risks carefully. It's not just about the immediate reward; it's about the long-term consequences. They need to be prepared for the possibility of getting caught and facing serious repercussions. If they're in it for the thrill, there are other ways to get that rush without breaking the law.
Author:	Let's talk about morality. How do you reconcile your actions with your sense of right and wrong?
Cybercriminal:	It's a complex issue. I don't see myself as a bad person. I view my actions as exploiting opportunities within a flawed system. If companies and individuals were more vigilant, they wouldn't fall victim to my schemes. In a way, I'm highlighting the weaknesses that need to be addressed.
Author:	Do you ever feel guilty about the impact your actions have on your victims?
Cybercriminal:	Not really. I try to detach myself from the personal side of things. It's easier to focus on the technical aspects and the challenge. If I thought too much about the people affected, it would make it harder to do what I do.
Author:	Can you give an example of a time when your actions had a significant impact on a victim?
Cybercriminal:	There was a case where I targeted a small organisation. They ended up losing a substantial amount of money, which

affected their operations for months. It was a wake-up call for them to improve their security, but it also caused a lot of stress and hardship for the owner and employees.

Author: Knowing the harm you cause, does it ever make you reconsider your actions?

Cybercriminal: Sometimes. There are moments when I think about the consequences and wonder if it's worth it. But the thrill and the rewards usually outweigh those doubts. It's a constant balancing act between my actions and their impact.

Author: How do you think your victims perceive you?

Cybercriminal: They probably see me as a villain, someone who caused them harm. And I understand that perspective. But from my point of view, I'm just exploiting vulnerabilities. It's a harsh reality, but it's part of the game.

Author: Do you ever think about the long-term effects on your victims?

Cybercriminal: Occasionally. I know that some organisations might never fully recover, and individuals might face significant financial and emotional stress. It's not something I dwell on, but I'm aware of the potential long-term impact.

Author: What would you say to your victims if you had the chance?

Cybercriminal: I'd tell them to take their security seriously. Learn from the experience and strengthen their defences. It's not personal—it's about the vulnerabilities in their systems. If they can improve their security, they'll be better protected in the future.

Author: Thank you for your time. This has been an eye-opening conversation.

Cybercriminal: My pleasure.

Interview with a cybercriminal 2

Next, we interviewed a second cybercriminal specialised in online fraud.

Author: Thank you for agreeing to this interview. Can you tell us a bit about yourself and how you got into cyber fraud?

Cybercriminal 2:   Well, I prefer to stay anonymous for obvious reasons. Let's just say I've always had a knack for computers and understanding how systems work. I started out with harmless hacking in my teens, but over time, I realised there was a lot of money to be made in exploiting vulnerabilities.

Author: What motivates you to target companies and their employees specifically?

Cybercriminal 2:   Companies often have more resources and data than individuals, making them lucrative targets. Employees are usually the weakest link in a company's security chain. They can be tricked into clicking on malicious links or sharing sensitive

	information, which opens the door for me to access the company's systems.
Author:	Can you walk us through a typical attack?
Cybercriminal 2:	Sure. It usually starts with reconnaissance. I gather as much information as I can about the company and its employees. Social media is a goldmine for this. Once I have enough data, I craft a phishing e-mail that looks legitimate and send it to targeted employees. If just one person takes the bait, I can install malware on their system and gain access to the company's network.
Author:	How do you stay ahead of cybersecurity measures?
Cybercriminal 2:	It's a constant game of cat and mouse. I keep up with the latest security trends and tools, and I also learn from other hackers. Sometimes, I even buy or trade exploits on the dark web. The key is to be adaptable and always look for new ways to bypass security measures.
Author:	What do you think companies can do to better protect themselves?
Cybercriminal 2:	Education is crucial. Employees need to be trained to recognize phishing attempts and other common scams. Companies should also invest in robust security systems and regularly update their software to patch vulnerabilities. And, of course, they should have a good incident response plan in place for when things go wrong.
Author:	Do you ever feel guilty about what you do?
Cybercriminal 2:	Not really. To me, it's just a job. Companies have insurance and can recover from most attacks. Plus, the way I see it, I'm exposing weaknesses that they need to fix. If they don't take security seriously, that's on them.
Author:	Let's delve a bit deeper into your psychology. What drives you to continue engaging in cyber fraud despite the risks involved?
Cybercriminal 2:	It's a combination of factors. The thrill of outsmarting security systems and the financial rewards are big motivators. There's also a sense of power that comes from being able to manipulate and control systems that are supposed to be secure. It's like a high-stakes game, and winning is addictive.
Author:	Do you ever worry about getting caught?
Cybercriminal 2:	Of course, there's always that risk. But I take precautions to minimize it. I use various anonymisation techniques, like VPNs and Tor, to hide my tracks. I also avoid targeting high-profile companies that might have the resources to track me down. It's about balancing risk and reward.
Author:	How do you justify your actions to yourself?

Cybercriminal 2:	I see it as a challenge and a way to test my skills. Plus, I believe that if companies can't protect their data, they deserve to be exposed. It's a harsh view, but in my world, it's survival of the fittest. If I didn't do it, someone else would.
Author:	Do you think there's a part of you that enjoys causing disruption?
Cybercriminal 2:	Maybe. There's definitely a sense of satisfaction in knowing that I've outsmarted a company's defences. But it's not about causing chaos for the sake of it. It's more about proving to myself and others that I can do it.
Author:	Have you ever considered using your skills for good, like working in cybersecurity?
Cybercriminal 2:	I've thought about it. The idea of being a white-hat hacker is appealing, but the corporate world doesn't suit me. I value my independence and the freedom to operate on my own terms. Plus, the financial incentives are much higher on the dark side.
Author:	What do you think it would take for you to leave this life behind?
Cybercriminal 2:	That's a tough question. It would probably take a significant life change, like starting a family or finding a passion that rivals the thrill of hacking. For now, though, this is what I do best, and I don't see that changing anytime soon.
Author:	Any advice for those who might be tempted to follow in your footsteps?
Cybercriminal 2:	Think long and hard about the risks. It's not a path to take lightly. The consequences of getting caught can be severe, and it's not a life for everyone. If you're truly skilled, there are legitimate ways to use those talents. But if you do choose this path, be smart and always stay one step ahead.
Author:	Let's explore more about why you choose to live this life as a Cybercriminal 2. What is it about this lifestyle that appeals to you?
Cybercriminal 2:	There are several aspects that make this lifestyle appealing. First and foremost, it's the freedom. I don't have to adhere to a 9-to-5 schedule or answer to a boss. I can work from anywhere in the world, as long as I have an internet connection. That kind of independence is hard to find in a traditional job.
Author:	How does the financial aspect play into your decision?
Cybercriminal 2:	The financial rewards are significant. Successful attacks can bring in a lot of money, much more than I could earn in a regular job. It's not just about the money, though. It's also about the challenge and the satisfaction of pulling off a successful operation. But yes, the financial aspect is definitely a big part of it.

Author:	Do you ever think about the impact your actions have on others?
Cybercriminal 2:	I try not to dwell on it too much. I know that what I do can cause problems for companies and individuals, but I rationalize it by thinking that it's part of the game. Companies need to be vigilant and protect themselves. If they don't, someone will exploit their weaknesses. It's a harsh reality, but it's the world we live in.
Author:	What about the personal risks? How do you cope with the constant threat of being caught?
Cybercriminal 2:	It's always in the back of my mind, but I've learned to manage the stress. I take precautions to protect my identity and avoid leaving traces that could lead back to me. It's a calculated risk, and I try to stay one step ahead of law enforcement and cybersecurity experts. The adrenaline rush from the risk is part of what makes it exciting.
Author:	Have you ever considered the possibility of changing your ways and leading a different life?
Cybercriminal 2:	Sometimes. There are moments when I think about what it would be like to have a more conventional life, maybe even using my skills for good. But the pull of this lifestyle is strong. The freedom, the challenge, and the financial rewards are hard to give up. It would take something significant to make me change course.
Author:	What do you think would be the tipping point for you to leave this life behind?
Cybercriminal 2:	It would probably take a major life event, like starting a family or finding a new passion that gives me the same sense of fulfilment. For now, though, this is what I know and what I'm good at. It's hard to imagine doing anything else.
Author:	Let's talk about the psychological toll this lifestyle might have on you. Do you ever feel stressed or anxious about your activities?
Cybercriminal 2:	Absolutely. The constant need to stay ahead of security measures and the fear of getting caught can be very stressful. There's always a level of anxiety that comes with this line of work. It's a high-pressure environment, and sometimes it can be overwhelming.
Author:	How do you manage that stress and anxiety?
Cybercriminal 2:	I have a few coping mechanisms. I try to maintain a healthy work-life balance, even though it can be challenging. Exercise helps a lot, as does having hobbies outside of hacking. I also make sure to take breaks and disconnect from the digital world when I can. It's important to have a support system,

even if it's just a few trusted friends who understand what I'm going through.

Author: Do you ever experience guilt or remorse for your actions?

Cybercriminal 2: There are moments when I feel a twinge of guilt, especially when I think about the individuals who might be affected by my actions. But I try to compartmentalize those feelings. I remind myself that it's a job and that companies should be better prepared. It's a way to rationalize my actions and keep moving forward.

Author: Has this lifestyle affected your personal relationships?

Cybercriminal 2: It has, to some extent. It's hard to maintain close relationships when you have to keep such a big part of your life secret. Trust can be an issue, and there's always the fear that someone might find out what I do. It can be isolating at times, but I've learned to live with it.

Author: Do you ever feel isolated or lonely because of your work?

Cybercriminal 2: Yes, there are definitely times when I feel isolated. It's not easy to connect with people when you can't be honest about your life. The online communities I'm part of help to some extent, but it's not the same as having real, face-to-face interactions. It's one of the downsides of this lifestyle.

Author: What keeps you going despite these challenges?

Cybercriminal 2: The thrill of the challenge and the financial rewards are big motivators. There's also a sense of pride in being able to outsmart sophisticated security systems. It's a complex mix of factors, but ultimately, it's the excitement and the sense of accomplishment that keep me going.

Author: Do you think you'll ever reach a point where the psychological toll outweighs the benefits?

Cybercriminal 2: It's possible. Everyone has their breaking point, and I'm no different. If the stress and isolation become too much, I might have to reconsider my choices. For now, though, I'm managing. But it's something I keep in mind and try to stay aware of.

Author: Any advice for others who might be struggling with similar issues?

Cybercriminal 2: Find healthy ways to cope with stress and make sure you have a support system, even if it's just a few trusted people. Don't be afraid to take breaks and disconnect when you need to. And always be mindful of the impact your actions have on your mental health. It's important to take care of yourself, no matter what line of work you're in.

Author: Let's delve deeper into how you handle guilt or remorse. Do you have any strategies for dealing with these emotions?

Cybercriminal 2:	It's not easy, but I've developed ways to manage those feelings. One strategy is compartmentalisation. I separate my work from my personal life as much as possible. When I'm working, I focus on the technical aspects and the challenge, rather than the potential consequences for others. It helps to keep those feelings at bay.
Author:	Do you ever find it difficult to separate your work from your personal life?
Cybercriminal 2:	Sometimes, yes. There are moments when the lines blur, especially if I've had a particularly challenging or stressful day. But I try to maintain a clear boundary. Having hobbies and interests outside of hacking helps. It gives me something else to focus on and provides a mental break.
Author:	How do you handle moments when guilt or remorse do surface?
Cybercriminal 2:	When those feelings do come up, I try to rationalize them. I remind myself that companies have the resources to recover and that my actions are exposing weaknesses they need to address. It's a way to justify my actions and lessen the emotional impact. I also talk to a few trusted friends who understand my world. It helps to have someone to vent to.
Author:	Do you ever feel that these emotions affect your performance?
Cybercriminal 2:	They can, but I've learned to manage them. If I'm feeling particularly guilty or stressed, I might take a break and step away from my work for a while. It's important to recognize when you need to recharge. Pushing through those emotions without addressing them can lead to mistakes, and in this line of work, mistakes can be costly.
Author:	Have you ever considered seeking professional help to deal with these emotions?
Cybercriminal 2:	I've thought about it, but it's complicated. Finding a therapist who understands the unique challenges of my lifestyle would be difficult. Plus, there's the risk of exposing my activities. For now, I rely on my own coping mechanisms and the support of a few trusted friends.
Author:	Any final thoughts or advice for our readers?
Cybercriminal 2:	Stay vigilant. Cyber threats are constantly evolving, and anyone can be a target. Always question unexpected e-mails and messages, and never share sensitive information unless you're absolutely sure it's safe.

Interview with a cybercriminal-turned-white-hat-hacker

Next, we interviewed a hacker who was convicted following a significant hacking attack on a well-known global firm. This was a serious and well-publicised event. They have asked to remain anonymous to be protected from any further legal implications.

Author: Thank you for agreeing to this interview. Please can you tell us about yourself?

Hacker: I'm just another geek. I was brought up in a small town.

Author: What was it like growing up?

Hacker: Dull. Most of the youth services were closed so there wasn't much for kids my age to do.

Author: Can you tell us about your early life? Do you think anything may have contributed to what happened?

Hacker: It was your typical small town upbringing. I guess I spent a lot of time on my own.

Author: Why was that?

Hacker: I guess I lacked some of the social skills that other children my age had.

Author: Would you mind sharing your health conditions?

Hacker: Yes it's okay, I have Autism and I also suffer from depression and anxiety.

Author: How do your conditions affect you?

Hacker: I have always been a bit of a loner. I preferred my own company. When something stresses me out it can cause me to spiral sometimes. I guess I fixate on things.

Author: Do you think your health contributed to the hack and your decision-making?

Hacker: Yes and no. Not the main reason. Around the time of the hack I'd lost a lot of weight as I was spending increasing amounts of time on my own so I'd just eat cereal or junk. But my decisions were a conscious choice.

Author: How did you learn hacking techniques?

Hacker: Fell into it at school and at home. There were cybercafés I'd visit at certain times.

Author: What do you feel were the main factors that led to you becoming a hacker?

Hacker: All that time I spent alone. I spent a lot of time on computers and on devices. When you spend so much time online I guess you'll find more ways keep yourself entertained. There were some people I interacted with online. You could call them friends. I had a lot of free time. I was a teenager and I was impressed by what these guys did. I fell in love with hacking. Hacking into servers and stealing information was fun.

Author: What did you find fun about hacking?

Hacker:	I had nothing better to do. I did a lot of research. I'm not going to pretend this was about anything other than my own personal gratification. I did it because it was a challenge. It was fun. I did it because I could.
Author:	What were your aims?
Hacker:	To crack their security. It was a challenge but mostly I just wanted to have fun.
Author:	Did your motivations for hacking ever change over time?
Hacker:	Yes. At the beginning it was just about having fun and learning. I then became a hacktivist and moved onto being a black hat for hire. I found ways to make some money along the way.
Author:	Were you ever part of a group or did you always act alone?
Hacker:	I'm not going to pretend I didn't interact with or learn from others. I wouldn't want to incriminate anybody. So with that in mind let's say I always acted alone.
Author:	What criminal offences have you committed with a computer?
Hacker:	I have broken laws related to gaining unauthorised access to computer systems and networks. I have stolen accounts and personal information and then sold them on. You could probably add money laundering to the list.
Author:	When did all this start? What was your first hack?
Hacker:	I loved computers. I wanted to study computer science. They let a load of thickos (slang word for idiots) on the course. But I didn't get in. So I decided to get revenge.
Author:	What was your motivation for the first hack?
Hacker:	If they had given me a place on the course none of this would have happened. I would have had a completely different life.
Author:	Does that justify what you did?
Hacker:	Nothing justifies what I did. But you know what happened... I got into hacking. I started with hacking computers belonging to people that had crossed my path over the years. It was payback time. I took their credit card details and had some fun. Other times I'd blackmail them to pay or I'd release their information on the dark web.
Author:	Did you consider the victims or the consequences?
Hacker:	No. Do they think about us? There were no consequences so I just kept hacking. I had a stash of credit card details... Thousands of people.
Author:	Did you have any other motivation?
Hacker:	No I'd made my mind up by that stage. Nothing could stop me. I had a point to prove. That was my sole motivation. I went further and hacked others.
Author:	Did laws or punishments against cybercrimes have a deterrent effect on you?
Hacker:	No. It didn't stop me the first time or afterwards. I went on to do my attack on the education organisation.
Author:	With the next hack on that organisation there were huge numbers of victims and stakeholders. Thousands lost in research. Partner

organisations in healthcare were affected and so many people had their sensitive health information laid bare. Do you have any regrets?

Hacker: If I was to say I regret it now it wouldn't be worth much. At the time this was just about me proving a point and they were just target practice.

Author: How did hacking make you feel?

Hacker: It made me feel empowered. It was fun. Proving you are smarter than them. Making them pay. Embarrassing them publicly. I was on bail and then looked at this erm... global organisation. I breached their website. I got hold of e-mail addresses and bank information. I tried to blackmail them to pay a ransom. They didn't cough up. So I shared the details with others.

Author: The hack caused tens of millions in costs to this organisation. It damaged their reputation as a global brand and affected so many innocent customers. Do you regret anything you did?

Hacker: No, not at the time. I did what I had to do. While they were trying to salvage their reputation I was far away, safe behind my computer screen. They traced who I was from IP addresses and some of my activities online and that was it. After the arrest I was dragged to Court with over a dozen charges. I was in my twenties but I was still just a kid.

Author: As well as the financial damage to the organisation, you were sentenced to many years in incarceration. Can you share how you felt during that experience?

Hacker: I was suffering from depression and was suicidal at that point so I wasn't fully present. The judge sentenced me and I got locked up. Their solution to all this was more time on my own. They could have avoided all that by just allowing me on the computer science course I wanted to do. Locking me up didn't change anything about the situation or the circumstances that caused it.

Author: Did time away reform you?

Hacker: No. The system isn't designed with any real rehabilitation. But over the years eventually I did begin to regret my actions and started to change my life.

Author: What was the catalyst that made you change your life?

Hacker: My company began to change. I spent more time with people who cared about me and encouraged me to see life from a different perspective. I then began using my time to help improve security. I'm no longer a hacker. I conduct research on security.

Author: You are now part of the solution?

Hacker: Yes I guess you could say that. I can see the industry is beginning to change. Security leaders like you are trying to open up pathways and pull people up. We need to allow more young people into Tech.

Author: There is a huge amount of talent. Is there anything else you'd like to share with us about your mindset throughout all this?

Hacker: We all need something to live on. A job, an income. When people are not given opportunities... When they are not heard... They get disillusioned.

Some people suffer from poor mental health and are easy prey. We get influenced online. If they don't get into hacking, it'll be some other type of criminality, extremism or terrorism. If we don't give people an opportunity and we don't give them a voice and listen to them they will protest one way or another. It's just a way for them to channel their frustration. Hackers come from all walks of life, all over the world. Some are protesting, while others are just getting paid. Either way, we are all part of systems of control. So you are fair game. That's all I have to say.

Author: Thank you for agreeing to be part of this. I appreciate this must have been difficult and I'm grateful that you shared your views. Hopefully this may help provide the readers some insight into the mindset of hackers and help them to understand some of the root causes.

Common themes

It was fascinating for us to hear directly from people who deliberately chose to carry out malicious cyber-attacks. Many aspects of the crime theories we described earlier came through in their responses. We did a short thematic analysis on these interviews to identify common themes in how these cybercriminals saw themselves and think about their behaviour.

Curing boredom

Two of the interviewees mentioned the "thrill" and "excitement" of learning to hack. They expressed being "left alone" and "bored" as a youngster. In relation to the crime triangle (Figure 1.1), the lack of a guardian facilitated them exploring hacking activities on their own and refraining from other legitimate activities, such as sports. We all need to feel excited by something in life to feel fulfilled in the end.

Loneliness

One person mentioned it is easy on the internet to engage with others who are already hacking. Indeed, various forums, including on the dark web, enable people to anonymously gather and discuss topics such as cyber-attacks. Especially youngsters who may feel left out in real life may feel at home in an online community with shared interests – in this case, hacking.

Genuine interest in computers

One of the interviewees said they always had an interest in understanding computer systems. And one way to test whether you really understand computer systems certainly is by trying to break into them.

Freedom and independence

A shared theme among the cybercriminals was the sense of control and freedom of operating as an independent actor. It comes with temporal and geographical flexibility, as well as nobody to report to. As one of them said, they only need their computer to work. Whether they open their laptop in Bali or in Alaska, cyber-attacks can be carried out from anywhere at any time.

Proving oneself and pride

Two of the interviewees mentioned taking pride in carrying out successful cyber-attacks. It gives them a sense of accomplishment. Especially the cybercriminal who was rejected from a university course they applied for felt the need to prove themselves by attacking the very university. Every time an attack turns out to be successful, it boosts hackers' confidence in their special abilities.

Staying anonymous

A situational factor that shone through in two of the interviews is the need and relative ease to be unidentifiable on the internet. Indeed, anonymity on the internet makes it more difficult for prosecutors to identify suspects, especially when per-petrators operate from outside the legislative area of the prosecutors. State-backed hackers, for instance, are especially difficult to arrest. Cybercriminals all capitalise on the internet's anonymity.

Financial gains

In terms of external motivators, they mentioned that the financial gains from being a black hat hacker can far outweigh those for white hat hackers.

Duty to expose vulnerabilities in "cat-and-mouse" game

Two of the cybercriminals used the term "cat-and-mouse" game to describe the role of cybersecurity and cyber-attacks. One of them alluded to a belief that, in fact, cyber-attacks are good for organisations, as they expose them to their vulnerabilities which forces them to take cybersecurity (more) seriously. This is an intriguing take, since in the same vein, just because your grandmother is suffering from dementia, does one need to exploit her memory loss to make her take her cognitive decline seriously?

Dealing with mental stress

All of the interviewees mentioned the mental toll that comes with their "job". One fully rationalised their actions and described various ways in which they distance themselves from the lives they are impacting with their attacks, such as exercising a lot and having other hobbies to distract their thoughts. The second person men-tioned having to take longer periods off. The third person admitted to feeling guilt, suffering from depression and anxiety, and possibly left their black hat behind to avoid the psychological toll it took on them.

Together, these themes align surprisingly well with academic studies pub-lished in the late 1990s and early 2000s on hackers [1], and show that various psychological and situational factors play important and consistent roles in shaping hackers' motivations. The thrill of a successful cyber-attack and the external rewards are answers to feelings of loneliness and boredom. The anonymous online community and ease of engaging in hacking in the absence of a guardian set a conducive backdrop for these cybercriminals to continue their nefarious activities. Again, note the striking similarity of their stories and themes with those of the notorious hackers described earlier, such as Kevin Mitnick's genuine fascination for computer network systems which these interviewees share.

Through these real-world examples, we identified how specific personal and contextual factors almost make it inevitable that certain individuals become black hat hackers. In the next chapter, we will dive even deeper into the lives of these people by describing how they carry out different types of cyber-attacks.

References

1 A. E. Adam, "Hacking into hacking: Gender and the hacker phenomenon," *ACM SIG-CAS Computers and Society*, vol. 33, no. 4, p. 3, 2003.
2 J. London, "Happy 60th birthday to the word 'hack.'" Accessed: February 06, 2025 [Online]. Available: https://alum.mit.edu/slice/happy-60th-birthday-word-hack#:~: text=But the more broad definition of hack%2C commonly,%28TMRC%2960yearsag oonApril5%2C195
3 T. Jordan and P. Taylor, "A sociology of hackers," *The Sociological Review*, vol. 46, no. 4, pp. 757–780, 2017.
4 K. D. Mitnick and W. L. Simon, *The Art of Deception: Controlling the Human Element of Security*. John Wiley & Sons, Australia, 2003.
5 O. Turgeman-Goldschmidt, "Meanings that hackers assign to their being a hacker," *International Journal of Cyber Criminology*, vol. 2, no. 2, pp. 382–396, 2008.
6 M. K. Rogers, "The psyche of cybercriminals: A psycho-social perspective," in *Cybercrimes: A Multidisciplinary Analysis*, G. Ghosh and E. Turrini, Eds. Berlin: Springer-Verlag, 2010, pp. 217–235.
7 S. Toupin, "Feminist hackerspaces: The synthesis of feminist and hacker cultures," *Journal of Peer Production*, vol. 5, no. 2014, pp. 1–11, 2014.
8 T. Singh, *Cybersecurity, Psychology and People Hacking*. Cham: Springer International Publishing Imprint, Palgrave Macmillan, 2025.
9 Aiken, M. P., Davidson, J., Amann, P. 'Youth Pathways into Cybercrime' (Report). 2016. Retrieved from
10 https://www.mdx.ac.uk/__data/assets/pdf_file/0025/245554/Pathways-White-Paper.pdf.
11 J. A. M. Schiks, Susanne van 't Hoff-de Goede & Rutger E. Leukfeldt. An alternative intervention for juvenile hackers? A qualitative evaluation of the Hack_Right intervention, *Journal of Crime and Justice*, 2023. DOI: 10.1080/0735648X.2023.2252394
12 https://www.nytimes.com/2023/07/20/technology/kevin-mitnick-dead-hacker.html
13 https://www.nytimes.com/2018/03/17/obituaries/adrian-lamo-dead.html
14 https://malicious.life/episode/us_vs_gary_mckinnon/
15 https://www.psychologytoday.com/intl/articles/200811/the-job-hacker-hunter
16 https://yourstory.com/2023/07/adrian-lamo-life-journey-impact-cybersecurity
17 https://www.psychologytoday.com/us/blog/stuck/200910/hacker-with-aspergers-fears-extradition-will-cause-his-suicide

3 How an attack is devised

So far, we have described how opportunity, ability, and desire give rise to different types of hackers. We gained a better understanding of what drives them, both psychologically and contextually. In this chapter, we will delve deeper into how they operate. In other words, the process of how they devise an attack.

The three broad functional steps in a cyber-attack are preparation, execution, and aftercare. Once a hacker decides to launch a new attack, whether for political, financial, trolling, or other personal reasons, they will have to decide whom specifically to target, what attack vector to use, how they would get to receive any monetary or other desired outcome, when to launch the attack, and how to avoid being caught. They need to research potential targets, choose which ones to focus on, procure software and other required tools, develop and test their specific attack setup, and ensure anonymity in the process. In evaluating their options, they will weigh up the potential rewards of a successful attack against the risks of detection and retaliation, akin to a cost-benefit analysis. A potential target's security posture and technical controls can determine the likelihood of success.

Although not every single cyber-attack may be deliberated to the same level of detail, organised crime groups and "professional" hackers will make their processes as watertight as possible. After all, to be prepared is half the battle. In the spirit of red teaming and to raise awareness, we will describe misconfiguration exploits, social engineering, and ransomware attacks in this chapter to illustrate each of these aspects. We will see that psychological factors play a critical role in these attacks, which makes it essential for cybersecurity professionals to understand how these tactics work and to develop effective countermeasures. But before that, we want to highlight how hackers select their target(s) and the skills (i.e., ability) required to execute cyber-attacks.

Selecting targets

Depending on the type of attack, hackers can be extremely strategic when selecting their targets, often employing a combination of research, reconnaissance, and psychological tactics. The first phase in the cyber-attack chain consists of reconnaissance and information gathering. Hackers may use open source intelligence (OSINT) to gather any publicly available details about potential targets.

DOI: 10.4324/9781003610533-4

This includes social media profiles, company websites, news articles, and public records. They may use automated tools like Nmap to scan networks on a large scale for open ports and vulnerabilities, identifying potential entry points. These include not only weak technical entry points such as outdated software, unpatched systems, and misconfigurations that can be exploited, but also individuals who could fall victim to social engineering tactics. To identify them, hackers analyse patterns in employee behaviour by monitoring and observing their online activities, work habits, and communication patterns to identify the best time and method for an attack.

Hackers will often profile and prioritise targets that offer the greatest potential reward, such as financial institutions, large corporations, and government agencies. It may depend on what they are primarily after: money or certain data, such as intellectual property or personal details of political adversaries. Sometimes, hackers go after low-hanging fruit – easier targets with known vulnerabilities, even if the potential reward is smaller. Another way to impact larger organisations is through third-party vendors or partners with weaker security measures to eventually gain access to a larger organisation. Hackers may identify insider threats and exploit disgruntled employees or those with access to sensitive information. By employing a combination of technical and psychological tactics, they increase their chances of a successful attack.

Skills that make attacks succeed

Skills that enable hackers to launch successful cyber-attacks rely on a combination of technical and non-technical skills. By combining skillsets, hacker groups can effectively identify and exploit vulnerabilities, making their attacks more impactful.

The bare minimum skills to exploit technical targets include programming and scripting. Proficiency in programming languages like Python, JavaScript, and SQL is crucial for writing exploits and automating tasks. Bash scripting is essential for automating system tasks and managing files. Knowledge of TCP/IP, DNS, HTTP, and other protocols is vital for identifying and exploiting network vulnerabilities, as well as skills in using tools like Nmap to scan and map networks for potential entry points. In terms of operating systems, proficiency in both Linux and Windows environments is necessary for navigating and exploiting different systems, and understanding system configurations and security settings to identify weaknesses.

A good understanding of web application security is also increasingly important. This includes knowledge of web technologies and vulnerabilities like Cross-Site Scripting (XSS) and SQL injection, and understanding how web applications are built to identify and exploit flaws. Understanding cryptographic principles is essential to both protect data and break weak encryption. Cryptanalysis, or skills in analysing and breaking cryptographic algorithms, is also important. The ability to deconstruct malware to understand its behaviour and develop countermeasures, as well as skills in reverse engineering binaries to find vulnerabilities are relevant too.

Non-technical skills to exploit human targets all focus on understanding human psychology: reading and understanding human behaviour, knowing how people think and behave in different contexts, and knowing their needs and motivations.

Building a (false) sense of trust helps to manipulate targets more effectively and typically rely on social engineering tactics: manipulation techniques whereby hackers use psychological strategies to trick individuals into revealing sensitive information. Skills in crafting convincing phishing messages, for instance, using generative artificial intelligence (AI), helps to persuade individuals to click malicious links and providing their personal details.

Other non-technical skills such as creativity, adaptability, and problem-solving help hackers develop innovative ways to bypass security measures and solve complex problems. Determination is a key personality trait among hackers to keep trying different approaches until a vulnerability is found. In terms of communication skills, persuasion is vital in convincing targets to take actions that compromise security. Clear communication is essential, as hackers come across a wide range of targets and attack affiliates. Successful hackers are excellent at security research and intelligence gathering from publicly available sources to plan attacks. They keep up with the latest security trends, vulnerabilities, and attack techniques, and adapt to new environments and technologies quickly. They have to continuously learn and update their skills to stay ahead of security defences.

These skills bear a striking similarity to what a robust cybersecurity team would need. Again, we see that when people have the same ability and opportunity to commit and protect against cyber-attacks, the only real difference between a legitimate cybersecurity professional and unethical hacker may be their desire to work for a bigger legitimate cause as opposed to personal gratification only.

Social engineering attacks: hacking people's minds

Hacking is not just about exploiting vulnerabilities in software or hardware. It is also about exploiting vulnerabilities in people. Social engineering attacks are a prime example of this, in which people are manipulated to divulge sensitive information or perform actions that they would not normally take. It is a common tactic used by hackers to gain access to systems, steal data, or spread malware, as it is relatively easier to exploit human vulnerabilities than it is to hack into a secure system. It can take many different forms, such as (spear)phishing, whaling, pretexting, baiting, tailgating, smishing, vishing (phone scams), business e-mail compromise, honeytraps (romance scams), scareware, and watering hole attacks. Essentially, they are all forms of lies and deception, but adapted to different communication contexts.

In a phishing attack, hackers send e-mails or messages that appear to be from a trusted source, such as a bank or a social media site. The goal is to trick the target into clicking a malicious link or downloading a malware-infected attachment. Spearphishing attacks occur when hackers target a specific individual or organisation. This way, hackers completed a \$1 billion heist spanning 40 countries in 2015. They sent bank employees phishing e-mails with an attachment to deploy Carbanak malware. Once clicked, the hackers could control the employees' workstations and were able to infect ATM servers remotely. A new take on spear phishing is called angler phishing. This occurs when scammers impersonate customer service accounts on social media with the goal of getting you to send them your login information.

Whaling is a term used to describe phishing attacks that target a specific, high-profile person – usually an executive, government official, or celebrity. The victims of whaling attacks are considered "big fish" to cybercriminals. These targets offer great potential to scammers with either large financial pay-outs or access to valuable data. In the case of hacked celebrities, scammers hope to find compromising photos that they can use to extort exorbitant ransoms. In another example, hackers send spoof e-mails to C-level employees that appear to come from within the victim's organisation. The sender claims to know confidential information about a co-worker, but is afraid to report the situation in person. Instead, they offer to share their evidence as a spreadsheet, PDF, or slide deck. But when victims click the link to the file, they are taken to a malicious website – or they try to open the attachment and malware infects their system and spreads to their network.

Pretexting is another type of social engineering attack where hackers create a false scenario to gain the target's trust. For example, a hacker might pretend to be a company's IT support to convince an employee to reveal their login credentials. Baiting involves leaving a tempting item, such as a USB drive, in a public place to entice people to pick it up and plug it into their computer. When they do, malicious software on the USB stick may exfiltrate data or infect their computer system with malware. Tailgating is when a hacker follows an employee into a restricted area without authorisation.

Smishing is the term used to describe phishing via the use of SMS text messages. Scammers purchase spoofed phone numbers and blast out messages containing malicious links. There's also vishing, which is the same as phishing but done over the phone. Vishing is especially widespread in organisations. Scammers will contact a company's front desk, customer service, human resources, or information technology (IT) and claim to need personal information about an employee. Lies range from mortgage lenders trying to "verify" e-mail addresses, to executive assistants requesting password changes on their manager's behalf.

Piggybacking or tailgating both refer to a type of attack in which an authorised person allows an unauthorised person access to a restricted area. This form of social engineering may happen at your place of work if you let someone follow you into the building or at your apartment building as you are leaving for the day. Social engineers (i.e., scammers) may be dressed as delivery drivers, say they forgot their IDs, or pretend that they are "new" in the area. Once inside, they can spy on people, access workstations, check the names on mailboxes, and more. Tailgating also includes giving unauthorised users (e.g. a co-worker or child) access to your company devices. They may put your device at risk and spread malicious code throughout the rest of your company.

Scareware, also known as fraudware, deception software, or rogue scanner software, tricks victims into believing they are under imminent threat. For example, you could receive a message saying that your device has been infected with a virus. Scareware often appears as pop-ups in your browser. It can also appear in spam e-mails. Victims are supposed to click on a button to either remove the virus or download software that will uninstall the malicious code. But doing so is what causes the actual malicious software to get in.

Watering hole attacks occur when hackers infect a site that they know you regularly visit. When you visit the site, you automatically download malware (known as a drive-by-download). Or you are taken to a fake version of the site that is designed to steal your credentials. For example, scammers could divert you away from a normal login page to one designed to steal your account name and password. It will look exactly the same. But anything you enter will go straight to the scammer. This is where having password management software can be so important. Even if a phishing website looks exactly like the real one, a password manager would not automatically enter your credentials.

Hackers are leveraging the recent advances in AI to create more sophisticated social engineering attacks [1]. As a result, individuals and organisations ought to improve their communication policies and processes for moving assets like budgets and sensitive data, and ability to recognise the psychological tactics used in social engineering attacks. You may be familiar with Robert Cialdini's six principles of persuasion [2] that are often applied here, for instance, to study the prevalence of different persuasion tactics in phishing e-mails [3].

One of these principles, social proof, involves using the opinions or actions of others to influence a target's behaviour. For example, a hacker might create fake social media profiles to make it appear that many people are using a particular product or service, to convince a target to use it as well. Another tactic is authority, where a hacker poses as a person of authority to gain the target's trust. For example, a hacker might pretend to be a police officer or a government official to convince a target to reveal sensitive information or pay outstanding charges.

Scarcity is another psychological tactic hackers use, where they create a sense of urgency or scarcity to motivate the target to act. For example, a hacker might send an e-mail claiming that the target's account has been compromised and that immediate action is required to prevent further damage. Alternatively, an attacker may pose as a colleague from the IT department and ask an employee to provide their login credentials. The employee may comply with the request, because they assume that the person is an authority figure and has a legitimate reason for the request. Individuals are generally more likely to comply with requests from authority figures, even if the request goes against their beliefs or values. In cybersecurity, the power of authority can be an often-exploited vulnerability.

Social identity is a social psychology concept that describes how individuals identify themselves as part of a group and how this group membership affects their behaviour. In cybersecurity, someone's social identity can be exploited, for example, when an attacker poses as a member of a trusted group, such as a partner or supplier, to gain access to an organisation's systems. The employee may comply with the request, because they assume the other person is a member of a trusted group.

Another psychological factor that cybercriminals often exploit is fear. Fear can be used to create urgency, which can lead people to make hasty decisions that can compromise their security. For example, a cybercriminal might send a phishing e-mail, claiming to be from a bank and warning the recipient that their account has been compromised. The e-mail might urge them to click a link and enter their login information to secure their account. In reality, the link leads to a fake website that steals their login information.

With openly available large language models, it has become trivial to create persuasive messages that employ various of the above persuasion tactics. The era of awkward phishing e-mails from Nigerian princes and grammatically flawed Microsoft security notices is over. Combined with the trove of personal data breached over the years and the information people publicly reveal about themselves online, an adversary could easily craft and automate the type of messages you normally may expect to receive. What sets successful social engineering attacks apart is the ability to build the infrastructure to mimic any legitimate organisational web domain or tone of voice. A recent example is when an employee at the finance department of the British engineering company Arup got scammed for $25 million over a deepfake video call with their ostensible chief finance officer and other colleagues [4]. The employee had fallen for a phishing e-mail and was convinced of the need for a secret transaction through the semblance of the deepfake personas in the Zoom call. Thus, by using AI, the attackers managed to obtain the employee's trust to perform an action they normally would not and cashed in the money.

We do not know Arup's organisational culture, but in addition to the sophisticated social engineering techniques, the employee's circumstances may have been especially conducive to falling for the attack. That is, the employee was based in Hong Kong and the phishing e-mail purported to be from the UK office. With remote working and internal communications dominated by the use of digital channels, it is not always straightforward to verify with colleagues in the physical world whether a request is legitimate. A cultural value of not questioning your superiors may also have played a role here, as Asian cultures generally tend to be more hierarchical than western ones. The perfect social engineering hacker would, indeed, be a sociopath with a heightened sensibility for a target's context, so they know what language to use to persuade them, without feeling remorse.

Ransomware attacks

To describe how ransomware attacks are devised, we will borrow another concept from crime science called *crime scripting*. Crime scripting is the process of documenting each step required to carry out a specific crime. Doing so helps us understand the types of deterrents or other interventions needed to thwart a specific step in a crime operation. This helps police and lawmakers create better crime prevention policies and legislation [5].

In a ransomware attack, hackers manage to execute malicious software on a target system that exfiltrates and encrypts data found on the target system. As a result, the system becomes unusable and the system user is asked to pay a ransom to receive the decryption key. If the victim does not comply, the adversaries will threaten to leak their data online and to the media. Matthijse and colleagues (2023) used crime script analysis on 44 court documents and 10 expert interviews to detail how ransomware attacks are executed, to help law enforcers and organisations develop situational crime prevention and adequate cybersecurity measures [6], which we describe below.

When starting from scratch (i.e., not buying "ransomware-as-a-service" from an underground supplier), the attack starts with the formation of a criminal group of hackers and affiliates. Since the development of ransomware and finding network vulnerabilities to get the ransomware delivered to the target are specialised skills, hackers will post recruitment advertisements on dark web forums and markets to find collaborators. When they agree to collaborate, they set up the infrastructure to host the ransomware, prepare databases to exhilarate stolen data to, and use virtual private networks, different communication channels, and false credentials to hide their true identities. The malware developers in the group will develop and test the ransomware, ensuring they fix any bugs and address any published ransomware software vulnerabilities. Once these critical preparation steps are complete, they may sell the ransomware or use it themselves. In the latter case, they need to agree on whom to target.

The study found that although ransomware initially was used to target individuals and consumers, attackers now only target organisations since they would be more profitable. Importantly, most ransomware attacks are not specific to one organisation only – in stark contrast to the social engineering attacks described above, but attackers will use it to cast a wide net and see whichever organisation gets trapped. To get the ransomware delivered to the target, they either use a phishing e-mail, or exploit remote desktop connections or security vulnerabilities. Instead of engineering this access oneself, the group may consult an access broker to execute this step for them.

When the group manages to gain access to a system, they will first expand access to other computers in the network, seek higher system privileges, ensure back-ups get encrypted too, scan the data on the system network, and research the victim to determine the ransom amount. They want to ensure their efforts are worth the potential value to be gained. To avoid detection, they may bypass the target's firewall and turn off antivirus software. Next or simultaneously, the attackers may exfiltrate the target's data or, instead, not exfiltrate threaten with General Data Protection Regulation fines from exposing personal customer and client information. Then, the encryption process starts, which may take hours up to several months. If the attackers manage to also encrypt the target's data back-ups, or if the target does not have a back-up, it makes them more likely to pay the ransom in the end.

Once the data are encrypted, the extortion and communication between the attackers and target start. How much the target is asked to pay is typically tailored to the organisation's annual turnover. Some of the interviewed experts said that it varies between 2% and 5% of annual revenue. Often, the stated ransom amount is in Bitcoin, allowing attackers to remain anonymous. Victims may then be led to a chat interface built into the ransomware, another website, or e-mail to interact with the attackers. This is where psychological negotiation skills can help to extend ransom payment deadlines, so the victim organisation buys themselves more time to assess the (potential) damage and decide how to act. But some experts also said further negotiation could result in a higher ransom amount and increased pressure on the victim to pay. Eventually, organisations who decided not to pay mentioned that they could not know whether the attackers actually exfiltrated any data, they had unaffected back-ups of data in place or they stood by the principle to not pay cybercriminals. Organisations that decided to pay typically lost access to critical files that were either not backed up or the back-up was also encrypted, the system's downtime would be too costly, having insurance to cover the ransom amount or to avoid leaking the stolen data.

To pay, the target has to transfer money to cryptocurrency wallets that may contain a mixture of flat and crypto currencies, or are pure crypto wallets. Once the ransom is received by the attackers, they do stick to their promise of decrypting the data for the sake of upholding the ransomware "organisation model". In some instances, the decryption process was faulty, however. If organisations did not pay, their data indeed get leaked online and the attackers may contact data protection authorities and media outlets about them.

In the last phase, attackers launder the money to disguise it came from a ransom payment. The proceeds are then divided among the crime group and reinvested in the ransomware infrastructure. If law enforcers manage to catch the offenders and convict them, they are forced to quit the ransomware attacks. But some experts noted that convicted offenders will continue after stopping for a little while and develop a new type of ransomware under a different brand. Others may quit because they obtained enough money.

It should have become clear from this crime script how important it is to have adequate basic cybersecurity measures in place such as data back-up and restore processes, but also how people's moral standpoint can affect the decision to pay a ransom, and how networks of hackers, brokers, and cybercriminals collaborate like a malicious software company to create ransomware attacks.

Exploiting misconfigurations

Misconfigurations are improperly configured devices, applications, or systems, which can lead to a variety of risks for organisations, including vulnerabilities that cybercriminals can exploit, data breaches, and errors and crashes that can lead to system downtime and lost revenue. Misconfigurations can be caused by technical misalignments and human error. For example, it can occur when a developer sets up a system improperly, when a user misconfigures a device or does not adequately install a software update. Misconfigurations can also happen when there are changes made to a (sub)system that make it incompatible with other dependencies or when a device is not properly maintained. Even system engineers with a thorough understanding of the intricate dependencies found in an IT infrastructure may overlook something or underestimate the risk of a known vulnerability. Cybercriminals and hackers use automated tools and keep a close eye on sources that publicise system vulnerabilities to find ways to exploit such misconfigurations. They will also learn from successful security and data breaches to see what hacking patterns may be replicated in future attacks.

Misconfigurations have in fact been a common cause of data breaches in recent years with severe potential consequences and pose easy targets for cybercriminals

[7], especially since many misconfigurations exist that are only waiting to be exploited [8]. For example, a misconfigured server led to the Equifax data breach in 2017, which exposed the personal information of over 143 million people from the United States, UK, and Canada. Another example is the Capital One data breach in 2019, which resulted in the theft of over 100 million customer records, significant reputational damage, regulatory scrutiny, and a $190 million settlement with affected customers [9]. The attacker, who turns out to be a transgender female hacker [10], was able to exploit a vulnerability in Capital One's systems that had been identified before, but not remediated. The team responsible for configuring a web application firewall likely underestimated the potential risks of not addressing the vulnerability – such as the attacker gaining access to the data stored on the server. This case highlights the importance of systematically managing access controls and vulnerabilities, where biased assumptions and erroneous beliefs embedded in the security organisation can lead to important misconfigurations staying unaddressed [9] – a topic we will elaborate on in *Chapter 6: Human fallacies and how to overcome them*. In addition to these high-profile breaches, other examples include the Target breach in 2013, and Yahoo data breaches in 2013 and 2014, which were caused by misconfigured servers and security settings, respectively.

We typically hear that exploitation of misconfigurations can be avoided by following best practices for cybersecurity [11]. But, using a holistic systems perspective on cybersecurity, others have started further emphasising the importance of operating on a security by design principle, and the negative influence of institutional, organisational, and personal factors on security decisions [7,9]. Indeed, the study by Constanze Dietrich and colleagues (2018) on system operators' experiences with misconfigurations led to a mostly non-technical set of recommendations that may also be known to organisations, but are often not implemented thoroughly: (i) keeping system documentation up to date and accurate, (ii) clearly define shared team responsibilities for device security, (iii) address systemic failures in post-mortem analysis instead of blaming the responsible people, (iv) plan any changes and avoid frequent configuration updates, (v) automate deployments and rollback plans in case of misconfigurations, and (vi) run cyber "fire drills" to improve staff awareness of security risks and what to do in those cases. These are all topics we will elaborate on in *Part 2: Inside the line of defence*.

References

1 T. Singh, Artificial Intelligence and Ethics: A Field Guide for Stakeholders. CRC Press, United Kingdom, 2024.

2 R. B. Cialdini and N. J. Goldstein, "Social influence: Compliance and conformity," Annual Review of Psychology, vol. 55, pp. 591–621, 2004, doi: 10.1146/annurev. psych.55.090902.142015.

3 A. Van Der Heijden and L. Allodi, "Cognitive triaging of phishing attacks," in Proceedings of the 28th USENIX Security Symposium, USENIX Association, United States, 2019, pp. 1309–1326.

4 CNN, "British engineering giant Arup revealed as $25 million deepfake scam victim," Accessed: February 11, 2025 [Online]. Available: https://edition.cnn.com/2024/05/16/ tech/arup-deepfake-scam-loss-hong-kong-intl-hnk/index.html

5   H. Dehghanniri and H. Borrion, "Crime scripting: A systematic review," European Journal of Criminology, vol. 18, no. 4, pp. 504–525, Jun. 2019, doi: 10.1177/1477370819850943.

6   S. R. Matthijsse, M. S. van 't Hoff-de Goede, and E. R. Leukfeldt, "Your files have been encrypted: A crime script analysis of ransomware attacks," Trends in Organized Crime, vol. 23, pp. 23–31, 2023, doi: 10.1007/s12117-023-09496-z.

7   S. Loureiro, "Security misconfigurations and how to prevent them," Network Security, vol. 2021, no. 5, pp. 13–16, May 2021, doi: 10.1016/S1353-4858(21)00053-2.

8   C. Dietrich, K. Krombholz, K. Borgolte, and T. Fiebig, "Investigating system operators' perspective on security misconfigurations," in Proceedings of the 2018 ACM SIGSAC Conference on Computer and Communications Security, in CCS '18, New York: Association for Computing Machinery, 2018, pp. 1272–1289, doi: 10.1145/3243734.3243794.

9   S. Khan, I. Kabanov, Y. Hua, and S. Madnick, "A systematic analysis of the Capital One data breach: Critical lessons learned," ACM Transactions on Privacy and Security, vol. 26, no. 1, pp. 1–29, Article No. 3, 2022, doi: 10.1145/3546068.

10   AP News, "Seattle woman gets probation for massive Capital One hack," Accessed: February 11, 2025 [Online]. Available: https://apnews.com/article/technology-business-seattle-sentencing-paige-thompson-6eab17de7a88d0c6a33d3f44dbfa4d2a?utm_source=copy&utm_medium=share

11   A non-exhaustive list of cybersecurity best practices that applies to virtually any threat prevention program: regularly updating software and security systems, implementing strong passwords and multi-factor authentication, monitoring systems for signs of suspicious activity, conducting regular security audits, using configuration management tools and patch management systems, anti-virus software, firewalls, intrusion detection and prevention systems, SIEM and vulnerability scanning tools and training employees on how to properly configure devices and systems.

4   Special cases

So far, we detailed in what circumstances ethical and unethical hackers arise, their motivations and desires, and gained an insight into how they devise various types of cyber-attacks. Security risks and cyber-attacks can, however, also be created by people who do not identify as hackers or cybercriminals. We distinguish three such special cases: insider threats, whistleblowers, and third party and supply chain risks.

Insider threats

One of the most concerning types of attack is one that originates from within an organisation. *Insider threats* occur when an employee intentionally or unintentionally causes harm to an organisation's systems or data. This can include stealing confidential information, such as customer data, trade secrets, financial information, copying data to a personal device or selling it to a third party, as well as introducing malware or sabotaging systems.

Insider threats are a growing and disturbing phenomenon [1]. Employee-related cybersecurity breaches are becoming more common and, like any other cyber-attack, can result in significant financial losses, reputational damage, and legal liabilities. According to a Cost of a Data Breach report by IBM in 2024, insider attacks are the most common and costliest form of cybercrime, with an average cost of $11.45 million per incident [2].

During our careers in cybersecurity, we have come across numerous examples where insider threats materialised with our clients. To share these stories, we will anonymise the organisations involved but describe what transpired.

One of our client organisations discovered that an employee was using company equipment to run a side business. The employee was using the company's internet connection to sell products on an online marketplace during work hours. The company's information technology (IT) department was able to detect the employee's activity and brought it to the attention of management. The employee was promptly terminated for violating the company's acceptable use policy.

In another case, an employee shared confidential company information with a competitor. The employee had access to sensitive data and was able to download and transfer it to a personal device. The company was able to trace the activity back

DOI: 10.4324/9781003610533-5

to the employee's computer and terminated the employee. The company also took legal action against the competitor.

A few years ago, we came across an organisation whose IT department discovered an employee had installed a keylogger on a company computer. The keylogger recorded everything the employee typed, including login credentials and confidential information. The IT department was able to remove the keylogger and the employee was reprimanded for violating the company's security policy.

We have also seen a situation where a former employee of a financial institution was charged with stealing confidential customer information. The employee worked in the IT department and had access to sensitive data such as credit card numbers, social security numbers, and bank account information. The employee used this information to create fake identities and obtain credit cards, which were then used to make fraudulent purchases.

Now, let us examine real-life cases of cybersecurity breaches caused by insiders in more detail that are in the public domain and explore what encouraged them to commit these nefarious actions. We will then provide prevention and mitigation strategies to minimise the risk of such incidents.

Case study 1: The Proofpoint intellectual property breach

The Proofpoint intellectual property theft stands out as an egregious example of a malicious insider threat. In 2019, Proofpoint, a leading cybersecurity company, discovered upon internal investigation that one of its former directors had stolen the company's trade secrets and shared them with a competitor. The former director, who had left Proofpoint to work for the competitor, was accused of stealing confidential customer information, sales data, and other proprietary information. Proofpoint immediately filed a lawsuit against them and the competitor, seeking to stop them from using the stolen information and to recover damages [3].

The case highlights the risks of insider attacks in the cybersecurity industry. Proofpoint is a trusted provider of cybersecurity solutions and its customers rely on it to protect their sensitive data. The fact that one of its own directors was able to steal valuable information and share it with a competitor shows that even the most trusted employees can pose a threat.

The Proofpoint breach happened because of the former director's greed and desire to benefit themselves and their new employer. They succumbed to the temptation of giving the competitor and himself an unfair advantage and stole the confidential information, believing they could get away with it. The breach also highlights the importance of employee training and monitoring. Proofpoint had policies and procedures in place to protect its information, but the former director was able to bypass them. This rendered their security policies and procedures ineffective, and more could have been done to prevent the breach.

Case study 2: The Intel breach

A high-profile case involved Intel, which filed a lawsuit in 2018 against one of its former employees, alleging that they had stolen confidential documents and trade secrets before leaving the company to work for a competitor. The former employee, who had worked for Intel for nearly 20 years and had access to highly sensitive information, was accused of downloading and copying confidential files onto a USB drive before resigning. Intel claimed that the stolen documents included details about its manufacturing processes and designs for future products [4]. According to court documents, the former employee took a job with a competitor and saw the stolen information as an opportunity to gain an advantage in their new role. That, combined with some weaknesses in Intel's security protocols allowed the former employee to commit an insider attack.

The lawsuit garnered a lot of media attention and highlighted the growing problem of insider attacks. Moreover, the breach was a significant blow to Intel, which had heavily invested in developing its manufacturing processes and designing new products in the highly competitive semiconductor industry. Apart from filing a lawsuit against the former employee, Intel implemented new security measures to prevent similar incidents from occurring in the future, including tighter access controls and improved monitoring of employee activity.

Case study 3: The Shopify breach

Another insider attack was the Shopify breach, which affected millions of customers. Shopify is a popular e-commerce platform used by over one million organisations worldwide. They were breached in September 2020, which impacted approximately 200 merchants using the platform. The attackers accessed customer data, including personal names, addresses, and order details, which they sold online for several months. Although no financial information was compromised, the breach still had a significant impact on affected organisations and their customers [5].

The breach turned out to be an insider attack by two employees who were solely incentivised by financial gain. They were tempted by a lucrative offer from cybercriminals in exchange for stealing transaction records of 200 online merchants and customer information. As they had legitimate access to Shopify's customer support platform, it was easy for them to obtain these data. They exported the data and sold them through a third-party service. The breach went undetected, until a security researcher discovered the stolen data being sold online. Shopify acted swiftly to contain the breach, notified the affected merchants, and worked with law enforcement to identify and apprehend the attackers. However, the damage was already done.

This case illustrates the importance of strong access controls and monitoring, especially for operationally critical data like customer and order details. It is absolutely essential to limit access to such sensitive data and monitor access for unusual activity. Another factor that contributed to the breach was lack of oversight. The attackers were able to carry out the attack for several months without being detected. This highlights the importance of regular security audits and monitoring, so to ensure security measures stay updated and effective.

Case study 4: The Pfizer breach

Pfizer is one of the world's largest pharmaceutical companies and has been at the forefront of developing vaccines and treatments for COVID-19. The company has invested billions of dollars in research and development to create safe and effective vaccines in record time. In October 2021, they experienced a major security breach. An employee who was with Pfizer for 15 years stole 12,000 highly sensitive documents related to the COVID-19 vaccine, the relationship between Pfizer and BioNTech and experimental monoclonal cancer treatment [6].

This breach is a textbook example of an insider attack, which means that it was carried out by someone with authorised access to company's information. In this case, sensitive e-mails, PowerPoint presentations, and Excel spreadsheets about Pfizer's partnership with BioNTech, the manufacturing of the COVID-19 vaccine, and the distribution of the vaccine to various countries. They allegedly stole the data over a period of months and then shared them with others. It is not clear who received the data or how they were used. The theft was discovered by Pfizer's cybersecurity team during routine monitoring. The employee was immediately terminated and the company began litigation against the former employee for uploading documents, including trade secrets, to Google Drive accounts and personal devices.

Several reasons may encourage employees to carry out insider attacks. These may include financial gain, revenge, ideology, and even plain curiosity. In this case, the motive behind the insider attack remained unclear. The employee had been with Pfizer for 15 years and had a good track record. It is possible they were paid to steal the data or were acting on behalf of a competitor. It is also possible that the employee was disgruntled or motivated by a personal grudge.

Case study 5: The Cash App breach

Many data breaches, like the Shopify breach, occur due to insider attacks. Another such case that caught our attention was the Cash App breach.

Cash App is a mobile payment service that allows users to send and receive money. It is a popular payment platform in the United States, with millions of users making transactions every day. In 2020, the platform suffered a major cybersecurity breach that compromised the personal data of many of its users [7]. It happened because a former employee of the company, who had access to sensitive data including customer information, had turned against Cash App. They had downloaded reports containing data on more than eight million Cash App customers, both past and present. They then sold the data to cybercriminals, who used the stolen data to carry out fraudulent activities, including unauthorised transactions and identity theft.

The breach was discovered after many users reported unauthorised transactions on their accounts. Upon investigation, the company discovered that their system had been compromised. They launched an investigation, which revealed that the breach was caused by an insider who had sold the company's data to cybercriminals.

The Cash App breach happened for several reasons. First, the company failed to properly vet its employees, including those who had access to sensitive data. The former employee who sold the data had a history of unethical behaviour, but the company failed to detect it during the hiring process. Second, the company had lax security measures in place. The former employee was able to access sensitive data without being detected and the company did not have proper monitoring tools in place to detect suspicious activity. Finally, the company did not have a proper incident response plan in place. When the breach was discovered, the company was slow to respond, which allowed the cybercriminals to carry out fraudulent activities for an extended period before the breach was contained.

The Cash App breach is a reminder that insider attacks can happen to any organisation, regardless of its size or industry. It is essential for organisations to take proactive steps to prevent insider attacks by properly vetting employees, implementing proper security measures, and having an incident response plan in place. By taking these steps, they can protect themselves and their customers better from the devastating consequences of insider attacks.

The impact of insider threats

The first thing we can learn from these cases is that threats posed by insiders are real. These cases all had significant impacts on the employees and organisations they worked for, were costly to deal with, ruined lives, and damaged company reputations, without the insider needing to invent some intricate hacking tactics to gain access. We have seen everything from loss of competitive market advantage, loss of trust from clients and customers, financial damage, compromised customer data, disclosure of intellectual property, regulatory fines, a fall in share prices to reputational damage – all as a result of an insider's legitimate access to internal systems. These are indeed some of the most challenging cybersecurity threats to detect and prevent. But by keeping the offender triangle in mind of opportunity, desire, and ability, we will argue that insider threats can be managed by (i) improving security as a whole to reduce opportunities for insider threat, and (ii) caring for employees' *psychological* needs and desires and desires.

As mentioned in the Intel, Pfizer, and Shopify breaches, implementing strong access controls and monitoring suspicious actions could have prevented the insiders from stealing data for a prolonged period of time. Security policies such as employee background checks must be thorough and technical monitoring of aberrant behaviour put in place.

Behavioural warning signs of insider risks include employee attempts to bypass security (both physical or digital), frequenting the office out of normal working hours, violation of corporate policies, employees discussing resigning or new employment opportunities, and personal grudges or displays of disgruntled behaviour towards co-workers or management. Evidence of malicious behaviour in the workplace can be a precursor, which includes false expense claims, aggressive behaviour, and any financial red flags identified in background checks.

Whistleblowers

Whereas insider threat attackers are typically terminated and fought in court, whistleblowers are insiders too, but without malicious intents. Insider threats refer to individuals within an organisation who pose a risk to its security, operations, or data. This could be due to malicious intent (like sabotaging or stealing information for personal gain), negligence (like mishandling data), or being manipulated by external entities. Insider threats are often covert and aim to harm the organisation from within. Whistleblowers on the other hand, are insiders who disclose information about illegal, unethical, or harmful activities within an organisation. Their intent is usually to expose wrongdoing and promote accountability for the greater good or to protect public interests.

Internal whistleblowing occurs when an employee reports the wrongdoing to their supervisor or another member of the company's management. External whistleblowing occurs when the whistleblower reports the wrongdoing to an outside organisation, such as a government agency or the media. Whistleblowers typically face significant personal and professional risks to reveal such information, and therewith also bear risks for the organisation they work for. They are sometimes protected by laws designed to shield them from retaliation. Thus, while insider threats aim to harm the organisation, whistleblowers seek to bring to light harmful practices within the organisation, often to enforce positive change. It is a matter of detrimental versus beneficial actions from within.

Whistleblowing can take many forms, including reporting fraud, corruption, discrimination, harassment, safety violations and environmental issues. In cybersecurity, it can involve reporting data breaches, security vulnerabilities, or other actions that could compromise the security of a company's systems or data. Whistleblowing is an essential component of cybersecurity, because it allows organisations to identify and address potential security threats before they become major issues. By reporting security vulnerabilities or breaches, whistleblowers can help prevent data loss, theft, or other types of cyberattacks, by making organisations aware of security issues before it is too late. In addition, whistleblowing can help organisations maintain their credibility by demonstrating their commitment to transparency and accountability.

There have been many high-profile cases of whistleblowing in cybersecurity in recent years. One notable example is Edward Snowden, a former National Security Agency (NSA) contractor who leaked classified information about the agency's surveillance activities. Snowden's actions raised important questions about the balance between privacy and national security, and sparked a global debate about government surveillance.

Another example of whistleblowing in cybersecurity is the case of Chelsea Manning, a former United States Army intelligence analyst who leaked classified information to WikiLeaks. Manning's actions led to her being charged with violating the Espionage Act and sentenced to 35 years in prison. However, her sentence was commuted by President Obama in 2017.

Whistleblowers in the United States are protected under various federal and state laws. The most well-known of these laws is the Whistleblower Protection Act, which protects federal employees who disclose information about fraud, waste, or abuse. Other federal laws, such as the Sarbanes-Oxley Act and the Dodd-Frank Wall Street Reform and Consumer Protection Act, provide additional protections for whistleblowers who report financial misconduct. In addition to federal laws, many states have their own whistleblower protection laws. These laws vary widely in terms of the protections they provide and the types of conduct they cover. Some states, such as California, have very strong whistleblower protection laws that cover a wide range of conduct, including violations of state and federal law.

Whistleblowing can raise a variety of ethical issues, including questions about loyalty, confidentiality, and the public interest. Some people argue that whistle-blowers have a moral duty to report illegal or unethical behaviour, regardless of the consequences. Others argue that whistleblowers are betraying their loyalty to their employer and violating the trust that is essential to the employment relationship.

There also is a debate about whether whistleblowers should be required to exhaust internal reporting channels before going public. Some argue that internal reporting is the best way to address wrongdoing, because it allows companies to address the issue without public scrutiny. Others argue that internal reporting channels are often ineffective or biased, and that whistleblowers should be allowed to go public if they believe it is necessary.

Whistleblowing can significantly affect organisations, both positively and negatively. On the positive side, whistleblowing can help organisations identify and address potential security threats, which can ultimately lead to improved cybersecurity and better protection for the company's systems and data. On the negative side, whistleblowing can damage an organisation's reputation, lead to legal liabilities, and create a culture of fear and mistrust among employees. In some cases, whistleblowers may face retaliation, such as termination or demotion, which can have a chilling effect on other employees who may consider reporting wrongdoing.

Organisations that receive whistleblowing complaints must take them seriously, and investigate them promptly and thoroughly. Failure to do so can lead to legal liabilities and damage the organisation's reputation. It is essential to have clear policies and procedures in place for handling whistleblowing complaints, including how to protect the whistleblower's identity and how to respond to retaliation. It is also important to communicate with employees about the organisation's commitment to transparency, accountability, and ethical behaviour. Employees should be encouraged to report any concerns they have about illegal or unethical behaviour, such as potential cyber threats, and they should feel confident that their concerns will be taken seriously and addressed appropriately.

Encouraging whistleblowing in the workplace can be challenging, but is relevant for maintaining the safety of organisational systems and data. It can indeed help identify cyber threats and strengthen the organisation's cybersecurity posture. Organisations should provide employees with clear channels for reporting concerns, and ensure that those channels are accessible, confidential, and free from retaliation.

Case study: Wikileaks and Chelsea Manning

Wikileaks was founded in 2006 by a group of hackers, journalists, and activists as an online platform that allowed whistleblowers to anonymously leak confidential information. Wikileaks became widely known in 2010 when they released a series of classified documents from the US government, including diplomatic cables, military reports, and videos. The release of these documents, which became known as Cablegate, sparked a global controversy, and put Wikileaks in the spotlight.

The release of sensitive information by Wikileaks has had a significant impact on cybersecurity. Governments and corporations around the world are now more aware of the potential for information leaks and are taking steps to protect their data. In response to the release of the diplomatic cables, the US government implemented new security measures to prevent similar leaks in the future.

However, the impact of Wikileaks on cybersecurity is not all positive. Some argue that the release of confidential information by Wikileaks could make it easier for hackers to access sensitive data. In addition, the release of confidential information could put individuals and organisations at risk, as their private information could be exposed [8].

Wikileaks has been embroiled in controversy since its inception. Many governments and organisations view Wikileaks as a threat to national security and have taken legal action to shut down the site. In addition, some argue that Wikileaks' actions are unethical, as the release of confidential information could put individuals at risk.

Wikileaks has also been accused of being biased in its releases. Some argue that Wikileaks has a political agenda and only releases information that supports its agenda. Others argue that Wikileaks is simply a neutral platform that allows whistleblowers to release information without fear of retaliation.

Wikileaks and its founder, Julian Assange, have faced numerous legal battles and arrests over the years. In 2010, Assange was arrested in the UK on charges of sexual assault. He fought extradition to Sweden, arguing that he would be extradited to the United States to face charges related to the release of classified information.

In 2019, Assange was arrested by UK authorities and charged with violating the Espionage Act of 1917. He was being held in a UK prison awaiting extradition to the United States for many years, but the case has since been settled.

In light of the impact of Wikileaks on cybersecurity, many organisations are taking steps to protect their data from leaks. One of the most effective measures is to implement strong encryption protocols. Encryption can help protect data from hackers and other malicious actors who may attempt to access confidential information. Organisations can implement access controls to limit who has access to confidential information. This can help prevent leaks from within the organisation. Data loss prevention tools can identify when data exfiltration is taking place.

The release of confidential information by Wikileaks raises numerous ethical questions. Some argue that the release of information can be justified if it exposes wrongdoing or corruption. Others argue that the release of confidential information is never justified and puts individuals at risk.

Wikileaks has had a significant impact on cybersecurity and has been at the centre of numerous controversies and legal battles. While the release of confidential information can be justified in some cases, it is important to consider the potential consequences and ethical implications. Organisations must take steps to protect their data from leaks, while also ensuring that whistleblowers have a safe and anonymous way to report wrongdoing.

To illustrate the controversial role of Wikileaks, let us consider the case of Chelsea Manning. She has been a polarising figure. Some see her as a hero who exposed government corruption and lies, while others see her as a traitor who endangered national security. However, regardless of one's opinion of Manning, it cannot be denied that her actions have had a profound impact on the world of cybersecurity and privacy [9].

Chelsea Manning was born Bradley Manning in Oklahoma in 1987. She enlisted in the US Army in 2007 and was trained as an intelligence analyst. Manning was deployed to Iraq in 2009, where she had access to classified information that would eventually lead to her arrest and imprisonment.

During her time in Iraq, Manning became disillusioned with the US military's actions and policies. She began to question the morality of the war and the government's justification for it. Manning's experiences in Iraq would ultimately lead her to become a whistleblower.

In 2010, Manning leaked classified documents to WikiLeaks. The documents included diplomatic cables, military logs, and videos that showed US military personnel killing civilians in Iraq. The release of this information caused an international uproar and led to Manning's arrest [10].

The leak was the largest in US military history and had far-reaching consequences. It led to the resignation of the US ambassador to Mexico and strained diplomatic relations between the United States and other countries. It also sparked debates about government transparency and the ethics of whistleblowing.

Manning was arrested in May 2010 and charged with 22 counts, including aiding the enemy and violating the Espionage Act. She was held in pretrial confinement for over three years, during which time she was subjected to harsh treatment, including solitary confinement, and forced nudity.

In 2013, Manning was convicted of 20 of the 22 charges against her and sentenced to 35 years in prison. Her sentence was commuted by President Barack Obama in 2017, and Manning was released from prison after serving seven years.

Manning's leak highlighted the vulnerabilities in government and corporate cybersecurity. It showed that even the most sensitive information is not always secure and can be accessed by insiders with the right clearance. The leak also underscored the need for better protection of whistleblowers and their rights.

Manning's case brought attention to the issue of government surveillance and the erosion of privacy rights in the digital age. It raised questions about the balance between national security and individual rights and freedoms.

Since her release, Manning has been a vocal advocate for government transparency, LGBTQ rights, and other progressive causes. She has spoken at conferences and rallies and has written op-eds for major publications.

Manning has also been involved in legal battles to protect the rights of whistleblowers and to challenge government surveillance programmes. Her activism has made her a target of government scrutiny and has landed her back in court on several occasions.

Manning's leak and subsequent imprisonment have been the subject of much controversy. Some see her as a hero who exposed government corruption and lies, while others see her as a traitor who endangered national security.

The leak has been criticised for putting US military personnel and foreign allies at risk and for damaging America's reputation abroad. Manning's treatment in prison has also been a source of controversy, with many human rights organisations condemning the harsh conditions she was subjected to.

Manning's release from prison in 2017 did not mark the end of her legal battles. She has continued to fight for her rights as a whistleblower and has been involved in several court cases related to government surveillance and the rights of transgender individuals.

In 2019, Manning was jailed for refusing to testify before a grand jury investigating WikiLeaks. She was released after 62 days when the grand jury's term expired. Manning has since been fined for her refusal to testify and has been threatened with further imprisonment.

Manning's treatment in prison and her subsequent legal battles have also brought attention to the need for better protection of whistleblowers and their rights. Her legacy will continue to shape the conversation around government transparency and the role of whistleblowers in holding those in power accountable.

Chelsea Manning's story is one of courage, controversy, and activism. Her leak of classified information to WikiLeaks has had a profound impact on the world of cybersecurity and privacy, and her subsequent legal battles have brought attention to the need for better protection of whistleblowers.

While opinions about Manning's actions may be divided, one thing is clear: her legacy will continue to shape the conversation around government transparency and the rights of individuals to speak out against corruption and injustice. This also has implications for those working in cybersecurity as we must encourage them to speak out against companies and executives that wilfully flout regulations or put sensitive information at risk.

Case study: Edward Snowden

Edward Snowden is one of the most controversial figures in modern history. He is a former NSA contractor who leaked classified information about the US government's surveillance programmes. Snowden's revelations have sparked a global debate about privacy, security, and government transparency. We will briefly explore the life of Edward Snowden, his motivations for disclosing classified information, and the impact of his actions on government surveillance and privacy.

Edward Joseph Snowden was born on 21 June 1983, in Elizabeth City, North Carolina. He grew up in a family of government employees and moved around frequently. He attended high school in Maryland and later went to Anne Arundel Community College. However, he did not complete his studies and instead joined the US Army in 2004. Snowden was eventually discharged from the army after breaking both of his legs in a training accident.

After leaving the army, Snowden began working for the CIA as a computer security specialist. He later moved to the NSA, where he worked as a contractor for several years. During his time at the NSA, Snowden became increasingly disillusioned with the government's surveillance programmes. He was disturbed by the scope of the NSA's data collection and the lack of oversight and accountability.

In 2013, Snowden began leaking classified information about the NSA's surveillance programmes to journalists. He revealed that the NSA was collecting vast amounts of data on American citizens, including phone records, internet activity, and e-mails. Snowden's disclosures also revealed that the NSA was conducting surveillance on foreign leaders, including allies like Germany and France.

Snowden's leaks caused a global uproar and triggered a debate about government surveillance and privacy. Many people criticised the government for its overreach and lack of transparency. Some argued that Snowden was a hero for exposing government abuses, while others saw him as a traitor who endangered national security.

The impact of Snowden's disclosures has been significant. His leaks led to reforms in the US government's surveillance programmes, including the end of the bulk collection of phone records. The disclosures also led to a renewed focus on privacy and cybersecurity. Many people became more aware of the risks of online surveillance and began taking steps to protect their digital privacy [11].

After leaking classified information, Snowden fled to Hong Kong and then to Moscow, where he was granted asylum. The US government charged him with espionage and theft of government property. Snowden has remained in Russia ever since, and his asylum status has been extended several times.

Snowden's actions have been controversial, and he has received criticism from many quarters. Some argue that his leaks endangered national security and put lives at risk. Others have criticised him for seeking asylum in Russia, a country with a poor record on human rights and free speech.

The Snowden effect has been significant. His disclosures have led to a surge in interest in privacy and cybersecurity. This has led to the development of new technologies and tools for securing online communications, but also a new pervasive form of economic exploitation with big technology companies like Google and Meta, termed "surveillance capitalism", that is difficult to counter [12].

Edward Snowden's disclosures have had a profound impact on government surveillance and privacy. As we move forward, it is essential to strike a balance between security and privacy and to ensure that government surveillance is transparent, accountable, and subject to oversight.

His leaks have led to a more informed public debate about the balance between security and privacy.

It brought attention to government surveillance and sparked a global conversation about privacy rights. It also led to changes in government policies, such as the USA Freedom Act, which placed limits on the government's ability to collect phone metadata.

Furthermore, the Snowden effect raised awareness about the importance of whistleblowers in holding the government accountable. It also highlighted the need for increased transparency and oversight of government agencies.

The Snowden effect would not have been possible without the role of the media. The leaked documents were first published by *The Guardian* and *The Washington Post*, which brought attention to the government's surveillance programmes and sparked a global conversation about privacy rights.

They played a critical role in shaping public opinion and bringing attention to government surveillance.

Whistleblowing plays an essential role in holding the government accountable and exposing wrongdoing. However, it is also a risky endeavour that can lead to severe consequences for the whistleblower.

The Snowden effect had a global impact, sparking conversations about government surveillance and privacy rights around the world. It also led to changes in government policies, such as the EU's General Data Protection Regulation, which placed stricter rules on data protection.

The Snowden effect also led to increased scrutiny of government agencies and their surveillance programmes around the world. It highlighted the importance of privacy rights and the need for increased transparency and oversight of government agencies.

As we move forward, it is essential to continue the conversation about the Snowden effect and its impact on society. We must continue to advocate for privacy rights, increased transparency, and protections for whistleblowers. The legacy of the Snowden effect will continue to shape our understanding of government surveillance, the balance we want to strike between privacy and security, and the role of whistleblowers in society.

Third party and supply chain risks

The supply chain is one of the most critical aspects of your operation [13]. The supply chain is the backbone of any organisation, and it is essential to manage and mitigate supply chain risks to ensure that your organisation runs smoothly. Supply chain risk encompasses the risks associated with the organisation's entire value chain.

The supply chain is a complex network that involves many different parties, and any disruption to the chain can have severe consequences. For instance, a natural disaster such as a hurricane or earthquake can disrupt the supply chain by causing delays in the transportation of goods, destruction of infrastructure, among other things. The COVID-19 pandemic is another example of how supply chain disruptions can impact organisations worldwide.

As the world becomes more connected, organisations are increasingly relying on vendors to provide services and products they need. *First party* refers to your organisation and information systems. If one of your employees can merge code, make a configuration change, spin up or wind down a service directly, then this is a first-party asset. However, these assets often contain third-party code and assets themselves [14].

Second party refers to your customers and their information systems. They compensate you, with money or data in exchange for a product or service.

Third party refers to people, organisations, and information systems with whom you have a direct relationship and on whom the confidentiality, integrity, or availability of your data relies but are not your employees or customers. Examples include contract developers, open source developers, and other software vendors.

Fourth parties are the same as third parties, except you do not have a direct relationship with them. For example, if you use Slack but have no direct relationship with Amazon Web Services (AWS), then AWS is the fourth party. That is because Slack runs on AWS. Some customers only learned about this when the former suffered downtime due to an outage with the latter.

From this point on we will refer to all relationships beyond third parties as having nth party relationships. An nth party relationship refers to the dependencies that exist beyond the third party in an organisation relationship. It explains the relationships between a company and its vendors, the vendors of those vendors, etc. For example, if Business X uses Vendor Y for IT services, and Vendor Y uses Vendor Z for cloud hosting, then Vendor Z is an nth party to Business X. Open source projects can represent an nth party, when your vendor uses the relevant library in their app. OpenAI customers learned about this the hard way in early 2023 [15].

Third-party risks include risks created by entities that an organisation is not directly purchasing from or selling to. Third-party risks come from actors that may have a direct or indirect influence on your organisation's IT environment. Managing such risks involves the assessment of a third party's cybersecurity practices and vulnerabilities to create and implement effective security strategies. Examples include government agencies, a service provider's connections, apps downloaded by employees, open source software and Freemium-as-a-Service.

We can see how third-party vendors can be a great way to save money and streamline operations, but it also comes with risks. One of the biggest risks is the possibility of a third-party vendor attack. Supply chain risk is distinctly separate from third-party risk, as it includes entities involved in the production and distribution of goods and services at any given level. It includes any nth party relationship. Such supply chain risks can lead to a variety of cybersecurity issues, like breaches, data leaks, or cyberattacks, via weaknesses or compromises in the products, software, or services provided by your suppliers and partners. Examples include customers, contractors, manufacturers, HR service providers, distributors, and vendors.

There are several techniques, tools, and technologies available to help organisations manage risk in the supply chain.

Vendor risk management (VRM) is targeted at specific third parties who vend things to you (the first party). Your organisation compensates them for doing something or giving you something. If you pay a partner organisation a commission on joint sales efforts, then they are your vendor. If the relationship is reversed, then they are likely your customer.

Third-party risk management (TPRM) is more nuanced. All vendors are third parties, but third parties can include many organisations and assets that are not vendors. For third parties who are not vendors, for example, open source developers, you rely on them, but do not have as much leverage over them. Much of your risk management efforts must rely on some combination of asking nicely, threatening to shame them, or offering to pay them (and making them a vendor).

Supply chain risk management (SCRM) is the most expansive discipline of all of these, beyond TPRM and VRM. This includes managing the risk not just from third parties but also from second and nth relationships. A customer, especially one of a software product, could accidentally or intentionally do something that allows a malicious actor to impact your data. For example, a customer might click on a phishing e-mail that allows cybercriminals to gain an entry point to your network. Or a malicious insider at a customer may intentionally use your software to conduct a denial of service attack impacting your organisation.

Let us initially consider VRM which helps in mitigating the risks associated with third-party vendors. VRM is critical for ensuring the security and resilience of an organisation's IT infrastructure [16]. The risks associated with vendors can range from data breaches to organisation disruptions and can have significant financial and reputational consequences.

One of the biggest challenges with VRM is that organisations often have a large number of vendors, and it can be difficult to keep track of all of them. In addition, many vendors have access to sensitive data or critical systems, which makes them a prime target for cybercriminals. Therefore, it is essential to have a robust VRM programme that includes regular assessments and monitoring of vendor activities.

In 2019, a major retailer experienced a cybersecurity incident that was caused by a third-party vendor. The vendor had access to the retailer's payment processing system and was responsible for managing the network that processed credit card transactions. The vendor's system was compromised by cybercriminals, who were able to steal the credit card information of millions of customers.

The impact of the incident was significant. The retailer faced regulatory fines, lawsuits, and a loss of customer trust. The cost of the incident was estimated to be in the hundreds of millions of dollars. The incident also highlighted the importance of VRM and the need for organisations to have a comprehensive programme in place.

The aftermath of the incident was a wake-up call for the retailer and other organisations that rely on third-party vendors. The retailer was forced to invest significant resources in mitigating the incident and rebuilding customer trust. This included hiring cybersecurity experts to investigate the incident, implementing new security controls, and offering free credit monitoring to affected customers.

The costs of the incident were significant and included regulatory fines, legal fees, and lost revenue due to a decline in customer confidence. The incident also had a lasting impact on the retailer's reputation, which can be difficult to quantify, but has long-term implications.

Preventing cybersecurity incidents caused by third-party vendors requires a comprehensive approach. Conduct due diligence during the vendor selection process to ensure that vendors have adequate security measures in place. Regularly assess vendor security controls to ensure that they are effective and up to date. Implement access controls to limit the amount of data and systems that vendors can access. Monitor vendor activities for signs of suspicious behaviour. Have an incident response plan in place that includes procedures for responding to vendor-related incidents.

Effective VRM requires a combination of policies, procedures, and tools. Establish a VRM programme that includes policies and procedures for vendor selection, assessment, and monitoring. Conduct regular risk assessments of vendors to identify potential risks and vulnerabilities. Communicate with vendors about security expectations and requirements. Implement security controls that are commensurate with the level of risk posed by vendors. Regularly monitor vendor activities for signs of suspicious behaviour.

There are many tools available to support VRM, including vendor risk assessment, monitoring, and scoring tools. These tools can help organisations streamline the VRM process and identify potential risks more efficiently. Vendor risk assessment software automates the process of assessing vendor security controls. Vendor monitoring tools track vendor activities and alert organisations to potential risks. Vendor scoring tools assign a risk score to each vendor based on their security posture.

Cybersecurity insurance can play an essential role in managing vendor risk. Cyber insurance policies can provide coverage for losses associated with cybersecurity incidents, including those caused by third-party vendors. However, it is important to note that cyber insurance policies vary widely in terms of coverage and exclusions. Therefore, it is essential to carefully review policies and understand what is covered and what is not.

Next, let us consider third-party risk management. This is crucial, as third-party vulnerabilities can have a devastating impact. Third-party vulnerabilities refer to vulnerabilities that exist in software or hardware components that are provided by a third-party vendor. These vulnerabilities can be exploited by attackers to gain unauthorised access to an organisation's systems and data. Third-party software and hardware components are often used in critical systems, such as payment processing and customer data management.

Third-party vulnerabilities can take many forms.

Unpatched vulnerabilities are vulnerabilities that have been discovered but not yet fixed by the third-party vendor. These vulnerabilities are often exploited by attackers to gain unauthorised access to the system.

Misconfigured components are components that have been configured incorrectly, leaving them open to exploitation by attackers. Misconfigured components are often the result of human error or lack of knowledge about how to properly configure the components.

Malicious components are components that have been intentionally designed to exploit vulnerabilities in the system. These components can be difficult to detect and can cause significant damage to an organisation's systems and data.

Third-party vulnerabilities can have significant impacts on organisations. Data breaches can occur when attackers exploit third-party vulnerabilities to gain access to sensitive data. Data breaches can lead to significant financial and reputational damage to an organisation. System compromise can take place when attackers exploit third-party vulnerabilities to gain access to an organisation's systems. This can lead to data theft, system downtime, and other significant impacts. Compliance issues are formed when an organisation is found to be in violation of regulatory requirements due to third-party vulnerabilities. This can lead to fines and other legal consequences.

There are several steps that organisations can take to mitigate third-party vulnerabilities. Regular vulnerability assessments can help to identify vulnerabilities in third-party components. These assessments should be conducted by a qualified cybersecurity professional. Ensure third-party components are patched and configured correctly. Organisations should ensure these are patched and configured correctly to prevent vulnerabilities from being exploited. A vulnerability management programme can help organisations to identify and manage third-party vulnerabilities. This programme should include regular assessments, patch management, and configuration management.

Organisations should follow best practices when managing third-party vulnerabilities. Organisations should maintain a comprehensive inventory of all third-party components used in their systems. This inventory should include information about the components and their potential vulnerabilities. Organisations should develop a vendor management programme to ensure that third-party vendors are properly vetted and monitored for security vulnerabilities. Organisations should conduct regular vulnerability assessments of third-party components to identify and mitigate potential vulnerabilities.

There are many tools available to help organisations manage third-party vulnerabilities. Vulnerability scanners can help organisations to identify vulnerabilities in third-party components. These scanners can be used to scan both internal and external systems. Configuration management tools can help organisations to ensure that third-party components are configured correctly and are not vulnerable to exploitation. Patch management tools can help organisations to ensure that third-party components are patched in a timely manner to prevent vulnerabilities from being exploited.

Regular third-party vulnerability assessments are critical to maintaining the security of an organisation's systems and data. These assessments can help to identify vulnerabilities before they can be exploited by attackers, reducing the risk of data breaches and other security incidents.

Collaboration with third-party providers is critical to preventing vulnerabilities. Organisations should work with their third-party providers to ensure that their products and services are secure and free from vulnerabilities.

This brings us to SCRM, the most expansive discipline. SCRM helps organisations to identify potential risks and develop strategies to mitigate them. By doing so, organisations can reduce the impact of risks and ensure that their supply chain remains operational even in the face of adversity.

Umoga and colleagues (2024) argue that the two most impactful security risks facing financial firms are supply chain attacks and artificial intelligence (AI)-driven cyber-attacks [17]. The supply chain is the network of companies, individuals, and activities involved in the creation and delivery of a product or service. SCRM involves identifying, assessing, and mitigating risks that could affect your supply chain.

Xu and colleagues (2024) contend that in typical supply chains, improvements in risk management depend on the degree of system interconnection and proportion of information shared. In large-scale supply chains where there is system independence, firms with high information-exchanging demand in the supply chain are more motivated to mutually make improvements and invest in cybersecurity [18].

There are several types of supply chain risks. Natural disasters such as hurricanes, earthquakes, floods, and wildfires can disrupt the supply chain by causing delays in the transportation of goods, destruction of infrastructure, among other things. Geopolitical risks such as trade wars, terrorism, and political instability can affect the supply chain by disrupting trade routes, causing delays in the delivery of goods, among other things. Economic risks such as recessions, inflation, and currency fluctuations can impact the supply chain by affecting demand and supply, causing price fluctuations, among other things. Cybersecurity risks such as data breaches, malware attacks, and phishing can disrupt the supply chain by compromising critical systems, stealing sensitive data, among other things.

The impact of cybersecurity risks on supply chain management can be severe. Cyber-attacks can cause delays in the delivery of goods, compromise critical systems, and steal sensitive data. These disruptions can have significant financial and reputational repercussions for organisations.

For instance, a cyber-attack that compromises a company's financial data could result in significant financial losses, legal and regulatory fines, and loss of customer trust. A cyber-attack that compromises a company's critical systems could result in prolonged downtime, which could affect the delivery of goods and services.

We must implement best practices in SCRM. We can do this by conducting risk assessments to identify potential risks and their potential impact on your supply chain. Develop a risk management plan that outlines strategies to mitigate potential risks. Establish clear communication channels with all parties involved in the supply chain to ensure that everyone is aware of potential risks and how to address them. Regularly review and update your risk management plan to ensure that it remains effective and relevant.

SCRM software helps organisations to identify potential risks, assess their impact, and develop strategies to mitigate them. The global positioning system tracking helps organisations to track the movement of goods and services in real time, which is essential for identifying potential risks and addressing them promptly. Blockchain technology provides a secure and transparent way to track the movement of goods and services, which is essential for supply chain management.

SCRM will become a key area of focus, with new technologies and strategies emerging to help organisations manage potential risks. For instance, AI applications can help organisations to identify potential risks and develop strategies to mitigate them. Blockchain technology is also expected to play a significant role in supply chain management by providing a secure and transparent way to track the movement of goods and services.

The human or behavioural aspects of cybersecurity risk are crucial but behavioural risks have attracted less attention due to a perceived bias towards technical (data, application, and network) risks. Hence, it is important when assessing supply chain risk to look at human behaviour, as it is vital to collaborate with your supply chain partners to raise risk awareness, standardise policies, strategies to encourage collaboration, and foster greater supply chain cyber-resilience [18].

We emphasise the importance of having a robust incident response plan in place. With the increasing number of data breaches and cyber-attacks, it has become essential for organisations to prepare for security incidents. Chief information security officers (CISOs) must consider incident response and cybersecurity, including the types of incidents and data breaches that can occur, cybersecurity threats and attack vectors and incident response planning. CISOs are responsible for ensuring that the incident response process is effective, that incident response team roles and responsibilities are clear and best practices for incident response and cybersecurity are being followed in reality. CISOs should also consider how to drive continuous improvement through more effective incident response tools and technologies, incident response and cybersecurity training, and cybersecurity services and solutions.

We have seen various types of cyber-attacks in real life and a supply chain attack is very dangerous. A supply chain attack in cybersecurity targets the weakest link in the supply chain to gain unauthorised access to the ultimate target. CISOs must address the likelihood of a supply chain attack and its impact. This is a strategic attack that aims to exploit the trust between the target and the third-party vendor. Cybercriminals can use various techniques to launch a supply chain attack, such as malware injection, man-in-the-middle attacks, and social engineering.

The goal of a supply chain attack is to gain access to sensitive data, steal intellectual property, or disrupt operations. This type of attack is very dangerous, because it can affect many organisations at once, and it can be challenging to detect and mitigate.

The impact of a supply chain attack can be severe and far-reaching. A successful supply chain attack can compromise the integrity of the entire supply chain, leading to data breaches, financial losses, and reputational damage. The impact can be even more significant if the ultimate target is a critical infrastructure, such as a power grid or a hospital.

The impact of a supply chain attack can also be long-lasting. It can take months or even years to detect and remediate a supply chain attack, and the costs can be astronomical. The average cost of a data breach in the United States is $8.64 million, and the cost of a supply chain attack can be even higher, as it typically affects a whole ecosystem.

Supply chain attacks are a growing concern for organisations and individuals alike. These attacks occur when a cybercriminal infiltrates a third-party vendor or supplier to access their clients' data or systems. We describe several real-life examples of supply chain attacks and the lessons we can learn from them.

Case study 1: The 2020 SolarWinds supply chain attack

One of the most impactful cyber-attacks in recent years was the 2020 SolarWinds case, a prime example of a supply chain attack. This attack targeted SolarWinds, a software company that provides IT management solutions. The attackers were able to compromise SolarWinds' software development process and insert malicious code into one of its products. This code was then distributed to SolarWinds' customers, including several US government agencies.

The SolarWinds attack highlights the importance of operational resilience in cybersecurity, which we will get back to in *Chapter 7: Operational resilience relies on adequate cybersecurity*. The attack was able to bypass many traditional cybersecurity measures that were in place, such as firewalls and antivirus software. However, the attack eventually was detected and contained, thanks in large part to SolarWinds' strong operational resilience. They responded quickly to the attack, taking its systems offline and working to remove the malicious code from its products. The company also worked closely with its customers to ensure that they were aware of the attack and had the necessary information to protect themselves. SolarWinds' strong operational resilience helped to minimise the impact of the attack and ensure that the company was able to continue operating.

We can learn several lessons from the SolarWinds attack. First, it underscores the importance of supply chain security. Companies need to be aware of the potential risks associated with their supply chain and take steps to mitigate these risks. This may include performing regular security assessments of suppliers and implementing strict security requirements for them. Second, the SolarWinds attack demonstrates the importance of having a strong incident response plan in place. An incident response plan should outline the steps that an organisation will take in the event of a cyber-attack, including how it will detect and contain the attack, as well as how it will communicate with its customers and other stakeholders. Finally, the SolarWinds attack underscores the importance of ongoing monitoring and testing of cybersecurity measures. Companies need to regularly assess their cybersecurity posture and test their systems to ensure that they are effective in detecting and responding to cyber-attacks.

Case study 2: The CCleaner breach

In 2017, CCleaner, a popular system optimisation tool, was breached by cybercriminals. The attackers inserted malicious code into CCleaner's software updates, which were then downloaded by over 2.27 million users. The malware allowed the attackers to gain control over the affected systems, steal data, and install additional malware.

The CCleaner breach was a supply chain attack, as the attackers targeted a trusted software vendor to gain access to its clients' systems. This breach highlights the importance of vetting third-party vendors and ensuring they have proper security measures in place. It also underscores the need for organisations to have robust incident response plans in place to quickly detect and mitigate attacks.

Case study 3: The Codecov breach

In April 2021, Codecov, a software auditing tool, was breached in a supply chain attack. The attackers gained access to Codecov's Bash Uploader script, which is used to upload code coverage reports to Codecov's servers. The script was modified to include a backdoor that allowed the attackers to access the systems of Codecov's clients and steal sensitive data.

The Codecov breach illustrates the importance of regularly reviewing and updating security protocols and thoroughly vetting third-party vendors. It also underscores the need for supply chain security to be a top priority for organisations of all sizes.

Case study 4: Volkswagen

In 2021, Volkswagen experienced a third-party vendor attack that exposed the personal data of over 3.3 million customers and prospective customers. The attack was carried out by an unauthorised third party who gained access to a vendor's system that Volkswagen was using for sales and marketing purposes. The data that was exposed included names, e-mail addresses, and phone numbers. Volkswagen immediately launched an investigation and informed affected customers of the attack.

The Volkswagen third-party vendor attack took place in March 2021, compromised the personal data of over 3.3 million Volkswagen customers in North America. The attack highlighted the importance of securing third-party vendor relationships and the potential consequences of failing to do so. We can dive into the Volkswagen third-party vendor attack, its consequences, Volkswagen's response, lessons learned, and future implications.

The Volkswagen attack was a result of a breach in one of its vendor's systems. The vendor, used by Volkswagen for data processing and storage, was compromised by attackers who gained access to the vendor's system using stolen login credentials. The attackers then exploited a vulnerability in the vendor's system to gain access to personal data of Volkswagen customers.

The attackers were able to access sensitive information, including driver's license numbers, social security numbers, and contact information. Volkswagen discovered the attack in March 2021 and immediately launched an investigation. The investigation found that the attackers had access to the vendor's system for over two years, from August 2019 to May 2021.

The Volkswagen third-party vendor attack had severe consequences for the company and its customers. The attack compromised the personal data of over 3.3 million customers in North America, including sensitive information such as social security numbers and driver's license numbers. The attack could lead to identity theft and financial fraud for affected customers.

The attack also damaged Volkswagen's reputation and eroded customer trust. Customers expect companies to keep their personal information safe, and the Volkswagen attack shows that the company failed to do so. The attack could lead to customer attrition and loss of revenue for the company.

Volkswagen's response to the attack involved notifying affected customers and offering them free credit monitoring and identity theft protection services. The company also launched an investigation into the attack and terminated its contract with the vendor responsible for the breach. Volkswagen also implemented additional security measures, including multi-factor authentication and increased monitoring of third-party vendor relationships.

Volkswagen's response to the attack was swift and comprehensive. The company took responsibility for the breach and took steps to mitigate the damage and prevent future attacks. However, the attack highlights the importance of proactive measures to prevent such attacks in the first place.

The Volkswagen third-party vendor attack provides several lessons for companies that rely on third-party vendors for data processing and storage. First, companies need to thoroughly vet and monitor their third-party vendors and ensure that they have adequate security measures in place. Second, companies need to implement multi-factor authentication and other security measures to protect against unauthorised access to sensitive data.

Third, companies need to have a plan in place to respond to security incidents promptly. A response plan should include steps to mitigate the damage, notify affected customers, and prevent future attacks. Fourth, companies need to provide regular security training to their employees and third-party vendors to ensure that they are aware of security risks and how to prevent them.

The Volkswagen third-party vendor attack highlights the risks associated with third-party vendor relationships and the potential consequences of failing to secure them adequately. The attack could lead to increased regulatory scrutiny of data privacy and security practices, and companies may face increased liability for breaches involving third-party vendors.

The attack also underscores the need for companies to take a proactive approach to cybersecurity and implement security measures to protect against third-party vendor attacks. Companies that fail to do so may face reputational damage, customer attrition, and financial losses.

The Volkswagen third-party vendor attack provides a cautionary tale for companies that rely on third-party vendors for data processing and storage. Companies need to take a proactive approach to cybersecurity and implement security measures to protect against unauthorised access to sensitive data. They also need to monitor their third-party vendors and establish clear security policies and procedures to prevent security incidents. The consequences of failing to do so can be severe.

Case study 5: PayPal

Another example of a third-party vendor attack occurred in 2017 when the popular payment processor, PayPal, suffered a breach that affected its subsidiary, TIO Networks. TIO Networks was a third-party vendor that PayPal had acquired, and it provided bill payment services for customers. The breach resulted in the exposure of the personal and financial information of 1.6 million TIO Networks customers.

The attack was carried out by a third party who was able to exploit a vulnerability in the TIO Networks payment platform. PayPal immediately took action to shut down the TIO Networks platform and notify affected customers. They also conducted a thorough investigation to determine the source of the attack and implemented additional security measures to prevent future attacks.

One of the lessons we can learn from this attack is the importance of regularly monitoring and testing third-party vendor systems. This includes conducting regular vulnerability scans and penetration testing to identify any weaknesses that could be exploited by attackers. It is also essential to have a process in place for addressing any vulnerabilities that are identified.

Lessons learned must be identified and documented. One of the lessons we can learn from these attacks is the importance of vetting third-party vendors thoroughly. It is essential to carefully evaluate vendors before granting them access to your systems and data. This includes conducting background checks, verifying their security practices, and ensuring that they have appropriate measures in place to protect your data.

Another lesson we can learn is the importance of having a robust incident response plan in place. In the case of Volkswagen, they were able to quickly identify and contain the attack, minimising the damage. This underscores the importance of having a clear plan in place for responding to security incidents, including identifying the source of the attack, containing it, and notifying affected parties.

Case study 6: Target

In 2013, Target experienced a massive data breach that affected over 40 million customers. The attack was carried out by a third party who gained access to Target's payment processing system through a vulnerability in its HVAC vendor's system. The attacker was able to install malware on Target's payment processing system, which allowed them to steal credit and debit card information.

The Target breach highlights the importance of ensuring that third-party vendors are following best practices for cybersecurity. In this case, the HVAC vendor had not implemented proper security measures, which allowed the attacker to gain access to Target's systems. This underscores the importance of evaluating vendors' security practices and ensuring that they are following best practices for cybersecurity.

Case Study 7: The Yahoo data breach

In 2013, Yahoo experienced a data breach that affected all three billion of its user accounts. The breach included names, email addresses, telephone numbers, birth dates, hashed passwords, and security questions and answers. The breach was not discovered until 2016, and Yahoo did not disclose the breach until September 2016.

The Yahoo data breach had a significant impact on relationships. Customers felt violated and betrayed, and many chose to close their accounts and take their business elsewhere. Yahoo faced legal action and was required to pay a $35 million fine for failing to disclose the breach in a timely manner.

Case Study 8: The Uber data breach

In 2016, Uber experienced a data breach that affected 57 million of its users and drivers. The breach included names, email addresses, and phone numbers. Uber paid the hackers $100,000 to delete the stolen data and keep the breach quiet. The breach was not disclosed until November 2017, over a year after it occurred.

The Uber data breach damaged trust. Customers and drivers felt violated and betrayed, and many chose to take legal action against the company. Uber faced significant fines and legal action for failing to disclose the breach in a timely manner.

Case Study 9: The Anthem data breach

In 2015, Anthem experienced a data breach that affected 78.8 million of its customers and employees. The breach included names, dates of birth, Social Security numbers, medical identification numbers, and other sensitive information. The breach was not discovered until January 2015, and Anthem did not disclose the breach until February 2015.

The Anthem data breach had a huge impact. Customers and employees felt violated and betrayed, and many chose to take legal action against the company. Anthem faced significant fines and legal action for failing to protect its customers' information.

Lessons learned

These supply chain attacks demonstrate the need for organisations to take a proactive approach to cybersecurity. It is essential to have a comprehensive security strategy that includes regular risk assessments, vulnerability scans, and incident response plans. Organisations should also have a system in place for vetting and monitoring third-party vendors and suppliers. Because indeed, supply chain attacks are a growing threat in our digital world. The CCleaner breach, the SolarWinds hack, and the Codecov breach are just a few examples of the devastating consequences of these attacks. To protect themselves from these risks, organisations must have a comprehensive approach to cybersecurity that includes regular risk assessments, vulnerability scans, and incident response plans. They must also prioritise supply chain security and work together to share information about potential threats. Companies should also establish clear security policies and procedures for their third-party vendors, including requirements for security audits and vulnerability assessments. Regular security training for employees and third-party vendors is also essential to prevent security incidents.

Another key takeaway from these attacks is the importance of threat intelligence and sharing information about potential threats across the industry. By working together to identify and mitigate potential risks, organisations can help prevent future supply chain attacks.

Impact of cyber-attacks on trust

More so than financial and material impacts, these case studies also illustrate the serious consequences of cyber-attacks on trust. They provide valuable lessons for organisations on how to minimise loss of trust and rebuild it, the most important one being the importance of timely and transparent communication. Organisations must notify their customers and clients as soon as possible after a cyber-attack occurs. They must also be transparent about what information was stolen and what steps they are taking to prevent future attacks.

Another lesson is the importance of investing in cybersecurity measures. Organisations should have robust security protocols in place to protect their customers' information. They should also conduct regular security audits to identify vulnerabilities and address them before they can be exploited.

Rebuilding trust after a cyber-attack can be a costly and time-consuming process. Organisations may need to implement new security measures, provide credit monitoring and other services to affected customers, and invest in marketing and public relations efforts to repair their reputation.

The cost of rebuilding trust can be significant. Organisations may lose revenue as customers take their organisation elsewhere. They may also face legal action and fines for failing to protect their customers' information.

There are several steps organisations can take to prevent cyber-attacks and maintain trust with their customers and clients. The first step is to invest in robust cybersecurity measures. This includes firewalls, encryption, and regular security audits.

Organisations should also have a plan in place in case of a cyber-attack. This plan should include steps for notifying customers and clients, providing credit monitoring and other services, and addressing any vulnerabilities that led to the attack.

Transparency is also important. Organisations should be transparent about their security measures and how they are protecting their customers' information. They should also be transparent about any past security incidents and what steps they have taken to prevent future incidents.

Transparency is crucial in rebuilding trust after a cyber-attack. Customers and clients want to know what steps an organisation is taking to prevent future attacks and how their information is being protected. Organisations should be transparent about their security measures and any vulnerabilities that led to the attack. They should also be transparent about what steps they are taking to prevent future incidents.

Transparency can also help organisations repair their reputation after a cyber-attack. By being open and honest about the incident and what they are doing to prevent future incidents, organisations can demonstrate their commitment to their customers' security and rebuild trust.

Trust is crucial in organisations and cannot be stressed enough, especially in the digital age where cybersecurity incidents can have a significant impact on these relationships. Organisations must invest in robust cybersecurity measures, have a plan in place in case of a cyber-attack, and be transparent about their security measures and any past security incidents. By doing so, they can maintain trust with their customers and clients and minimise the impact of any future cybersecurity incidents.

Now we have a better understanding of how cybercriminals think and how various types of cyber-attacks can come about, we continue our journey to the people working on the defence line.

References

1 M. Maasberg, C. Van Slyke, S. Ellis, and N. Beebe, "The dark triad and insider threats in cyber security," *Communications of the ACM*, vol. 63, no. 12, pp. 64–80, 2020, doi: 10.1145/3408864.

2 https://www.ibm.com/reports/data-breach

3 https://www.crn.com/news/security/vade-secure-to-pay-proofpoint-14m-for-trade-secret-theft-jury

4 https://www.itpro.com/hardware/358548/intel-sues-former-engineer-for-stealing-trade-secrets-to-help-microsoft

5 https://www.cshub.com/attacks/articles/incident-of-the-week-shopify-internal-data-breach-exemplifies-insider-threat-trend

6 https://www.reuters.com/business/healthcare-pharmaceuticals/pfizer-sues-departing-employee-it-says-stole-covid-19-vaccine-secrets-2021-11-24/

7 https://www.cybertalk.org/2022/04/05/cash-app-breach-involves-informing-millions-about-ex-employees-actions/

8 https://www.britannica.com/topic/WikiLeaks

9 https://yalereview.org/article/whistleblower-traitor-soldier-queer

10 https://www.npr.org/2022/10/17/1129416671/chelsea-manning-wikileaks-memoir-readme

11 https://www.whistleblowers.org/news/the-case-of-edward-snowden/

12 S. Zuboff, *The Age of Surveillance Capitalism*. Profile Books, United Kingdom, 2019.

13 A. Ghadge, M. Weiß, N. D. Caldwell, and R. Wilding, "Managing cyber risk in supply chains: A review and research agenda," *Supply Chain Management*, vol. 25, no. 2, pp. 223–240, 2020, doi: 10.1108/SCM-10-2018-0357.

14 https://blog.stackaware.com/p/what-is-the-difference-between-supply

15 T. Singh, *Artificial Intelligence and Ethics: A Field Guide for Stakeholders*. CRC Press, United Kingdom, 2024.

16 T. Singh, *Digital Resilience, Cybersecurity and Supply Chains*, 1st ed. Routledge, 2025, United Kingdom, doi: 10.4324/9781003604969.

17 U. J. Umoga, E. O. Sodiya, O. O. Amoo, and A. Atadoga, et al., "A critical review of emerging cybersecurity threats in financial technologies," *International Journal of Science and Research Archive*, vol. 11, no. 1, pp. 1810–1817, 2024.

18 L. Xu, Y. Li, Y. Lin, C. Tang, and Q. Yao, "Supply chain cybersecurity investments with interdependent risks under different information exchange modes," *International Journal of Production Research*, vol. 62, no. 6, pp. 2034–2059, 2024, doi: 10.1080/00207543.2023.2206923.

Part 2

Inside the line of defence

5 Operational cybersecurity context

Without victims, we would not need cybersecurity. Yet, with cybersecurity, we may still have victims. There is a natural imbalance between the risk of a cyber-attack and the effort required to marginalise that risk. Current industry estimates of the number of cyber-attacks in the world on an average day range from 2000 up to hundreds of millions [1]. Even if our system captured 99% of all attacks, we still have at least 20 cyber-attacks that materialise somewhere every single day. Of course, we are making some assumptions here on temporal linearity and detection rates. The point is, cybersecurity can be an incredibly high-pressure, fast-paced, and critical environment to work in.

It should thus come as no surprise that balancing work and personal life can be particularly daunting in this industry. Cybersecurity is not for everyone and the stresses that come with the field can especially be conducive to cognitive biases. We, therefore, want to highlight the typical psychological powers at play, so you are aware of the pitfalls and reality of this noble profession.

We start in this chapter with the reasons people leave and stay in the field in this chapter. In *Chapter 6: Human fallacies and how to overcome them,* we describe what cognitive biases and psychological fallacies operational cybersecurity professionals should watch out for. *Chapter 7: Operational resilience relies on adequate cybersecurity* then talks about the importance of operational resilience and a practical framework to build it. *Chapter 8: Organisational psychology* highlights the role of organisational psychology in fostering cybersecurity culture, and in *Chapter 9: Improving organisational cybersecurity,* we describe the latest ideas and research on human-centred cybersecurity measures.

Pressures of the job

Akin to a medical emergency centre, operational cybersecurity requires constant vigilance, quick judgement and decision-making, and swiftly treating new incidents.

Emergency healthcare professionals are masters in triaging. They quickly assess the core symptoms of each incoming patient to determine who gets treated next. As a team, they form a medical diagnosis system on steroids. Since seconds could determine someone's life or death, they do not want to permit any mistake.

DOI: 10.4324/9781003610533-7

Whatever treatment is deemed necessary has to be available immediately and everyone needs to know their role in every type of procedure. Working in cybersecurity operations can feel just like this [2].

Not patients, but a constant supply of (potential) cyber-attacks is coming in. The stakes are high and the damage may already be done. Now you need to find the right remedies to relief your organisation from their impact and recover as efficiently as possible. You start performing diagnostic tests on your systems to understand what is happening. It is a race against the clock to identify the cause of the abnormal symptoms you are seeing in your network. When you find out an employee has downloaded ransomware through a phishing campaign, you activate the ransomware response plan. Your team isolates the affected user system and briefs the executive board on what happened so that they can decide on whether to pay the ransom, while other teams rush to ensure other organisation-critical systems are not affected. You feel responsible for preventing your organisation from going under, as ransomware attacks could pose major financial, operational, and reputational blows to your organisation – as well as cost you your job.

Situations like these can be especially exhausting and rob people from mental downtime. Various studies that surveyed information security professionals and analysts in security operations centres (SOCs) confirm the stresses and higher risk of burnout in this field [3,4,5]. Reasons include the high degree of complexity that cybersecurity professionals need to understand and grapple with.

No matter how sophisticated the security measures are, they can be easily compromised by human error or negligence [6]. Stress, burnout, and security fatigue continue to be key problems in the cybersecurity industry. Stress and burnout are major causes of short tenures in senior roles for security executives [7].

Modern IT infrastructures are incredibly complex, with numerous interconnected systems. Navigating these complexities requires deep technical knowledge and expertise. Moreover, the cybersecurity landscape is always changing. Professionals must constantly update their skills and knowledge to stay ahead of emerging threats and technologies – and be able to communicate about them effectively with non-technical stakeholders. A single miscommunication with relevant stakeholders can cost you their trust and support. The need to continuously learn can quickly become a burden.

Since cyber threats do not adhere to a 9-to-5 schedule, the need for 24/7 monitoring and responding to emergencies can lead to long working hours and feeling perpetually on-call. We personally know stories from senior cybersecurity leaders of large multinational organisations who have been called at any moment of a day, on weekends, while trying to catch up with a friend over lunch and having to postpone non-urgent meetings countless times. Combined with a deep sense of responsibility for any potential failure, this can pose a significant mental toll. Despite the efforts, cybersecurity work can also often go unnoticed until something goes wrong. This lack of recognition can be demotivating. As a consequence, we have seen a significant number of people leave the cybersecurity sector, particularly those in SOCs or leadership roles.

Cybersecurity needs diversity

Apart from the described stresses in this profession, another point for concern is the field's lack of diversity. As in other science, technology and engineering subjects, there is a disproportionally low number of women in cybersecurity worldwide [8,9]. This is a problem, because certain cybercrime may indeed be highly targeted at women, for example, sextortion, online stalking, romance scams, and (online) harassment. Moreover, organisations could simply not afford ignoring half the target population if they want to enhance their cybersecurity and reduce cybercrime.

We need to start by acknowledging the contributions that women can and have made in this field, notably to cryptography. For example, female intelligence helped to obtain critical information during military operations, with more than 17,000 women in the United States and UK deciphering secret messages sent by Nazis during the Second World War. Women were even referred to as "computers" during those times. They were essential in establishing the science of cryptography and doing the mathematical computations that helped the United States land people on the moon in the 1950s [8]. But the argument for more diversity extends well beyond gender.

Groupthink is a phenomenon where a group of people makes decisions that are not necessarily rational or optimal, but rather based on conformity and consensus. When people are part of a group, they often feel pressure to conform to the group's opinions and beliefs. This can lead to a situation where individuals don't express their own ideas or opinions, and instead go along with the group's decision. This can be a problem when it comes to cybersecurity, as a group's consensus could lead to poor decision-making that puts an organisation at risk.

For example, in a workplace setting, a group of employees might feel pressure to conform to their manager's decisions about cybersecurity, even if they don't agree with them. This can lead to a lack of critical thinking and analysis, which can ultimately result in a security breach. Groupthink can also occur in online communities, where group members can be influenced by the opinions of others without fully considering the potential consequences.

Groupthink can have a significant impact on cybersecurity. When individuals are part of a group that shares a common social identity, they may be more likely to overlook potential risks or vulnerabilities. This can lead to a false sense of security, where individuals feel that their group is invincible and that they don't need to take extra precautions to protect themselves. For example, a group of employees may feel that their organisation is safe from cyber threats because of their robust security measures, even though these measures may not be enough to protect against advanced threats.

Imagine having a team of cybersecurity analysts who all think the same way. They receive an alert of a potential hacking attempt on their systems. The very next thing they have to do is examine whether it is indeed a threat. All of them have the same hypotheses, all of them conduct the same diagnostic tests. All of them think it is a false alarm and tell you there is nothing to worry about there. Now imagine having a diverse team of analysts that each bring their unique viewpoints and experiences. The same alert comes in. Each of the analysts approaches their attack analysis differently. Each test out different possible scenarios. Two of them conclude there are system vulnerabilities that need to be investigated further. Not only did the more diverse team arrive at a different conclusion, they were also quicker at testing more possibilities and prevented a new type of exploit.

Diversity thus is not just about male and female perspectives. It consists of the whole range of experiences, representations, and backgrounds that will make a team more resilient, more innovative, more creative, and better at understanding different threats and attack vectors. The better your workforce reflects the global nature of the internet, the better you will be at capturing new threats that can come from any part of the world. Whereas a homogenous team risks having blind spots, a diverse team will more quickly identify and mitigate such biases. Something basic such as the (natural and programming) languages your team speaks can be a critical differentiator.

The side effect is that promoting diversity in the workplace stimulates an inclusive working environment. This may in turn improve job satisfaction, which may then mediate the perceived job stress so typical of this field, reduce employee turnover rates, and reduce rehiring costs [4]. It would also help attract a broader talent pool to address the skills gap in cybersecurity and demonstrate an organisation's commitment to best practices. Coming back to the gender, as well as race disparity in this domain, organisations are missing out specifically on talented people from underrepresented groups.

Doing so starts by addressing deeply rooted beliefs about the capabilities of such groups that may not look like stereotyped white males that wear hoodies and write computer programmes in the dark. Because beliefs that, for instance, women or people of certain colours are "not supposed to do" or "inherently incapable of" intricate, technical jobs like working in cybersecurity are exactly the ones that create the toxic work environments that keep diverse talents undiscovered. Organisations need to challenge such beliefs by celebrating the achievements of underrepresented, female and non-white cybersecurity professionals, and acknowledging that better cybersecurity relies on creative problem-solving skills that only a diverse workforce can bring.

You may wonder now, what are the reasons then for people to stay in this high-pressure, unpredictable domain?

Why work in cybersecurity

First and foremost, people continue working in cybersecurity, because it provides a clear sense of purpose. Protecting individuals, organisations, and even nations from cyber threats can be incredibly fulfilling. The impact of this work is clear and significant, which makes it worth the associated stresses. There are many other high-pressure jobs with long working hours, short delivery deadlines, and lack of recognition in which people do not see any bigger purpose of their work beyond a pay check. Preventing cyber-attacks can thus be a personally gratifying experience and a highly respectable profession to be in. It can give people a great sense of accomplishment, personal validation, and boost their confidence.

Second, there is great job security. Cybersecurity professionals are in high demand due to the increasing number of cyber threats. This leads to good job security and competitive salaries, numerous career paths with plenty of opportunities for career advancement and specialisation in areas that people enjoy working in [10].

Many people here are also excited by working with cutting-edge technologies and staying at the forefront of innovation. The dynamic nature of cybersecurity ensures there always is something new to learn. Professionals who stay in the field enjoy the challenge and this opportunity for continuous development. Lastly, cybersecurity typically involves a lot of teamwork and collaboration, both within an organisation and with the broader cybersecurity community. There usually is a strong sense of camaraderie that keeps people engaged and motivated.

Leaders in organisations need to highlight these factors to appeal to skilled professionals and keep them in the cybersecurity field. They also need to provide attractive secondary job conditions that enable employees to manage the stressful parts of the job described earlier. Ideas could be wellness and wellbeing perks, mental health support, and generous overtime compensation. Ultimately, by caring for your (cybersecurity) workforce, you care for the long-term survival of your organisation in this modern world of ever-evolving cyber threats.

References

1   BT, "Cybercrime: More than 500 potential attacks clocked every second," 2023. Available at: https://newsroom.bt.com/cybercrime-more-than-500-potential-attacks-clocked-every-second/; Microsoft, "Microsoft digital defense report 2024," 2024. Available at: https://www.microsoft.com/en-us/security/security-insider/intelligence-reports/microsoft-digital-defense-report-2024; Nivedita James Palatty, "How many cyber attacks per day: The latest stats and impacts in 2025," astra Security Audit, 2025. Available at: https://www.getastra.com/blog/security-audit/how-many-cyber-attacks-per-day/; SentinelOne, "Key cyber security statistics for 2025," 2024. Available at: https://www.sentinelone.com/cybersecurity-101/cybersecurity/cyber-security-statistics/; University of North Georgia, "Cybersecurity: A global priority and career opportunity," 2025. Available at: https://ung.edu/continuing-education/news-and-media/cybersecurity.php.

2   T. Singh, *Cybersecurity, Psychology and People Hacking.* Cham: Springer International Publishing Imprint, Palgrave Macmillan, 2025.

3   J. Cho, J. Yoo, and J. I. Lim, "Analysis of job stress's impact on job performance and turnover of cybersecurity professionals," *ICIC Express Letters*, vol. 14, no. 4, pp. 409–415, 2020, doi: 10.24507/ICICEL.14.04.409.

4   H. C. Pham, "Information security burnout: Identification of sources and mitigating factors from security demands and resources," *Journal of Information Security and Applications*, vol. 46, pp. 96–107, 2019, doi: 10.1016/j.jisa.2019.03.012.

5   B. Adetoye and R. C. Fong, "Building a resilient cybersecurity workforce: A multidisciplinary solution to the problem of high turnover of cybersecurity analysts," in *Cybersecurity in the Age of Smart Societies*, H. Jahankhani, Ed., Cham: Springer International Publishing, 2023, pp. 61–87.

6   N. Robinson, "Human factors security engineering: The future of cybersecurity teams," *EDPACS*, vol. 67, no. 5, pp. 1–17, 2023, doi: 10.1080/07366981.2023.2211429.

7   C. Nobles, "Stress, burnout, and security fatigue in cybersecurity: A human factors problem," *HOLISTICA – Journal of Business and Public Administration*, vol. 13, no. 1, 2022, pp. 49–72, doi: 10.2478/hjbpa-2022-0003.

8   W. R. Poster, "Cybersecurity needs women," *Nature*, vol. 555, pp. 577–580, 2018, doi: 10.1038/d41586-018-03327-w.

9   S. L. James, "The underrepresentation of females in the United States cybersecurity workforce: A multiple-case study," Capella University PP – United States – Minnesota, United States – Minnesota, 2019.

10 Besides the operational cybersecurity context focused on here, there are of course plenty of roles in cybersecurity-adjacent fields such as risk and compliance, internal communications, legal and data protection that typically do not come with the same critical time scales and stresses, but do have to stay up to date with bigger trends in the cyber domain.

6 Human fallacies and how to overcome them

If you often feel stressed or dissatisfied at work, your brain gets depleted of resources more quickly. It then likely becomes prone to making more biased judgements and decisions. Given the (operational) cybersecurity context outlined above, it is not difficult to imagine how the pressures in this field could affect people and play into the hands of cybercriminals. In this chapter, we will take a closer look at common biases that are especially relevant in cybersecurity, and consider strategies to overcome them.

There are two main activities cybersecurity professionals find themselves doing most of the time. One is analysing potential cyber-attacks and system vulnerabilities, the other is deciding how to manage any identified risks. Accordingly, there are cognitive biases related to information-seeking and biases in decision-making that may affect the quality of each respective activity. The first category taps into the way we divide our attention, memorise information and (subconscious) prejudices. The second category relates to our general attitudes towards ourselves and others.

Biases affecting threat analysis

When we receive an alert that something in our system may be off, the first thing we naturally do is gather information. We need to know where the alert came from, what (sub)system(s) may be impacted, whether it is in an organisation-critical component, who may have triggered it, when the source of the alert was last updated, whether similar cases have been dealt with before – and so on. We want to know all the details as quickly as possible, but we can only look at one thing at a time. A trained professional may know what type of information is needed, like the emergency doctor who knows what symptoms to check first, but deciding where to look for that information and how much time to spend on each avenue can take many years of experience to become proficient at. This is where biases can hamper the analysis.

Various psychological and neuroscience studies have shown how our judgements are impacted by our own behaviour. When we are sad, we interpret the world more negatively. When we are happy, we see the world in a more positive light. This effect is one manifestation of a psychological phenomenon termed "self-projection" [1]. When we are highly stressed and afraid of a potential cyber-attack,

DOI: 10.4324/9781003610533-8

it can cloud our ability to objectively assess information. It may result in false positives – raising a false alarm and wasting time on irrelevant analysis, but also misplaced optimism (i.e., downplaying or ignoring potential threats and risks).

When we are experiencing significantly positive or negative emotions, the antidote is to be aware thereof and find a way to release any emotional overload. There should be no shame in acknowledging how we feel. We may be going through a divorce, we may have lost a beloved pet, or received a medical scare – such situations are all part of life. Knowing, expressing and managing our emotional states can thus be an appropriate way to mitigate bias before even starting any analyses.

Another way self-projection can play out during information assessments is when we register a behaviour that we would not engage in ourselves. We all have been in situations at some point when we asked ourselves "why would anyone do that?". It is a direct result of us projecting what we would not do onto others and judging them for it. When we start seeing a pattern of alerts coming from a subsystem that we think would not at all be helpful or valuable to an attacker, we may discard it as not worth our time. But just because you would not do something does not mean someone else would not either. We have to keep an open mind. There are frameworks like the Risk Management Framework (RMF) and NIST guidelines, as well as peer review processes to ensure our judgements and decisions are based on systematic analysis. Moreover, having a diverse team with different vantage points can help address this bias.

Now say we start the actual information gathering and analysis process. The first place we decide to run diagnostic tests may be our web integration with a third-party payment provider, because the alert concerned a high number of failed transactions on our organisation's paid subscriptions page that recently had an issue – albeit unrelated to security. The other issue may still be fresh in our mind, which makes us jump to the conclusion that "something dodgy *must* be going on with this service integration". In other words, the information readily available in our mind concerned an irrelevant issue to the current alert. This availability heuristic [2] can result in overlooking less obvious, but more critical aspects of systems potentially implied in an alert.

Strategies to overcome acting on an availability heuristic include implementing a comprehensive risk assessment framework that considers a wide range of potential threats and scenarios. Leveraging advanced analytics and machine learning can help identify and predict patterns from past threats. These technologies can provide a more comprehensive view of the threat landscape than human intuition alone. We also need to conduct post-mortem analyses of past incidents to understand what was missed and why. This can provide valuable lessons and help improve future threat analyses and risk management.

Two other biases that may appear during the information-seeking and analysis phase of a potential cyber threat are the anchoring effect and confirmatory bias. The anchoring effect has often been studied in experiments where participants were asked to guess or estimate something after getting to know someone else's guess [3]. When we say we think about ten employees click on a phishing link every week in a large enterprise (i.e., the "anchoring" number), the likelihood you say you estimate the number to be 200 – a completely different order of magnitude – will be very low.

But when we said we think this number is about 100, you may be more inclined to say something much higher than what you would have said without hearing our thought. When we estimate the potential impact of the cyber-attack we are analysing, we may be biased by what colleagues tell us or the information we find about similar past incidents. This, in turn, can lead to outdated or inadequate security policies.

We can overcome this by including periodically reviewing and updating security policies based on the latest threat intelligence. There needs to be a decision-making process that is structured to reduce reliance on anchors. Aforementioned RMF frameworks and NIST guidelines for systematic analyses also apply here. Incorporating peer reviews and red teaming (i.e., where a group simulates an attack to test defences) to challenge assumptions and initial decisions will also help overcome the anchoring effect.

The confirmatory bias happens when we seek out information that confirms pre-existing beliefs. This can lead to ignoring or downplaying evidence of emerging threats that is counter to what we believe to be the case. Although many people show this bias, we can overcome it by encouraging an open culture of critical thinking and peer review, where team members feel safe challenging each other's assumptions. Moreover, relating back to *Chapter 5: Operational cybersecurity context*, working with diverse teams brings varied viewpoints that can help challenge assumptions and reduce confirmatory bias. We also need to conduct regular scenario planning and simulation exercises to test assumptions and prepare for a range of potential threats.

Biases affecting risk management

When we reach the conclusion after analysing all the information available to us at the time of a potential threat, we need to decide how to act. How teams and organisations are structured, as well as organisational culture play important roles in this process. With this, we refer to factors like authoritativeness, norms embedded in organisational systems, fault tolerance, and pride.

During review and decision-making processes, we may put greater weight to the views of more experienced, senior colleagues. It is natural for us to do so, until it comes to the point that you blindly believe your seniors are correct and succumbed to authority bias. It can also work in a negative direction, where you place less trust in the accuracy of someone, for instance, if your boss is female and you associate women with less authority [4]. In both cases, objectivity in the risk management process gets undermined. Experienced staff need to ensure each member of their team feels and gets heard to foster the belief that their individual contributions are valued. In the negative case, seniors may want to address any unhelpful beliefs such as "women are less capable of technical things and thus less accurate and thus deserve less respect" directly with their staff and make them aware that such biases can lead to detrimental outcomes – both to their job and the organisation's cybersecurity.

Another common bias that affects men more than women is overconfidence [5]. It can be defined as a general certainty of one's own excellence in terms of one's judgement accuracy, technical capability, potential, and so on that does not reflect reality. The reason this bias exists may be because it could help people take more risks, and try and discover new things. In technical fields that typically are male-dominated, however, mistakes happen regularly. Several studies with software developers, for example, showed that the majority of them, regardless of their years of experience and whether they use static analysis tools, make at least one mistake that exposes their programme to cybersecurity vulnerabilities [6,7]. It is thus extremely important to implement good coding practices, including code reviews, comprehensive testing protocols, and programme analysis tools to manage overconfidence and marginalise the risk of building insecure systems.

Overconfidence in the general public may show in a lack of understanding the consequences of a cyber-attack until they experience it themselves. They may not realise the financial and emotional toll it can take, or the damage it can do to their reputation. This sense of "but we would not be targeted by cyber-attacks" can make it difficult to convince people to take cybersecurity more seriously and adopt the necessary precautions to protect themselves.

A closely related phenomenon is the Dunning–Kruger effect, which describes how newcomers to a field at first feel (overly) confident in their knowledge about this new field, but lose that confidence as time progresses when they discover all the subfields and nuances in the field they did not know when starting out – only to regain confidence again and stabilise at a comfortable level much later about their newly developed expertise [8]. Accordingly, people who just started in cybersecurity may overestimate their skills and knowledge, and risk making more mistakes.

Basic mitigations for this effect are ensuring only qualified professionals make critical security decisions, providing ongoing education and certification programmes, and encouraging team members to acknowledge their limitations and seek advice or second opinions from more experienced colleagues. Establishing a mentorship programme can help, where less experienced employees can learn from seasoned professionals, as well as the beforementioned peer review process that can help address people's knowledge gaps.

Another way overconfidence can impact cybersecurity risk management is when it leads to a false sense of security. People who are overly confident in the security of their systems may be less careful and make more insecure decisions, assuming their technical system or organisation is well capable of mitigating cyber risks. When something then goes wrong, for instance, if an alert was misinterpreted or an employee fell for a phishing campaign that slipped through the automated e-mail filters, and an organisation becomes compromised, the organisational culture can go into a downward spiral.

The person or team who made the mistake could be named, blamed, and shamed for the incident. "How could they have missed that, they are so stupid and incompetent!" – as noted previously in Part 1's *Impact of cyber-attacks on trust*. But mistakes are always the result of both people and situational factors. Systemic issues in the technology stack, structural under-resourcing, and hostile working environments could drastically increase the likelihood of someone overlooking or misinterpreting a risk [9]. Attributing mistakes to personal flaws instead of acknowledging the wider context in which a person or team was working in is known as the fundamental attribution error [10]. We can overcome this by implementing a systemic approach to cybersecurity that focuses on process improvements and technological solutions, and not on human error.

The three final biases we will discuss here relate to inertia and resistance to change: the sunk cost fallacy, status quo bias, and herd mentality. The sunk cost fallacy could reveal itself as continuing investments in outdated or ineffective security solutions due to previous investments in those systems. Working with legacy IT infrastructure will likely leave an organisation vulnerable to cyber threats. Organisations thus need to prioritise current and future IT needs over past investments, and schedule regular reviews of security measures. Without regular review, outdated solutions may continue to receive investment.

We always need to reassess the effectiveness and relevance of current solutions based on evolving threats and technologies. Adopting a fail-fast approach can help with quickly identifying ineffective solutions, so they can be abandoned. This approach encourages experimentation and rapid iteration while minimising wasting resources. Furthermore, it is among the chief information security officer's (CISO) responsibilities to develop a strategic roadmap that outlines future cybersecurity investments and goals, establish clear performance metrics to evaluate the effectiveness of cybersecurity investments, and use these metrics to guide decisions about continuing or discontinuing investments. We will come back to this topic in *Chapter 12: Responsibilities of a CISO.*

Status quo bias can prevent adoption of new technologies or processes that could enhance security. Various reasons may underlie this resistance – perceiving no or low risk, idleness, a demotivated workforce (ironically). On the other end of the spectrum, herd mentality is when we follow whatever most people are doing. In cybersecurity, people may simply follow industry trends without critically evaluating whether certain security measures would suit their organisation's unique needs.

To manage these biases, we need to strike a balance between promoting a culture of continuous improvement and innovation, and thorough risk assessments of new security strategies. Open discussion and a culture where assumptions can comfortably be questioned will reduce herd mentality and allow opportunities for strategic new security approaches. Simulating various scenarios and scenario planning will help identify potential gaps and tailor solutions to the organisation's specific context.

Of course, this is not an exhaustive list of biases that cybersecurity professionals may experience. Indeed, there are other human fallacies not described here that may just signify our own bias. Nonetheless, the given examples are meant to demonstrate the importance of implementing the right organisational processes and security measures to minimise the risk of making biased decisions. And it will not be the last time to point out we often first need to acknowledge the cognitive biases we hold ourselves, to see the importance of organisational culture and systematic implementation of cybersecurity measures.

References

1 R. L. Buckner and D. C. Carroll, "Self-projection and the brain," *Trends in Cognitive Sciences*, vol. 11, no. 2, pp. 49–57, Feb. 2007, doi: 10.1016/J.TICS.2006.11.004.

2   T. Pachur, R. Hertwig, and F. Steinmann, "How do people judge risks: Availability heuristic, affect heuristic, or both?," *Journal of Experimental Psychology: Applied*, vol. 18, no. 3, p. 314, 2012.

3   A. Furnham and H. C. Boo, "A literature review of the anchoring effect," *The Journal of Socio-Economics*, vol. 40, no. 1, pp. 35–42, Feb. 2011, doi: 10.1016/J. SOCEC.2010.10.008.

4   L. A. Rudman and S. E. Kilianski, "Implicit and explicit attitudes toward female authority," *Personality and Social Psychology Bulletin*, vol. 26, no. 11, pp. 1315–1328, 2000. https://doi.org/10.1177/0146167200263001.

5   L. Dahlbom, A. Jakobsson, N. Jakobsson, and A. Kotsadam, "Gender and overconfidence: Are girls really overconfident?," *Applied Economics Letters*, vol. 18, no. 4, pp. 325–327, 2011; B. M. Barber and T. Odean, "Boys will be boys: Gender, overconfidence, and common stock investment," *The Quarterly Journal of Economics*, vol. 116, no. 1, pp. 261–292, 2001; A. Adamecz-Völgyi and N. Shure, "The gender gap in top jobs – The role of overconfidence," *Labour Economics*, vol. 79, p. 102283, Dec. 2022, doi: 10.1016/J.LABECO.2022.102283.

6   C. Weir, B. Hermann, and S. Fahl, "From needs to actions to secure apps? The effect of requirements and developer practices on app security," in *29th USENIX Security Symposium (USENIX Security 20)*, USENIX Association, Aug. 2020, pp. 289–305; D. Votipka, K. R. Fulton, J. Parker, M. Hou, M. L. Mazurek, and M. Hicks, "Understanding security mistakes developers make: Qualitative analysis from build it, break it, fix it," in *Proceedings of the 29th USENIX Security Symposium*, 2020, pp. 109–126; M. Tahaei, K. Vaniea, K. (Kosta) Beznosov, and M. K. Wolters, "Security notifications in static analysis tools: Developers' attitudes, comprehension, and ability to act on them," in *Proceedings of the 2021 CHI Conference on Human Factors in Computing Systems*, in CHI '21, New York: Association for Computing Machinery, 2021, doi: 10.1145/3411764.3445616; L. Geierhaas, A.-M. Ortloff, M. Smith, and A. Naiakshina, "Let's hash: Helping developers with password security," in *Eighteenth Symposium on Usable Privacy and Security (SOUPS 2022)*, Boston, MA: USENIX Association, Aug. 2022, pp. 503–522.

7   It will be interesting to see how new AI-based coding tools may help software developers create more secure programs, depending on how much programmers are willing to trust and rely on such systems. However, this increases the potential for generating insecure code due to data poisoning in the training data, lack of understanding of context by the AI, potential for malicious actors to manipulate the model, and the risk of inadvertently leaking sensitive information through the generated code; so it is vital to carefully review and audit any AI-generated code before deployment to mitigate security risks.

8   D. Dunning, "The Dunning–Kruger effect: On being ignorant of one's own ignorance," *Advances in Experimental Social Psychology*, vol. 44, pp. 247–296, Jan. 2011, doi: 10.1016/B978-0-12-385522-0.00005-6; T. Schlösser, D. Dunning, K. L. Johnson, and J. Kruger, "How unaware are the unskilled? Empirical tests of the 'signal extraction' counterexplanation for the Dunning–Kruger effect in self-evaluation of performance," *Journal of Economic Psychology*, vol. 39, pp. 85–100, Dec. 2013, doi: 10.1016/J. JOEP.2013.07.004.

9   T. Singh, *Cybersecurity, Psychology and People Hacking*. Cham: Springer International Publishing Imprint, Palgrave Macmillan, 2025.

10 L. Ross, "From the fundamental attribution error to the truly fundamental attribution error and beyond: My research journey," *Perspectives on Psychological Science*, vol. 13, no. 6, pp. 750–769, 2018.

7 Operational resilience

One often overlooked, but critical aspect of cybersecurity is operational resilience: an organisation's ability to withstand and recover from disruptions in their operations, such as cyber threats. Acting on this aspect requires liaising with other parts of an organisation to develop an organisation-wide strategy for operational resilience. Cybersecurity leaders must be able to relay the importance of this to, for example, customer-facing and production units, marketing and communications, and the executive board – people who tend to be of non-technical backgrounds. To help you make that case, operational resilience from a cybersecurity point of view should be regarded as essential to an organisation's bottom line [1].

A phrase that was popularised since the 2000s is "data is the new gold". Data contain information, usually related to people's behaviour, that can be leveraged for commercial, political, and criminal ends. Financial value can now be expressed in terms of how much quality data you can move around. The increasing pace of digitisation around the globe means we are both generating an exponential amount of data, as well as completely reliant on it. It has simply become impossible to run a modern organisation without appropriate information and communication technology systems that allow people to interact with this wealth of data. Information and communications technology and the security thereof should thus not be seen as necessary evils, but are absolutely essential enablers for any organisation's mandate – be it commercial, governmental, or not-for-profit.

We described in *Part 1: Enter the world of cybercrime* how debilitating cyber-attacks can be. They are devised precisely to disrupt organisation operations, cause financial losses, and damage organisations' reputations. For example, Target suffered a massive data breach in 2013 that resulted in the theft of millions of customers' personal and financial information. The breach was caused by a vulnerability in Target's payment system, which cybercriminals then exploited. In 2017, Maersk, the world's largest shipping company, suffered a cyber-attack that disrupted its operations worldwide. The attack caused significant financial losses and disrupted global trade. The difference between these two cases is that Target's operational resilience programme was slow and ineffective in detecting and responding to the breach, leading to significant financial losses and damage to the company's reputation. These could partially have been contained if they had implemented better

DOI: 10.4324/9781003610533-9

operational resilience measures. In contrast, Maersk's operational resilience programme was effective in mitigating the impact of the attack and recovered relatively quickly.

Operational resilience thus allows organisations to continue functioning, despite dealing with cyber threats and recover efficiently from any disruptions. Operational resilience is also important, because it provides a holistic approach to cybersecurity. Many organisations have a fragmented approach to cybersecurity, leading to gaps in their security posture. Operational resilience instead considers *all* aspects of an organisation's operations, including people, processes, and technology, which extends beyond traditional cybersecurity paradigms [2].

To this end, organisations must identify their critical systems and data, develop and test organisation continuity plans, implement incident response plans, and train employees. By following best practices and leveraging tools and technologies, organisations can improve their operational resilience and protect their systems and data from cyber-attacks. The following components are essential parts of an operational cybersecurity resilience framework:

People

Employee training: Employees are an essential part of an organisation's operational resilience programme. Organisations should *train employees* on usable and evidence-based cybersecurity practices, including identifying and reporting incidents, and making them aware of what to do in the (hopefully) rare case of a cyber-attack. Understanding people's psychology in various operational contexts is crucial in doing this well.

Communication plan: An adequate communication plan ensures that stakeholders stay informed during a disruption. Stakeholders naturally include the executive team and the directly affected organisational units, but in more severe cases may include the whole organisation and external parties, suppliers and other dependencies. The communication plan should include procedures for communicating with employees, customers, the media, and possibly law enforcers to report the incident to.

Processes

Risk Management: Organisations must identify and assess their operational risks and implement controls to mitigate them, which will improve their cybersecurity maturity [3]. Risk management should be a continuous process that considers the evolving threat landscape and changing organisation operations. Accordingly, organisations should regularly update their risk assessments to ensure they are identifying and assessing the latest cyber threats.

IT Incident Management: The process of detecting, analysing, and responding to incidents that could have operational impact on an organisation. Incident management should include procedures for reporting incidents, analysing their impact, and responding to them.

Crisis Management: The process of managing a crisis that could impact an organisation's operations. Crisis management should include procedures for activating crisis management teams, communicating with stakeholders, and preventing any further escalations of the attack.

Business Continuity Planning: The process of developing strategies to ensure that critical organisational functions can continue *during and after* a disruption. Business continuity planning should include procedures for backup and recovery of critical systems and data, communication plans, and incident response plans. These plans need to be regularly updated and tested to ensure their effectiveness.

Security Incident Response Management: The process of identifying, analysing, and responding to security incidents in an organisation. It involves a coordinated effort to minimise the damage caused by an incident and to restore normal organisation operations as quickly as possible. Cybersecurity, on the other hand, refers to the practice of protecting computer systems, networks, and data from unauthorised access, theft, and damage. Cybersecurity is an essential component of incident response, as it helps organisations prevent security incidents from occurring in the first place.

Incident response planning is essential for organisations to minimise the impact of security incidents. A well-designed incident response plan includes a step-by-step guide for responding to security incidents, identifies the roles and responsibilities of incident response team members, and outlines communication protocols. Incident response planning should be a collaborative effort involving various departments within an organisation, including information technology (IT), legal, and human resources.

The incident response process involves several steps, including preparation, identification, containment, eradication, and recovery. In the preparation phase, organisations develop an incident response plan and train employees on incident response procedures. In the identification phase, organisations detect and analyse security incidents. In the containment phase, organisations take steps to contain the incident and prevent it from spreading. In the eradication phase, organisations remove the threat and restore normal organisation operations. In the recovery phase, organisations evaluate the incident response process and make improvements where necessary.

The roles and responsibilities for the incident response team must be clear. An incident response team typically includes representatives from various departments within an organisation, including IT, legal, human resources, and public relations. The incident response team has several roles and responsibilities, including incident management, technical analysis, communication, and documentation. The incident response team should have clear guidelines for communication, including who to contact and how to report incidents.

There are several best practices that organisations can follow to improve their incident response and cybersecurity efforts. These include conducting regular risk assessments, implementing strong access controls, using encryption to protect sensitive data, and providing employee training on cybersecurity awareness. Organisations should also have a robust incident response plan in place and regularly test and update it.

There are several incident response tools and technologies that organisations can use to improve their incident response capabilities. These include security information and event management (SIEM) solutions, intrusion detection systems, and vulnerability scanners. Incident response teams should also have access to forensic analysis tools, network analysis tools, and malware analysis tools.

Incident response and cybersecurity training and certification can help organisations ensure that their incident response teams are prepared to respond to security incidents effectively. Certification programmes such as Certified Information Systems Security Professional(CISSP) and Certified Ethical Hacker(CEH) provide incident response professionals with the knowledge and skills needed to detect, analyse, and respond to security incidents.

Cybersecurity services and solutions can help organisations improve their incident response and cybersecurity efforts. These include managed security services, threat intelligence services, and penetration testing services. Organisations can also implement security solutions such as firewalls, antivirus software, and intrusion prevention systems to protect their systems and data from cyber threats.

Incident response and cybersecurity are critical components of any organisation's security strategy. By understanding the types of incidents and data breaches, cybersecurity threats and attack vectors, incident response planning, incident response process, incident response team roles and responsibilities, best practices for incident response and cybersecurity, incident response tools and technologies, incident response and cybersecurity training and certification, and cybersecurity services and solutions, organisations can better prepare for security incidents and minimise their impact. It is essential for organisations to take a proactive approach to incident response and cybersecurity to protect their systems, data, and reputation.

Configuration management is the process of identifying, tracking, and controlling all components within an IT system, including hardware, software, and network settings, to ensure consistency, maintain a documented baseline, and manage changes effectively throughout the system's lifecycle; essentially, it is a method to keep all aspects of an IT infrastructure organised and in a known state. Woods and Seymour (2024) argue that attack surface management and patch cadence are crucial in improving cybersecurity. They contend these are consistently the most effective interventions [4].

One of the most common misconfiguration mistakes is a lack of configuration management. Configuration management involves tracking and controlling changes to IT systems to ensure they remain secure. Without proper configuration management, changes can be made that leave systems vulnerable to attack. To avoid this mistake, organisations should implement a configuration management process and ensure that it is followed.

Cloud services are becoming increasingly popular, but they can also be a source of misconfiguration. In many cases, cloud services come with default settings that are not secure enough. Organisations should take the time to configure cloud services properly and ensure that they are secured before deploying them. Regular security audits can also help identify any misconfigurations.

Misconfigurations can also happen due to human error. This can occur when employees do not follow security protocols, or when they make changes to systems without fully understanding the consequences. To avoid this mistake, organisations should conduct regular security training for employees and ensure that they understand the importance of security protocols.

Preventing misconfigurations requires a proactive approach to cybersecurity. Employees are often the weakest link in cybersecurity. Employee training is crucial to prevent misconfigurations caused by human error or neglect. Employees should be trained to recognise and report potential security threats, follow best practices for password management, and understand the importance of cybersecurity.

Changes to systems, networks, or applications should be properly planned and tested before implementation. Change management processes should be established to ensure that changes are properly authorised and documented.

Security controls should be implemented to prevent misconfigurations. This includes proper access control, network segmentation, and monitoring for vulnerabilities and threats. Security risk increases where the protocols are inadequate or not properly enforced by the organisation.

There are several techniques that organisations must use to identify misconfigurations. Vulnerability scanning tools can scan systems, networks, or applications for known vulnerabilities and misconfigurations. The results of the scan can be used to prioritise remediation efforts and prevent cybersecurity breaches.

Penetration testing involves simulating a cyber-attack to identify vulnerabilities and misconfigurations. The results of the penetration test can be used to improve security controls and prevent cybersecurity breaches.

Configuration management tools can be used to manage the configuration of systems, networks, or applications. These tools can ensure that configurations are standardised, documented, and properly secured.

Regular audits and assessments are crucial to maintaining effective cybersecurity. Audits and assessments can identify vulnerabilities and misconfigurations that may have been missed during regular monitoring. They can also provide valuable feedback on the effectiveness of cybersecurity controls and help identify areas for improvement.

As noted in *Chapter 3: How an attack is devised*, misconfigurations can have devastating consequences for organisations. Cybercriminals are constantly looking for vulnerabilities to exploit, and misconfigurations provide an easy target. Misconfigurations are a common cause of cybersecurity breaches, and organisations need to take a proactive approach to prevent them. While it is impossible to eliminate all risks, organisations can reduce their likelihood by implementing proper configuration management processes, configuring cloud services securely, and conducting regular employee training. Effective change management, security controls, vulnerability scanning, penetration testing, and regular audits and assessments are all important measures in preventing misconfigurations. By implementing these measures, organisations can protect themselves from the costly consequences of misconfigurations.

Technology

Tools and technologies: Almost needless to say, organisations should implement cybersecurity tools and technologies to protect their systems and data. This includes firewalls, intrusion detection systems, and antivirus software. Specifically, SIEM systems that collect and analyse security events from various sources allow organisations to detect and respond to incidents quickly. Disaster Recovery as a Service provides organisations with a secure and scalable disaster recovery solution that ensures their critical systems and data are protected. Endpoint Detection and Response tools provide organisations with real-time visibility into their endpoints, allowing them to detect and respond to threats quickly.

Note that the role of cloud computing, artificial intelligence (AI), and machine learning (ML) in operational resilience is becoming more important. Organisations must ensure that their cloud infrastructure is secure and resilient to cyber threats, and will increasingly need to use AI to automate detecting *and* responding efficiently to incidents.

As with most cybersecurity measures, organisations should regularly test their operational resilience programme to ensure its effectiveness. This includes testing organisation continuity plans, incident response plans, and crisis management plans as summed up above.

One of the biggest problems in cybersecurity is a lack of understanding. Many people do not fully understand the risks associated with using technology or the importance of protecting sensitive information. This lack of understanding can lead to careless behaviour, such as using weak passwords or failing to keep software up to date, which can leave individuals and businesses vulnerable to cyber-attacks.

In addition, many people do not understand the consequences of a cyber-attack until it happens to them. They may not realise the financial and emotional toll it can take or the damage it can do to their reputation. This lack of understanding can make it difficult to convince people to take cybersecurity seriously and take the necessary precautions to protect themselves.

Another issue in cybersecurity is desensitisation. As cyber-attacks become more common, people may become desensitised to the risks and fail to take the necessary precautions. This desensitisation can lead to complacency and a false sense of security.

As technology continues to advance, cyber threats continue to increase. But technology is also making it easier to incorporate psychology in cybersecurity measures. For example, ML algorithms can be used to analyse user behaviour and detect anomalies that may indicate a cyber-attack. Psychology has a crucial role here in the identification of negative cybercriminal or malicious patterns of behaviour. We expect psychological knowledge to play an increasingly significant role in the development of AI and ML solutions, including for cybersecurity applications. These technologies can help detect and prevent cyber-attacks, although these technologies are only as good as the data they are trained on. By incorporating basic psychological principles into the interpretation and development of these technologies, cybersecurity professionals may achieve more effective solutions.

Indeed, the cybersecurity research community is growing interdisciplinary work between, for example, psychologists and technologists to improve our understanding of the root causes of poor security. We believe this is an exciting field with many open questions that will ultimately help individuals and businesses develop more effective cybersecurity measures that are more usable and less vulnerable to attacks.

Business continuity

We will take a brief moment here to highlight the importance of a business continuity plan (BCP) in cybersecurity. The BCP outlines the steps you can take to ensure that your organisation stays afloat during and beyond a disruptive event – whether the disruption is a natural disaster, cyber-attack, or human error.

First, it is essential to conduct a business impact analysis (BIA). A BIA is a process that identifies your organisation's critical organisation functions and the impact that a disruption would have on these functions. The BIA helps to prioritise recovery efforts and ensure that the most critical functions are restored first. Moreover, it helps ensure that your organisation continuity plan is tailored to your organisation's specific needs.

After the BIA, it is time to develop and implement your BCP. It will consist of the steps that your organisation will take to ensure that critical organisation functions can continue in the event of a disruption. The plan should include procedures for backup and recovery, communication, crisis management, and aftercare. It is essential to involve all stakeholders in the development of the BCP and ensure it is regularly reviewed, tested, and updated. Regular testing can help with identifying weaknesses in the plan and allows for adjustments to be made. It is essential to involve all stakeholders in the testing process and update the plan to reflect any changes in the organisation environment.

Employees play a critical role in organisation continuity. It is essential to provide employee recurring training to ensure that all of them are aware of the BCP and their role in its implementation. Employees need to know what to do in the event of a disruption, especially if they are working in organisation-critical functions. It remains important to encourage employees to report any security incidents or breaches promptly. One could compare this to running regular fire drills – but then for the organisation's digital assets.

Relating back to *Chapter 6: Human fallacies and how to overcome them*, the BCP and operational resilience strategy need to address how they want to address incidents caused by human error. You need to be aware if any particular biases in the cybersecurity strategy may have played a role. You will want to address any unhelpful characteristics of the organisational culture, and review flaws in testing and review processes. Many studies have pointed out how victims of various social engineering attacks typically feel deeply ashamed, guilt, stupid, and frustrated, apart from the material losses such attacks may have incurred [5]. Research on victims of rape or sexual abuse has shown they often do not report such incidents due to intense feelings of shame [6]. It is conceivable that employees may not want to report cyber incidents because of the very same reason – feeling deeply ashamed.

In this vein, Karen Renaud and colleagues surveyed 107 American individuals on their experience of causing cybersecurity incidents in their job. The shame they described from blaming oneself, blame from colleagues, and feeling judged all exacerbated the psychological burden on these employees, resulting in withdrawal, silence, and damaged work relationships [7]. Respondents who did not go down the same negative spiral, however, worked for organisations that showed a level of understanding, focused on lessons learned and repairing any flaws.

Simply blaming people and relating mistakes to job security is thus not going to benefit organisational resilience and therewith the bottom line in the long run. Any systemic biases and hostile organisational traits need to be resolved first instead of resorting to drastic finger-pointing at "the culprit", as unaddressed biases will lead to similar mistakes in the future. A BCP may, therefore, even specify mental health guidance for employees who felt responsible for the disruption and a clear path for how to improve. Karen Renaud and colleagues from the above study outlined five recommendations to effectively manage employees impacted by cyber incidents [7]:

1. **Recognise that mistakes can happen** by implementing a "no-blame" security incident reporting system;
2. **Keep employees informed and listen** to them during and after an incident;
3. **Implement creative employee training programmes** that go beyond "check-in-the-box" types of exercises – we will elaborate on this in *Chapter 9: Improving organisational cybersecurity*;
4. **Managers need to recognise that mistakes are not intentional** and part of human nature, and de-escalate any blame games;
5. **Do not exploit shame** to test new cybersecurity measures, as shame has a long-term adverse impact on people.

References

1   T. Singh, *Digital Resilience, Cybersecurity and Supply Chains*, 1st ed. Routledge, 2025, doi: 10.4324/9781003604969.
2   A. AL-Hawamleh, "Cyber resilience framework: Strengthening defenses and enhancing continuity in business security," *International Journal of Computing and Digital Systems*, vol. 15, no. 1, pp. 1315–1331, 2024.
3   E. Joko Wibowo and K. Ramli, "Impact of implementation of information security risk management and security controls on cyber security maturity (a case study at data management applications of XYZ Institute)," *Jurnal Sistem Informasi*, vol. 18, no. 2, pp. 1–17, 2022, doi: 10.21609/jsi.v18i2.1146.
4   D. W. Woods and S. Seymour, "Evidence-based cybersecurity policy? A meta-review of security control effectiveness," *Journal of Cyber Policy*, vol. 8, no. 3, pp. 365–383, 2023, doi: 10.1080/23738871.2024.2335461.
5   C. Cross, "No laughing matter: Blaming the victim of online fraud," *International Review of Victimology*, vol. 21, no. 2, pp. 187–204, 2015, doi: 10.1177/0269758015571471; Y. Hanoch and S. Wood, "The scams among us: Who falls prey and why," *Current*

Directions in Psychological Science, vol. 30, no. 3, pp. 260–266, 2021, doi: 10.1177/ 0963721421995489; K. R. Gould, J.-Y. J. Carminati, and J. L. Ponsford, "Neuropsychological rehabilitation 'They just say how stupid I was for being conned'. Cyberscams and acquired brain injury: A qualitative exploration of the lived experience of survivors and close others," *Neuropsychological rehabilitation*, vol. 33, no. 2, pp. 325–345, 2021, doi: 10.1080/09602011.2021.2016447; M. Finnemore and D. B. Hollis, "Beyond naming and shaming: Accusations and international law in cybersecurity," *The European Journal of International Law*, vol. 31, no. 3, pp. 969–1003, 2020, doi: 10.1093/ ejil/chaa056.

6 K. G. Weiss, "Deconstructing the shame of sexual victimization," *Feminist Criminology*, vol. 5, no. 3, pp. 286–310, doi: 10.1177/1557085110376343.

7 K. Renaud, R. Searle, and M. Dupuis, "Shame in cyber security: Effective behavior modification tool or counterproductive foil?," *Proceedings of the 2021 New Security Paradigms Workshop*, pp. 70–87, 2021, doi: 10.1145/3498891.3498896.

8 Organisational psychology

One of the key challenges in cybersecurity is that it is often seen as a technical issue that can be solved with better technology. However, many cyber-attacks are actually the result of malicious insider activity or human error as discussed in *Chapter 4: Special cases* and *Chapter 6: Human fallacies and how to overcome them*. Organisational psychologists can play an important role in identifying these human factors and developing strategies to address them. As a result, they will help improve both cybersecurity and organisational culture.

Organisational psychology studies human behaviour in organisations, and how it can be used to improve productivity, job satisfaction, and overall organisational effectiveness. One of the key benefits is that it can help organisations identify and address issues that may be hindering their success. For example, if a company is struggling with high turnover rates, an organisational psychologist can help identify the root causes of the problem and develop strategies to address it. This may involve improving employee engagement, providing better training and development opportunities, or addressing communication breakdowns within the organisation. As such, organisational psychology is also implied in the realm of cybersecurity [1]. With each new cyber threat and technological advance, simply implementing the latest technology solutions is not enough. Organisations also need to consider the human factor in cybersecurity, which is where organisational psychology comes in.

While cybersecurity can impact organisational psychology, organisational psychology can also impact cybersecurity. For example, if an organisation experiences a significant cyber-attack, it can have a profound impact on employee morale and job satisfaction. Employees may feel that their work is no longer safe or that their employer is not doing enough to protect them. This can lead to increased stress, decreased productivity, and even staff turnover. Moreover, customers may become hesitant to do business with the organisation. On the other hand, if an organisation takes a proactive approach to cybersecurity, it can actually improve employee morale and job satisfaction. Employees are likely to feel more secure in their jobs if they know that their employer is taking steps to protect their sensitive information.

Organisational psychology can help organisations address the psychological impact of cybersecurity breaches. This can be achieved through communication strategies that are transparent and honest about cybersecurity incidents, counselling

DOI: 10.4324/9781003610533-10

services for affected employees, and strategies to rebuild trust and confidence in the organisation. Organisational psychology can also help organisations understand how employees perceive cybersecurity and the role they play in keeping the organisation secure. Therewith, it can help organisations develop strategies to improve employee awareness and behaviour regarding cybersecurity. For example, an organisational psychologist may work with an organisation to develop a training programme that helps employees identify and avoid phishing scams. Or they may help an organisation develop policies and procedures that reduce the risk of insider threats. Put simply, organisational psychologists can help organisations develop and implement effective cybersecurity strategies by understanding and addressing the human factors that contribute to cyber risk.

Organisational psychology strategies in cybersecurity will need to evolve significantly over the next decade, driven by advancements in technology, changing threat landscapes, and translating insights from research on human behaviour to actionable cybersecurity measures.

Training programmes will have to become more personalised and adapt to changing contexts, leveraging data analytics to tailor content to individual learning styles and needs. Gamification and immersive technologies like VR and AR could make training more engaging and effective. Pioneering studies using VR to research crime, for instance, show how these technologies can enhance our understanding of how security risks can be exploited and thus help improve (cyber) security measures [2].

Organisations may increasingly need to use behavioural analytics to detect anomalies in user behaviour that may indicate a security threat, especially against the backdrop of increased remote working. By understanding typical user patterns, companies can identify potential breaches more quickly and accurately. We will briefly return to this topic in light of the data privacy considerations around such practice in *Part 4 The Psychoogy of a Chief Information Security Officer (CISO)*.

Cyberpsychology will need to play a more prominent role in cybersecurity strategies, too. Understanding how and why people make security-related decisions will help in designing better security protocols and reducing human error.

There will be a greater emphasis on fostering a security-first culture within organisations. This includes promoting security awareness at all levels, encouraging open communication about security issues, and recognising and rewarding secure behaviours. More diverse teams could help bring a variety of perspectives and problem-solving approaches, which could help enhance cybersecurity efforts. Organisations will work to create more inclusive environments that leverage the strengths of a diverse workforce.

Threat intelligence will become more sophisticated, incorporating AI and machine learning to predict and respond to emerging threats. This will enable organisations to stay ahead of cybercriminals and adapt their defences in real time. Incident response strategies will become more streamlined and efficient, with a focus on minimising downtime and reducing the impact of breaches. This will involve better coordination between different departments and the use of automated response tools.

The cybersecurity landscape is constantly evolving, and so must the strategies used to protect against threats. Organisations will need to prioritise continuous learning and adaptation, ensuring that their security measures remain effective against new and emerging threats.

There are several challenges that must be addressed to realise the full potential of organisational psychology in cybersecurity. One of them is a lack of awareness among organisations about the role of organisational psychology in this area. Many organisations still view cybersecurity as a purely technical issue and do not fully appreciate the importance of addressing the human factors that contribute to cyber risk. Another challenge is a lack of resources and expertise in this area. Organisational psychologists with expertise in cybersecurity are still relatively rare. Thus, there is a need for more training and development opportunities in this area, such as certification programmes in organisational psychology and cybersecurity. These programmes can provide employees with the knowledge and skills needed to improve both organisational psychology and cybersecurity. Certification programmes can also help organisations in demonstrating their commitment to cybersecurity to customers and other stakeholders.

Another way to improve organisational psychology and cybersecurity is by regularly surveying employees to gather feedback on organisational culture and cybersecurity awareness. This can help organisations with identifying areas where improvement is needed and develop targeted strategies to address these areas. Another way is using gamification to improve cybersecurity awareness and behaviour. Gamification involves using game-like elements such as points, badges and leaderboards to encourage employees to adopt good cybersecurity habits.

We will now further explore psychological strategies to improve organisational cybersecurity in *Chapter 9: Improving organisational cybersecurity*.

References

1 T. Singh, *Cybersecurity, Psychology and People Hacking*. Cham: Springer International Publishing Imprint, Palgrave Macmillan, 2025.
2 Van Gelder, J.L., Nee, C., Otte, M., Demetriou, A., Van Sintemaartensdijk, I. and Van Prooijen, J.W., Virtual burglary: Exploring the potential of virtual reality to study burglary in action. *Journal of Research in Crime and Delinquency*, vol. 54, no. 1, pp. 29–62, 2017.

9 Improving organisational cybersecurity

This book would not be complete without discussing how we can improve an organisation's cybersecurity from a human perspective. Just as the hackers described in *Chapter 2: Hackers: the good, the bad and the ugly*, people on the defence side need to stay up to date with the latest technological and regulatory developments too. That way, we know of newfound software vulnerabilities that may apply to our organisational systems, new anomaly and intrusion detection tools, industry best practices, and so on.

Frequenting cybersecurity conferences, professional community events, and internal knowledge sharing seminars are important ways to do so. We have to take care of ourselves to ensure we can manage the mental load that comes with working in the cybersecurity domain, as discussed in *Chapter 5: Operational cybersecurity context*, and are aware of our cognitive biases. But when it comes to the wider organisational context, we often find we have to communicate differently to get our message across to people outside our field.

We may have successfully deployed a new multi-factor authentication system that is technically brilliant, but getting everyone to use it adequately requires a different set of skills. This goes beyond network activity monitoring, encrypting and backing up data, penetration testing, implementing access controls, developing incident response plans, updating software, and regularly conducting security audits. Rather, organisational cybersecurity also requires people-oriented strategies for taking everyone on the same journey to better protecting your organisation. This entails (i) good governance, (ii) providing effective training and education programmes, (iii) implementing a "security by design" (SbD) approach that involves usability as a key performance indicator for organisational security tools, and (iv) shaping a positive organisational cybersecurity culture.

Before we delve into each of these approaches, it is worth noting that the often mentioned problem with people as "the last line of defence" is not that they do not care. We know from numerous studies and reports that cyber incidents due to human error lead to feelings of stupidity, shame, regret, guilt, and even fear of repercussions to one's career – feelings and situations that people want to avoid. Just from the countless breaches that happened in recent years, most people have an intuitive understanding that cybersecurity is important. But, in our day-to-day (work) life, we primarily care about "getting our job done", where security behaviour is

DOI: 10.4324/9781003610533-11

a secondary aspect of the job. If your goal is to get people in your organisation to act more securely, you need to create the circumstances for them to do so. That is where seemingly less tangible measures such as good governance, investing in organisational culture, and SbD enter the picture.

Good governance

Similar to the debunked idea that only certain types of people become criminals, as implied in *Chapter 1: Most cybercriminals are made, not born*, another attributional bias many people have is that they think only certain types of people fall for cyber-attacks, such as the elderly, females, or the non-technically schooled. Research studies do not show consistent evidence to support any such claims [1,2]. For instance, the idea that elderly people are most likely to fall for scams is more likely because they have more to lose on average. As a result, when they fall for a scam, the impact likely is greater than a 17-year old getting defrauded via Instagram for Taylor Swift concert tickets. Elderly who got scammed may thus tend to generate more "news-worthy" items. Yet, the latter type of scam with younger people also happens all the time. Indeed, recent estimates from the UK and United States say that billions of pounds and dollars have been lost year on year to scams, which is certainly not merely driven by the elderly getting defrauded [3]. Similarly, data breaches from small companies likely happen every week without our knowledge due to their small scale, whereas cyber-attacks that led to major impacts typically on large organisations tend to receive much more media coverage. This may in fact feed into the availability heuristic mentioned in *Chapter 6: Human fallacies and how to overcome them* that makes information about elderly and major financial losses to scams more prevalent in our worldview, compared to the myriad smaller-scale breaches and scams out there.

Technical people are not immune to falling for social engineering attacks either. This was famously demonstrated when John Podesta, the lead for Hillary Clinton's presidential campaign in 2016 fell for a phishing e-mail. The e-mail purported to be from Google, notifying him of the need for a password reset. He even forwarded the e-mail to the campaign's information technology (IT) team to check if it was a legitimate e-mail, who e-mailed back "This is a legitimate email. John needs to change his password immediately" [4]. Consequently, Russian hackers had access to sensitive campaign information shared through Clinton's team's personal e-mails. John Podesta's e-mails later got published on WikiLeaks [5].

There are several qualitative studies with technically educated participants that show they do not consistently follow their own cybersecurity advice on how to detect phishing e-mails, that is, by hovering over links and checking sender e-mail addresses [1,6] – let alone we expect non-technical people to do so. Anecdotal evidence we hear from chief information security officers (CISOs) who run simulated phishing tests on their senior management say the same. Just like people outside the cybersecurity domain, technical and cybersecurity professionals likely seem to follow the natural workings of our human brains – a topic we will elaborate on in *Part 3: The target's perspective*. Hence, the idea that certain people are more or less vulnerable to falling for cyber-attacks than others is flawed. We need to take into account the *contexts* they operate in.

We see a strong parallel here with the development in crime science that shifted from researching what dispositions determine people to become criminals, to how people interact with situational crime facilitators. This had big implications for how the police and law enforcers operate. As we described in *Chapter 1: Most cybercriminals are made, not born*, situational factors that create opportunities for crime are at least as important as having the desire and ability to engage in certain crime. When we think of who gets targeted with cyber-attacks and when, we need to take into account those same situational factors and not fixate on finding certain demographics that we believe form a bigger risk group. Instead, we need to consider the situations that facilitate cyber-attacks and adapt organisational cybersecurity measures accordingly. In other words, good governance requires organisational cybersecurity policies to be *context-aware*.

That said, we suggest that cybersecurity governance should have the following objectives:

1. Encourage people to report suspicious activity promptly, and recognise and address situations where organisation goals may clash with cybersecurity policies.
2. Tailor cybersecurity policies and runbooks to the specific risks of the organisation, and regularly update them to reflect the latest threats and vulnerabilities. Accordingly, any training, education, and awareness campaigns should address the vulnerabilities in human behaviour and the wider organisation that cyber-attackers seek to exploit.
3. Set up and maintain organisational policies for handling sensitive data. For instance, always involve at least one extra pair of eyes when receiving requests that involve moving or providing information and/or finances.
4. Make it clear to employees *who* the final decision-makers are in the organisation, *what requests* they are authorised to make, and *how* decision-making processes are run.
5. Reward secure, desired behaviour and create disincentives for insecure, undesired behaviour.

One key to achieving these objectives is through effective storytelling. Powerful stories on the impact of insecure behaviour through case studies and examples could help raise awareness. For example, the Dridex malware cases showed how Word and Excel macros should not mindlessly be downloaded and activated. Victims were sent phishing e-mails with malicious attachments that facilitated cyber-criminals to steal their bank details and fraudulently transfer millions of dollars [7]. The next step is to translate awareness into adequate cybersecurity behaviour.

Awareness does not equate behaviour

Let us say you implemented all the technical cybersecurity measures mentioned earlier, your security operations centre (SOC) is smoothly parrying 99% of all incoming attacks, and your risk and compliance teams have done all they could to set up the required organisational cybersecurity policies. Your cybersecurity teams are prepared for any type of attack. Now you just need the rest of the workforce to keep the organisation secure.

Cybersecurity training and awareness campaigns are argued to be among the most critical components of ensuring the effectiveness of cybersecurity governance. A lack of awareness or training can leave employees vulnerable to cyberattacks and lead to delayed responses to cyber threats [8,9]. The typical objectives of cybersecurity training and awareness campaigns are:

- Guide people through how to use relevant security tools and follow security procedures, and to ensure they have the skills to apply adequate cyber hygiene. They should understand the importance of reporting suspicious activity, how to deal with security incidents, and how to use more robust authentication methods.
- Help employees recognise and respond appropriately to requests, understand when and why they need authorisation for certain actions, and who to ask for help. Employees who are members of a trusted group need to know what requests they are authorised to make and what responsibilities come with this.
- Make people aware of social engineering techniques such as phishing campaigns, and what to do when they receive requests for information or certain actions. Training and awareness programmes need to be updated to reflect the latest threats and vulnerabilities, and be tailored to employees' specific risks and needs.

We emphasise here how important the behavioural components are in each of these objectives. Being aware of cybersecurity policies is not enough. Getting people to consistently act accordingly is the ultimate goal with all these efforts. Awareness should then not (just) be scoring 100% on five multiple choice questions in an annual online training programme. Critical behaviours that people should avoid could be detected through behavioural analytics software and automatically trigger a review process. The first time people set up their work accounts, prompt them to directly create secure pass phrases, and implement multi-factor authentication. Akin to fire drills, you might want to test your incident response plan by simulating a cyber-attack for certain departments or even the whole organisation on a regular basis.

Defining the objectives of your organisation's awareness and training programmes once again depends on your specific context. You first need to have an answer to the questions what it means for an employee to be "aware" or "unaware". What measurable behaviours do they display? What other indicators can you use to measure this? How much could you risk having an "unaware" workforce? What language should you use to relay these objectives to different staff contexts? In reflecting on these questions, topics such as the "privacy versus security" paradox and safety versus security may come up, which we will discuss later in this chapter.

We first turn to research on the effectiveness of cybersecurity training and education, often measured through phishing click rates.

Uniform cybersecurity recommendations do not exist

One pitfall related to the herd mentality bias described in *Chapter 6: Human fallacies and how to overcome them* is when organisations blindly adopt cybersecurity recommendations without considering their specific context. There are general best practices in every field. In cybersecurity, they may be using strong authentication methods, using a SIEM system, backing up data, using encryption et cetera, but their specific implementation will have to be tailored to your organisation's context. Take a multinational organisation like Visa – the primary credit card provider in the world. Each country and region they operate in will have its own regulatory requirements, both in terms of financial regulations and cybersecurity(-related) topics. This leads to a patchwork of regulations and system configurations that can be difficult to harmonise.

A local importer in agricultural products will have very different organisational needs and cyber risks compared to Visa. To start with, they will have an IT system tailored to their specific organisation operations with different service level expectations compared to Visa's high-speed, marginal-risk tolerance IT infrastructure. Thus, apart from their size and industry, their completely different technological landscape further complicates applying uniform cybersecurity recommendations.

Then, what would be recommended today may not be relevant anymore tomorrow. Cyber threats are constantly evolving, which makes it challenging to create static, one-size-fits-all recommendations. This is one of the biggest reasons we must adapt to better understand these cyber risks and ensure we don't leave weaknesses in controls. We also need to adapt cyber controls to enable the organisation to achieve its growth and transformation aspirations. This involves a constant need to review controls to ensure they are well-balanced and based on deliberate, contextually informed decisions. In short, "uniform cybersecurity recommendation" do not exist and organisations need to be aware of this. The good news is that the principle of situational awareness interwoven throughout this book can help address this, starting with context-aware policies.

Policies consistent with an organisation's (regional) context help enhance their security posture. They address specific contextual risks and threats, and reduce the risk of gaps and vulnerabilities. They provide clear guidelines for incident response, ensuring that all team members know their roles and responsibilities during a security incident. Ultimately, we must ensure the organisation has a more effective and targeted approach to cybersecurity. Having a context-aware policy framework simplifies compliance efforts, improves efficiency, makes it easier for organisations to meet regulatory requirements and enhances the organisation's cybersecurity scaling potential as it grows. Finally, we need to educate employees about these policies and foster a culture of security awareness – a topic we will return to later in this chapter.

Information privacy regulations

As more and more of our lives and organisations move online, information privacy has become a top priority for organisations worldwide. Information privacy refers to the right of an individual to control the collection, use, and dissemination of their personal information. Organisations need to understand the significance of information privacy, the (local) regulations and laws that govern it, common threats to information privacy, the impact of information privacy breaches, the benefits of information security, best practices for information security, and the future of information privacy controls.

Various regulations and laws govern information privacy at federal, state, and international levels. One of the most significant federal laws in the United States is the Health Insurance Portability and Accountability Act, which regulates the privacy and security of medical information. Other federal laws include the Children's Online Privacy Protection Act and the Gramm-Leach-Bliley Act, which regulate the collection and use of personal information by financial institutions. At the state level, California's Consumer Privacy Act and Virginia's Consumer Data Protection Act regulate the collection and use of personal information by organisations. In China, information privacy and data protection are regulated through the Personal Information Protection Law. Internationally, the European Union's (EU) General Data Protection Regulation has significant implications for organisations that collect and use data from EU citizens.

Attackers may attempt to corrupt information privacy for various different reasons, as described in *Part 1: Enter the world of cybercrime.* To ensure effective information security, organisations must implement regular security audits, employee training, and risk assessments. Regular security audits can help identify vulnerabilities in an organisation's security measures, while employee security education and awareness training can help prevent phishing attacks and other social engineering tactics. Risk assessments can help organisations identify potential security risks and develop strategies to mitigate them.

The future of information privacy controls is likely to involve increased regulation and stricter enforcement of existing laws. This trend is particularly evident in the United States, with several states passing new data privacy laws in recent years. The future of information privacy controls is also likely to involve increased use of artificial intelligence (AI), such as machine learning algorithms to detect and prevent security breaches [10]. Organisations need to watch these developments closely and big tech are certainly lobbying with regulators to establish a balance between commercial and privacy objectives.

Better training and education

Improving cybersecurity training and education programmes starts with acknowledging there is no single group that is de facto more or less likely to fall for a cyber-attack than others. This is to say that motivated attackers will tailor their tactics to their target (group), likely using widely available generative AI tools that make conventional phishing detection advice obsolete. Whether they are local security guards or the chief executive officer, everyone would benefit from adequate cybersecurity training and education.

Although most people agree it is good practice to have cybersecurity education, we know from our own experience and recent academic studies that despite such programmes, people still repeatedly click on phishing links [11,12] and download insecure freeware. There are several possible reasons for why security information may not "stick". One is that people tend to perceive mandatory training as time-consuming, not providing them with new knowledge and cumbersome, which likely makes them less engaged with the actual training content. Another is that certain security behaviours regularly taught in these programmes are not practical or even not useful.

To illustrate the latter, we return to research on detecting phishing links. Most, if not all, phishing detection training programmes will tell you that you should hover over links in e-mails to check whether the actual websites they lead to are legitimate. This requires a computer user to accurately interpret URLs. A study by Sara Albakry and colleagues (2020) showed that more than 90% of the study participants can not consistently distinguish URL domains [13]. They presented 1,929 participants with URLs such as https://profile.facebook.com, https://facebook.profile.com and https://twitter.com/facebook and asked them to indicate what website would open, if they were to type the link in their web browser. Many participants responded with the first recognisable name in the provided links and not the actual domains. If people are so bad at reading URLs, why do we keep telling them to hover over links in e-mails to check for phishing? Moreover, other studies, including our own, have shown that even technical professionals do not always hover over links to see whether an e-mail might be a phishing attempt [1,2]. The same can be said of disallowing tailgating, using unique passwords for every account and rejecting tracking cookies – they are security behaviours that most people find difficult to adhere to.

To know how effective a training or education programme is, we typically assess people on the knowledge they were intended to gain. Mandatory cybersecurity programmes typically only include a few multiple-choice questions at the end of the course material that allow multiple attempts. People are not alerted in their day-to-day work when they need to, for example, create a new unique password when creating a new account or how they are supposed to share confidential documents. Out of all aspects of cybersecurity training and education, one of the few that has a clear, measurable performance indicator is phishing detection.

Although phishing detection may not be representative of the effectiveness of all cybersecurity training and education, research on this topic suggests a ceiling effect of current cybersecurity training and education efforts. Ask any cybersecurity training provider and they will show you dramatic reductions in phishing click rates after implementing their training compared to before. What they will not show you is that by the third completed training or so, people's average click rates tend to stagnate. That is, they do not improve much more over time, as various independent studies are starting to show [11,12].

Researchers in Switzerland collaborated with a large enterprise to investigate the effectiveness of phishing training and simulations. They measured the likelihood that someone will click again on a simulated phishing link and enter personal information on a phishing website after previously receiving "embedded training" [12]. Their findings from over 14,000 employees showed that providing information on how to detect phishing e-mails after people clicked on simulated phishing attacks relates to even higher phishing susceptibility!

Organisations need to first ask themselves what they want to achieve with mandatory cybersecurity courses. Is it cybersecurity awareness? If so, what does cybersecurity awareness mean, what does it look like? How can it be measured? Or is it increasing the number of people reporting phishing campaigns? If it is about achieving any real behavioural change, providing an annual online training module is possibly not going to cut it. That is, cybersecurity is not just a "tick in the box" exercise. If you want to stay on top of the game, you will need to continuously seek ways to improve your operations. This likely includes regular cybersecurity training and education, but could also involve user studies on how people adopt security tools you want them to use (we will return to this topic in the next section), defining contextual communication policies that facilitate more secure interactions, organisation-wide red teaming events, "cyber fire drills" as part of operational resilience training, and putting signs in the digital workplace that encourage cyber hygiene.

In all cases, we have to start with a good understanding of how people think and what they do. A promising alternative approach to phishing detection training, for instance, is what we called "adversarial training" [14] that was borne out of a better understanding of how people suspect lies. In this training, we did not tell people what technical indicators to check when receiving e-mail, such as sender e-mail and URL domains, as in most current phishing education. Instead, we first showed people a unique five-minute video of an actor dressed up as a louche persona who explained precisely how they would prepare and deliver a spear-phishing attack. It included screen recordings of fictive LinkedIn profiles of potential targets, a hypothetical conference, and how they would write the actual phishing e-mail. We then asked the study participants to write three spear-phishing e-mails themselves and nudged them with instructions on using a well-faked e-mail address from which the hypothetical e-mail would be sent from. Two weeks later, we sent them a simulated phishing e-mail and compared their victimisation rate with that of a group that received no or a conventional type of phishing education. The result was quite remarkable: those in the adversarial training group had a victimisation rate of around 5%, whereas the conventional training group had a victimisation rate of around 14% [14]. The secondary outcome was that people were made aware of how easily a convincing phishing message could be created that will likely make them more cautious the next times they check their e-mail.

Two psychological insights inspired us to create this training. First, studies on lying and lie detection found that most people are mostly honest [15]. Second, in another set of experiments we did on the factors that drive human suspicion, we found that the more dishonest people were themselves, the more they suspected others of being dishonest, too [16]. We then wondered, could it be that people who find it difficult to detect phishing e-mails could just not imagine anyone would send them phishing e-mails, precisely because they never engage in such deceitful activities themselves? With the adversarial training, we thus aimed to let people think like a cybercriminal and gain an intuitive understanding of the digital deception tactics often employed in phishing campaigns. We did not tell people "check the sender's e-mail address to see if it a legitimate e-mail", but let people come up with fake e-mail addresses themselves during the training.

There were some notes of caution, however. First, some people believe we should not teach people how to write phishing e-mails. Although this is an understandable viewpoint, the idea of pretending to be a cybercriminal is not new to the cybersecurity domain. Red teaming is a regular, if not absolutely necessary practice to discover system vulnerabilities. Moreover, the training does not teach people how to conduct successful phishing campaigns, which requires further technical expertise. Second, more studies are needed to see how these first results on a relatively small group of people in an academic institute generalise to different types of organisations, populations, and even different social engineering contexts.

Third, even with the large difference in victimisation rates in this study, the adversarial training did not drive the rate down to near zero. This triggers the basic question whether there is a natural maximum detection rate. That is, we may have to expect that we all have a non-zero chance of falling for a social engineering attack at some point during our lifetime. Aiming for eradicating phishing victimisation altogether may not be possible – we can only try to marginalise the victimisation rate by using all the possible tools we have and being prepared for any potential incidents as outlined in *Chapter 7: Operational resilience relies on adequate cybersecurity*. Nevertheless, this study exemplifies how we can leverage knowledge about human psychology to develop better cybersecurity measures and hope it encourages practitioners to start testing alternative training and education approaches in their own organisations.

Security by design

SbD is a principle that emphasises integrating security measures into every stage of the software development lifecycle. Instead of treating security as an afterthought or add-on, it is woven into the fabric of software design, development, and deployment processes.

One way individual developers may do so is using the OWASP Top Ten list [17] with guidelines on preventing the most critical web application security risks. Developers integrate these best practices from the outset, such as protecting against cross-site scripting and cross-site request forgery. In product development, we see that payment processors like PayPal and Stripe design their systems with tokenisation, end-to-end encryption, and stringent compliance with standards like the Payment Card Industry Data Security Standard to protect financial transactions and customer data.

Essential SbD practices include any of the following:

- **The least privilege principle**: limiting user and system access rights to the minimum necessary to perform their functions. In an enterprise environment, a junior developer should only be given access to the components of the codebase they need to work on, rather than the entire system.
- **Threat modelling**: to identify potential security threats and vulnerabilities during the design phase. When designing a banking application, developers create scenarios where attackers might try to compromise user accounts or financial transactions. They then design countermeasures to mitigate these risks.
- **Secure defaults**: configuring systems with secure settings by default. An example is a cloud storage service defaults to encrypting data at rest and in transit, instead of requiring users to opt in to encryption.
- **Secure coding practices**: writing code in a way that inherently reduces vulnerabilities. An example would be using input validation to prevent SQL injection attacks or implementing encryption for data storage and transmission.
- **Good patch management**: ensuring that software is regularly updated to fix security vulnerabilities. An example is a web application framework provides regular patches to address newly discovered vulnerabilities and developers ensure these updates are applied promptly.
- **Regular security testing**: conducting continuous testing to identify and fix security issues. For example, incorporating automated security testing tools like Static Application Security Testing and Dynamic Application Security Testing into the continuous integration and continuous delivery pipeline to catch vulnerabilities early.

Apart from technical tests, we argue here that usability tests are crucial too. If a piece of software is not usable, that is, cumbersome or difficult to use correctly, people will find ways to circumvent it or make it easier to use. This can compromise security. Take authentication with passwords, for instance. People often find it difficult to come up with unique, memorable, "strong" passwords. The technical implementation of password authentication software may be fool proof, but the low usability of passwords may still jeopardise security.

To test for usability, organisations have to direct human–computer interaction specialists, such as user experience developers and user interface designers, to research how laypeople or a representative group of end users interact with the specified software before it gets deployed. For instance, through observational studies, beta testing, A/B testing, and contextual interviewing, you will identify how people will use and potentially misuse the software in practice. By making usability testing part of your SbD processes, we can prevent more cyber incidents resulting from human error.

Organisational cybersecurity culture

The Merriam-Webster dictionary defines culture as "the set of shared attitudes, values, goals, and practices that characterises an institution or organisation".

Often, culture is regarded as the invisible thread that binds us to the groups we identify with. Cybersecurity culture, then, refers to the set of attitudes, values, goals, and practices that people of an organisation have towards cybersecurity. In organisations, culture gets shaped top-down from the leadership level. They set examples for how to conduct oneself, appropriate personal and professional boundaries, and norms around what is considered relevant and valuable. Indeed, culture can greatly affect the ability of CISOs to act as a change agent and thereby influence the behaviours of employees across an entire organisation. Improving organisational cybersecurity culture thus requires a long-term commitment from the organisation's leadership.

We may say organisations with a strong cybersecurity culture have a critical number of staff with positive attitudes towards security behaviour, believes cybersecurity is important (i.e., value), wants the organisation to be secure (i.e., goal), and knows how to respond to potential risks (i.e., practice). Their leaders prioritise cybersecurity and communicate its importance to employees. They invest in cybersecurity training and awareness programmes, and hold employees accountable for their role in protecting the organisation from cyber-attacks.

In contrast, organisations with weak cybersecurity cultures view cybersecurity as an afterthought, and employees lack the necessary knowledge and skills to protect the organisation from cyber-attacks. They are characterised by a lack of leadership commitment to cybersecurity. Leaders may view cybersecurity as an IT issue and fail to recognise its role in the organisation's overall success. They may not invest sufficient resources in cybersecurity programmes, leaving employees ill-equipped to identify and respond to threats.

The Equifax breach from 2017 showed how a weak cybersecurity culture made a large multinational corporation vulnerable to cyber-attacks. Equifax suffered a major cybersecurity breach that compromised the personal information of millions of customers. The breach was caused by an employee who fell victim to a phishing attack and unwittingly gave access to the company's network to a hacker. The hacker then used this access to steal sensitive information [18]. Upon investigation, it was found that the company had a weak cybersecurity culture± the company had not invested enough in cybersecurity training and awareness programmes for employees, and there was a lack of accountability for cybersecurity incidents. The company's leadership had also failed to prioritise cybersecurity, and there was a disconnect between the IT department and the rest of the organisation. This lack of a cybersecurity culture resulted in significant financial and reputational damage to the company.

What makes embedding cybersecurity in organisational culture especially a daunting and never-ending task is due to several, mostly human factors. Poor security awareness is rife, and many employees may not fully understand the importance of cybersecurity or how their actions can impact the organisation's security. Resistance to change is common, as described in *Chapter 6: Human fallacies and how to overcome them*, and employees might be resistant to adopting new security practices and unlearning insecure behaviour, especially if they feel it adds extra work or complexity to their daily tasks. In this vein, Kim et al. (2024) argue we cannot underestimate the influence of work overload on cybersecurity behaviour.

Employees who feel the executive team are just pushing more and more work on them experience a psychological contract breach and burnout. This has a direct impact on them adopting insecure behaviours [19].

Implementing comprehensive cybersecurity measures also often requires significant investments in technology, training, and personnel. which some organisations may struggle to afford due to resource constraints. Moreover, the constantly evolving nature of cyber threats means that organisations must continuously update and adapt their security measures, which can be difficult to keep up with. Different departments or teams within an organisation may have varying attitudes towards cybersecurity, making it hard to establish a unified approach. The role of executive boards is crucial in overcoming these challenges.

A "bad" executive board can deplete the cybersecurity function of resources, seeing security purely as headcount. They can undermine cybersecurity initiatives and ask employees to prioritise organisation transformation initiatives instead. In this scenario, the security leader is merely seen as a person to blame in the event of a security incident. In the event of a major security incident, a bad executive board can quickly look for "heads to roll" to avoid accountability from regulators or shareholders. This creates a negative environment not just for the cybersecurity function, but anyone in a technology role. They know they are under huge pressure to deliver organisation transformation, but also that their feet will be held to the fire any time they make a mistake.

A "good" executive board can set the tone by prioritising cybersecurity and leading by example. Executives need to acknowledge the importance of cybersecurity to the entire organisation and integrate it into the organisation's values. The straightforward way to do so is by allocating adequate resources for cybersecurity initiatives, which include budget, personnel, and technology. Boards can also develop and enforce policies that promote a culture of security, such as tailored training and awareness programmes, rewards for secure behaviours, more collaboration across functional teams to build up a coherent security culture, and testing incident response plans. Executives can encourage open communication about cybersecurity issues that can help identify and address vulnerabilities more quickly. Finally, boards should regularly review and assess the organisation's cybersecurity measures to ensure they remain effective and up-to-date.

All these efforts are meant to create a security-first mindset that encourages employees to think about security in everything they do. To gauge and encourage an organisation's cybersecurity culture, one initiative that has recently been popularised with organisations is setting up a cybersecurity champions programme.

Cybersecurity champions

The idea for a cybersecurity champions programme comes from a desire to close the gap between cybersecurity teams and non-cybersecurity employees in an organisation. Its promise is that it will bolster organisational security through spreading awareness, increasing cybersecurity engagement, making security practices more engrained in the company culture, and acting more efficiently on suspicious activities.

The programme typically revolves around a group of "regular" employees, not necessarily of any particular background but from different parts of the organisation, who volunteer to be the cybersecurity champions in their organisation. They receive regular training on how to implement various secure behaviours, which they can then show to their colleagues in their respective teams. This makes them role models for non-technical colleagues to whom they may be better capable of relaying security concepts compared to cybersecurity professionals. As in a hub-and-spoke model, the cybersecurity team is the hub and the champions function as the spokes. They are like security antennae that extend into all areas of the organisation without significant additional resources. They provide feedback to the cybersecurity team on what they observed, what they have done, any security issues they found, and how the organisation could better tailor training and other cybersecurity measures.

We are often asked whether a strategy of having cybersecurity champions works in practice. Our answer is it probably depends on a wide variety of factors, including the organisation, the industry sector, the corporate culture, resources allocated to the champions group, levels of training and support, and the fit between the champions' expectations and their motivations. It is crucial to tailor the programme to fit the organisation's specific needs and resources – although this complicates evaluating the overall effectiveness of cybersecurity champions programmes across organisations.

Peers could have more immediate impact on awareness and security behaviour, as studies by Rick Wash and colleagues have found that people often learn about security decisions through stories told by family, friends, and peers [20,21]. The impact of such stories can be large, as people tend to share these stories with more than one person. Still, one of these studies also found that "facts-and-advice" type of training on phishing link detection by a security expert was more effective than a story told by a peer [20]. This implies that the potential impact of champions, whom usually are direct peers, sharing security knowledge may be overestimated.

Other factors that challenge the effectiveness of cybersecurity champions programmes are champions' varying levels of cybersecurity knowledge, risk of burnout, compromising the quality of employees' primary roles, appropriate incentive structures, and the long-term maintenance of hub-and-spoke interactions. Champions likely have different levels of cybersecurity knowledge, which could lead to inconsistent messaging across teams and modelling insecure behaviour. For example, champions handling sensitive information might inadvertently create privacy concerns if proper protocols are not followed. If champions leave the organisation or change roles, the cybersecurity culture may weaken, unless there is a structured programme in place for training new champions. Champions might already have demanding primary roles. Adding cybersecurity responsibilities could, therefore, lead to burnout or decreased effectiveness in both roles. Besides, employees may not see any immediate benefits or recognition from being a champion. Ensuring all champions are aligned and coordinating effectively with the central cybersecurity team can also be difficult, especially in larger organisations.

To begin with, organisations need to clearly define the champions' roles and responsibilities, agree on realistic expectations and set clear incentives in the form of recognition, bonuses, or career advancement opportunities. Then they need to provide standardised training to bring all new champions up to the same base level of knowledge, as well as regular ongoing training and support. The champions need to know the reporting pathways, how to best handle sensitive information and following privacy protocols to mitigate any privacy concerns. From an organisational point of view, any externally provided training needs to align with internal security policies. One study by Uta Menges and colleagues (2023) conducted with a German organisation found that the training provided to the cybersecurity champions contradicted with internal security policies [22]. Implementation issues like these can easily be overlooked and require more careful designing and planning of the programme.

This does require resources that may strain especially smaller organisations. Having a dedicated budget agreed for training and supporting champions could help address this issue. It is also important to establish clear communication channels between champions and the central cybersecurity team to ensure alignment and coordination. This could include regular meetings, newsletters, or an online portal for sharing information.

In summary, we need further studies to examine the effectiveness of cybersecurity champions programmes. Meanwhile, provided there is careful planning and support, many organisations find the potential benefits of having a cybersecurity champions programme worth exploring.

Nudge programmes

A "nudge programme" is a tactic to subtly influence people's behaviour by carefully designing the way choices are presented to them – essentially "nudging" them towards a desired action, without restricting their freedom of choice. This is based on the principles of behavioural economics and "nudge theory" developed by Richard Thaler and Cass Sunstein [23].

Practical examples of cybersecurity nudge programmes include security update reminders, warning banners on e-mails flagged as potential phishing campaigns [6], and authentication interfaces that offer users enabling of two-factor authentication when they are about to access a sensitive account. These nudges may help prevent users from clicking on malicious links, ensure their software is up to date, and help users implement more secure authentication methods.

Another example is a password strength metre, so that when employees are creating a new password, a visual indicator displays the password strength (weak, medium, strong) to encourage users to choose a more complex password. Suspicious activity alerts are good at nudging where unusual login attempts are detected, such as from a new location. Then, a notification is sent to the user that prompts them to review their recent activity and potentially change their password.

Although the validity of the concept of nudges as behavioural change interventions is unclear [24], there are relatively few studies on nudges in the security domain. The concept requires further exploration to evaluate its specific efficacy in cybersecurity.

Situational crime prevention

As some bonus material to inspire you to think creatively about how to facilitate security behaviour in your organisation, we want to point out a comprehensive set of 25 situational crime prevention techniques published by Cornish and Clarke in 2003 [25]. It is a widely used resource by law enforcers and policymakers to design (new) measures to reduce crime, rooted in the crime theory described in *Chapter 1: Most cybercriminals are made, not born* that underscores the role of situational factors in the prevalence of crime. Accordingly, the authors distinguish five situational crime prevention principles to reduce the likelihood that someone would seize a crime opportunity [26]:

1. **Measures to increase the effort** required to commit a crime, such as controlling access to facilities;
2. **Increasing the risks** of getting caught, such as reducing anonymity;
3. **Reducing the rewards** associated with the crime, such as removing targets from likely crime scenes;
4. **Reducing provocations** to engage in criminal behaviour, such as neutralising peer pressure;
5. **Removing excuses** that make it unlikely people were not aware of what criminal behaviour to avoid, such as placing warnings and instructions.

Table 9.1 shows the full list of prevention techniques. Some of these may be useful in devising measures to prevent cybercriminals from launching cyber-attacks on organisations. Currently, most organisational cybersecurity measures are focused on "increasing the effort". For instance, firewalls relate to technique 1 ("harden target"), authentication and authorisation methods relate to technique 2 ("control access to facilities"), anomaly detection systems relate to technique 10 ("strengthen formal surveillance"), data encryption relates to technique 11 ("conceal targets"), and data back-up and restore systems relate to technique 15 ("deny benefits") in the case of a ransomware attack. The anonymous nature of the internet and individualistic setting of working on a personal computer make prevention measures based on "increasing the risks", "reducing provocation", and "removing excuses" more difficult. People are free to browse what they want on the internet and can easily create digital aliases. Unless a watchful parent restricts their child from certain online spaces and influence from bad peers and role models, that kid may be tempted to explore hacking without much resistance. There are no "traffic signs" on the internet that warn people of undesirable, criminal content. Proponents of the "free" internet in fact take pride in the fact that it is a largely unregulated place. So, if situational crime prevention measures are difficult to implement in the current internet setup, we might as well turn the framework around to discourage insecure and encourage secure behaviour in our employees.

Of course, we are not suggesting to view secure or insecure employee behaviours as criminal offences. We are presenting this framework to encourage you to reflect on how you can change your organisational circumstances to encourage

Table 9.1 Twenty-five situational crime prevention techniques from Cornish and Clarke (2003) [27]

Increase the effort	Increase the risks	Reduce the rewards	Reduce provocation	Remove excuses
1. Harden target	6. Extend guardianship	11. Conceal targets	16. Reduce frustrations and stress	21. Set rules
2. Control access to facilities	7. Assist natural surveillance	12. Remove targets	17. Avoid disputes	22. Post instructions
3. Screen exits	8. Reduce anonymity	13. Identify property	18. Reduce emotional arousal	23. Alert conscience
4. Deflect offenders	9. Utilise place managers	14. Disrupt markets	19. Neutralise peer pressure	24. Assist compliance
5. Control tools/ weapons	10. Strengthen formal surveillance	15. Deny benefits	20. Discourage imitation	25. Control drugs and alcohol

desired and discourage undesired, insecure behaviours. Because these techniques likely apply well beyond crime to influence human behaviour in general. Viewed this way, they can be excellent starting points for organisations seeking new ways to promote cybersecurity.

For example, to increase the effort of performing an insecure action, such as sharing confidential documents with external parties, organisations could think of disallowing downloading those documents (i.e., "harden target") and sending managers a notification whenever a user attempts to download such documents (i.e., "screen exits"). To increase the risk of and remove excuses for clicking on a phishing link, organisations could design social nudges in its organisational e-mail interface that remind people of double checking unsolicited requests with a colleague from a different department before they click any link. Reducing rewards could mean removing an end-of-year bonus or withholding a promotion for those who cause cyber incidents (i.e., "deny benefits"). Investing in mental wellbeing and creating acknowledgement programmes could help reduce frustrations and stress at work as a way of reducing provocation of insider threat – related to techniques 16 and 17. There are many different ways in which these 25 techniques could be adopted by any organisation. It just takes a willingness to think "outside the box" and courage to try something new in the cybersecurity field.

References

1 R. Wash, "How experts detect phishing scam emails," *Proceedings of the ACM on Human-Computer Interaction*, vol. 4, no. CSCW2, pp. 1–28, 2020, doi: 10.1145/3415231.

2 S. Y. Zheng and I. Becker, "Presenting suspicious details in {user-facing} e-mail headers does not improve phishing detection," in *Eighteenth Symposium on Usable Privacy and Security (SOUPS 2022)*, Boston, MA: USENIX Association, 2022, pp. 253–271.

3 Cifas, "Scammers stole £11.4 billion from UK people in last 12 months." Accessed: January 30, 2025 [Online]. Available: https://www.cifas.org.uk/newsroom/gasa-stateofscamsuk2024; Feedzai, "Report: More than US$1 trillion lost to scams in one year." Accessed: January 30, 2025 [Online]. Available: https://www.feedzai.com/pressrelease/report-more-than-us1-trillion-lost-to-scams-in-one-year/; U. S. F. T. Commission, "As nationwide fraud losses top $10 billion in 2023, FTC steps up efforts to protect the public." Accessed: January 30, 2025 [Online]. Available: https://www.ftc.gov/news-events/news/press-releases/2024/02/nationwide-fraud-losses-top-10-billion-2023-ftc-steps-efforts-protect-public; UK Finance, "Fraud remains a major problem as over £1 billion is stolen by criminals in 2023." Accessed: January 30, 2025 [Online]. Available: https://www.ukfinance.org.uk/news-and-insight/press-release/fraud-remains-major-problem-over-ps1-billion-stolen-criminals-in

4 S. Sjouwerman, "How Podesta got hacked: HelpDesk said 'Password' phishing email was real," KnowBe4. Accessed: February 24, 2025. Available at: https://blog.knowbe4.com/it-told-podesta-to-click-the-link

5 See https://wikileaks.org/podesta-emails/

6 S. Y. Zheng and I. Becker, "Checking, nudging or scoring? Evaluating e-mail user security tools," in *Nineteenth Symposium on Usable Privacy and Security (SOUPS 2023)*, Anaheim, CA: USENIX Association, pp. 57–76, Aug. 2023.

7 C. C. Ife, Y. Shen, S. J. Murdoch, and G. Stringhini, "Marked for disruption: Tracing the evolution of malware delivery operations targeted for takedown," in *Proceedings of the 24th International Symposium on Research in Attacks, Intrusions and Defenses*, San Sebastian, Spain, pp. 340–353, 2021, doi: 10.1145/3471621.3471844.

8 A. AL-Hawamleh, "Cyber resilience framework: Strengthening defenses and enhancing continuity in business security," *International Journal of Computing and Digital Systems*, vol. 15, no. 1, pp. 1315–1331, 2024.

9 M. M. Willie, "The role of organizational culture in cybersecurity: Building a security-first culture," *Journal of Research, Innovation and Technologies*, vol. II, no. 4, pp. 179–198, 2023, doi: 10.57017/jorit.v2.2(4).05.

10 T. Singh, *Artificial Intelligence and Ethics: A Field Guide for Stakeholders.* CRC Press, Abingdon, Oxon, 2024.

11 B. Reinheimer, L. Aldag, P. Mayer, M. Mossano, R. Duezguen, B. Lofthouse, T. Von Landesberger, and M. Volkamer, "An investigation of phishing awareness and education over time: When and how to best remind users," in *Proceedings of the 16th Symposium on Usable Privacy and Security, SOUPS 2020*, Virtual Conference, pp. 259–284, 2020.

12 D. Lain, K. Kostiainen, and S. Čapkun, "Phishing in organizations: Findings from a large-scale and long-term study," in *2022 IEEE Symposium on Security and Privacy (S\&P)*, San Francisco, CA, US, pp. 842–859, 2022.

13 S. Albakry, K. Vaniea, and M. K. Wolters, "What is this URL's Destination? Empirical Evaluation of Users' URL Reading," in *Conference on Human Factors in Computing Systems - Proceedings, Association for Computing Machinery*, Honolulu HI, USA, pp.1–12, Apr 2020, doi: 10.1145/3313831.3376168.

14 S. Y. Zheng and I. Becker, "Phishing to improve detection," in *Proceedings of the 2023 European Symposium on Usable Security*, 2023, Copenhagen, Denmark, pp. 334–343, 2023.

15 B. DePaulo, "The many faces of lies," *The social psychology of good and evil*, New York: Guilford Press. Chapter 12, pp. 303–326, 2004.

16 S. Y. Zheng, L. Rozenkrantz, and T. Sharot, "Poor lie detection related to an under-reliance on statistical cues and overreliance on own behaviour," *Communications Psychology*, vol. 2, no. 1, p. 21, 2024, doi: 10.1038/s44271-024-00068-7.

17 See https://owasp.org/www-project-top-ten/

18 https://www.csoonline.com/article/534628/the-biggest-data-breaches-of-the-21st-century.html

19 B.-J. Kim and M.-J. Kim, "The influence of work overload on cybersecurity behavior: A moderated mediation model of psychological contract breach, burnout, and self-efficacy in AI learning such as ChatGPT," *Technology in Society*, vol. 77, p. 102543, 2024.

20 R. Wash and M. M. Cooper, "Who provides phishing training? Facts, stories, and people like me," in *Conference on Human Factors in Computing Systems - Proceedings*, New York: Association for Computing Machinery, Montréal, QC, Canada, Apr. 2018. doi: 10.1145/3173574.3174066.

21 E. Rader, R. Wash, and B. Brooks, "Stories as informal lessons about security." In symposium on Usable Privacy and Security (SOUPS) 2012, July 11-13, 2012, Washington, DC, USA.

22 U. Menges, J. Hielscher, L. Kocksch, A. Kluge, and M. A. Sasse, "Caring not scaring-An evaluation of a workshop to train apprentices as security champions," in *Proceedings of the 2023 European Symposium on Usable Security*, 2023, Copenhagen, Denmark, pp. 237–252.

23 https://www.mitre.org/resources/mitre-nudge-research#:~:text=Nudges%20help%20people%20make%20better,as%20MITRE's%20Nudge%20Lab%20demonstrates

24 M. Maier, F. Bartoš, T. D. Stanley, D. R. Shanks, A. J. L. Harris, and E.-J. Wagenmakers, "No evidence for nudging after adjusting for publication bias," *Proceedings of the National Academy of Sciences*, vol. 119, no. 31, p. e2200300119, 2022, doi: 10.1073/pnas.2200300119.

25 A. A. Braga, *Problem-Oriented Policing and Crime Prevention*, vol. 2. Monsey, NY: Criminal Justice Press, 2008.

26 https://popcenter.asu.edu/sites/default/files/twenty_five_techniques_of_situational_prevention.pdf

27 D. B. Cornish and R. V. Clarke, "Opportunities, precipitators and criminal decisions: A reply to Wortley's critique of situational crime prevention," *Crime Prevention Studies*, vol. 16, pp. 41–96, 2003.

Part 3

The target's perspective

10 Psychology applied in cybersecurity

Let us imagine that a cybercriminal created a targeted social engineering campaign for you. They first message you through LinkedIn, presenting themselves as a head-hunter for technical talent. You say you are interested and give them your professional e-mail address to continue the application process. Soon after, you receive an e-mail from them with a link to a malicious programming assessment. You are now the "last line of defence" for your organisation. If you click the link and complete the challenge, you may just have facilitated a $308m worth Bitcoin transaction to North Korea – as happened to an employee of a Japanese crypto-currency software firm in 2024 [1]. As a result, the organisation might collapse, people may lose their jobs and you have to live with the memory of that fateful "job offer".

People are often referred to as the "weakest link" in security [2], because we can easily (and cheaply) be tricked into falling for a cyber-attack. Indeed, even technical cybersecurity professionals and senior executives have fallen for well-crafted social engineering attacks. How is this possible? If we want to create more effective, *human-in-the-loop* cybersecurity measures, we need to understand what people think and do when they are faced with a potential cyber-attack. How do they decide what is true and what to trust? How are we persuaded to carry out tasks we normally would not do? What can we do to make more secure decisions?

To answer these questions, we turn to the field of neuropsychology. In this and the following chapter, we will take a quick tour through the faculties of our mind to understand how our brains construct our worldview – including the psychological pitfalls as a result of how our brains cope with the large volumes of information to process.

Opening the black box

The human brain has long been among the most mysterious parts of our bodies. The knowledge we gathered about this plump slimy mass of grey and white matter is the result of mostly the past 100 years. Techniques such as brain scanning, genetic modification, and computational models of how people make decisions are slowly revealing answers to big questions, such as what consciousness and intelligence are, and how the brain protects us from emotional distress. The promise

DOI: 10.4324/9781003610533-13

Figure 10.1 Black box as metaphor for what happens in our brains that gives rise to our psychology.

of this exciting field of research is a deeper understanding of ourselves – why we think, feel, and do what we think, feel, and do.

When one of the authors started their undergraduate in psychology, an introductory lecture explained the study of human behaviour with a diagram like the one shown in Figure 10.1.

Here, *stimuli* are the objects and physical phenomena in the world around us ("input"), the big *black box* refers to all the information processing in our brains about those stimuli, which then results in observable *behaviour* – the movements we produce with our physical bodies ("output"). At this meta level, we are just like a computing system. Where a computer relies on binary input data, we see, hear, smell, touch, and taste the world around us. Whereas a computer processes data through its electronic circuit boards, our eyes, ears, nose, tongue, and skin send biochemical data to the central nervous system – our brains and spinal cord. After processing all the input data, the computer outputs a deterministic decision, and the human brain may decide it is too hot in the room and send concerted signals to the body's eyes, neck, and leg muscles to walk over to the thermostat in the room and, once arrived, carefully activate the finger muscles to rotate the thermostat about 40 degrees anti-clockwise to reduce the heating. That is an observable "output" behaviour. Figuring out how the initial sensory data were weighted and combined in the person's brain that led to the conclusion "body too hot, reduce heating through thermostat" is the art of behaviour science. It is precisely how a bunch of biochemical signals give rise to our conscious experience of being that we refer to here as the "black box".

From ancient times, philosophers have been trying to open the black box through ways of reflective reasoning. Then from the 1800s, founding psychologists started creating clever, highly controlled experiments to infer the many qualities of our brains. They started carefully studying how people respond to deliberately manipulated stimuli, for instance, using psychometric questionnaires and experimental games. To this day, psychological and neuroscience research relies on this basic concept to explain both "normal" and maladaptive behaviour. Now, coupled with modern brain imaging and recording techniques, it is only a matter of time for us to fully open the black box that shapes our mind.

Since recent years, social scientists started applying the same psychological research methods to study how we can improve people's cybersecurity behaviour.

This field, known as *usable security,* aims to identify human factors to explain insecure and encourage secure behaviour. The research community is small, especially compared to traditionally cybersecurity-related disciplines like computer science, but is attracting many interdisciplinary collaborations, for example, between psychologists and engineers.

Many early works looked into ways to teach computer users basic cybersecurity concepts to, for instance, encrypt e-mails [3] and use more secure passwords [4]. These studies uncovered that insecure behaviour, such as wrongly using encryption tools and clicking on phishing links, stem from people's flawed ideas of how computer systems work. Naturally, many following studies tested ways to correct those misunderstandings – for instance, getting people to adopt different mental models and using behavioural change theories [5].

Unfortunately, these studies have not produced convincing long-term improvements in people's security behaviour [6]. What makes this especially difficult to achieve is that people do not easily change habits – certainly not after an annual mandated cybersecurity training, as discussed in *Chapter 9: Improving organisational cybersecurity.* Much of the current workforce did not grow up with personal computers all around, let alone were educated from childhood on how to adequately use computers or understanding how the internet works. The now 50+ year old generation had to figure out their own idiosyncratic computer habits to get their increasingly digitalised work done. In contrast, more and more countries are teaching children computer science subjects as part of primary and secondary school curricula. Time will tell if this leads to more secure future generations.

One could use this line of research to argue that we, in fact, need to keep humans *out* of the loop and automate cybersecurity as much as possible. Assuming we want to marginalise any risk from cyber-attacks, this is only an option if we can guarantee 100% accurate automated detection. That, or the idea that we can live in a world where nobody commits cyber-attacks, is a utopia. We should neither forget that we created computer systems precisely because they help us, humans, do things better. With our growing dependency on digital communication tools, it is becoming impossible to see computer systems as separate from ourselves, which brings us back to the starting point of this chapter. Even with a nearly perfect cyber-attack detection system, a 0.1% false negative rate combined with a large total volume of daily cyber-attacks still warrants taking the common individual's potential for unintentionally misusing computer systems seriously. Usable security research is thus set to continue growing its relevance to the cybersecurity practice.

Perhaps the essential reason to do usable security research is precisely to point out to cybersecurity engineers what does and does not work for most people. To illustrate this, let us consider recent developments in authentication methods that do not rely on memorising many unique, difficult passwords for many accounts. It was known by the 1950s through psychological experiments that our capacity for remembering things is limited to approximately seven items [7]. Most of us now have more than seven accounts on various e-commerce and government websites, in addition to personal and work e-mail addresses. This makes it humanly impossible to have unique passwords for each account, even though common cybersecurity advice will have you come up with a new password every time you create an account [8]. By knowing (the limitations of) our human psychology, we can thus anticipate what cybersecurity measures would be adopted by people and which behaviours likely would not. Authentication researchers who acknowledged this are now working on exciting alternatives such as methods based on physical keys [9] and electric muscle stimulation [10] that, apart from the technical perspective, also optimise for usability.

That said, we will now dive deeper into the key workings of our minds. Since many cyber-attacks involve a social engineering component, it is worth expanding further on the psychological phenomena that may explain why people fall for them. A solid understanding of how people form beliefs on what is true and whom to trust can then help us improve our defences against social engineering attacks.

Brains: natural prediction machines

The past decades of neuroscience research have led to the idea that our brains are natural prediction machines that are constantly estimating what we are seeing, hearing, smelling, touching, and tasting [11]. As we grow older, it learns a model of the physical world we find ourselves in, so it can explain, predict, and respond better to what is around us. This system probably gave us an evolutionary advantage, meaning our bodies have a higher chance of survival with a nervous system that senses and coordinates movements via electric pulses that allows us to respond faster to potential threats. Our thoughts, then, are just iterating over possible future scenarios and help us anticipate our response in each scenario.

A common, simple example is that when we stare at a bright green wall and then look at a white wall, we see a green haze on this white wall for a short while. This happens, because the nervous system does not want to waste energy on encoding redundant information. It makes its best guess about the world around us and sticks to it until it detects a change. When we are staring at the green wall, the cone cells in our retinas are at first continuously telling our brains "green!". Since the colour does not change for a while, our brain keeps thinking, or in other words, predicting "green". Then, when our eyes move to see the white wall, our brains are still predicting "green" for a little while, until enough information from our retinas has gone through to tell our brains the wall is white. Afterward, you may wonder about the future possibilities, such as "what would happen if I stare at a red wall and then a blue one?", and your thoughts will try to predict it in your mind.

The same prediction process is happening when we are talking with someone. When we listen to someone speak, our brains are constantly trying to predict the next words the other person will say [12]. When the movements of the other person's lips and sound from their voice do not align with the predicted words, something termed a "prediction error" occurs. Accordingly, we can think of the brain as a system that aims to minimise prediction error. It is constantly trying to make sense of the world by building a representation of the world that is as close to reality as possible [13]. Our brains are generally pretty good at doing this for things that are explicit and tangible to us, like colours, sounds, and textures. They are objectively measurable qualities. But less obvious, intangible things like what the person next to us in a meeting is feeling or whether an e-mail may be a social engineering attack, are progressively harder for our brains to build models and make predictions for, because indicators for how someone feels and phishing e-mails, respectively, are often not as straightforward as what colour an object has [14]. So how do we do it?

There are at least three types of cues the brain relies on: external event likelihoods, reward contingencies, and theory of mind. Event likelihoods relate to how often we sense and experience something from the outside world [15]. For example, if your boss always e-mails you about project deadlines, chances are that the next time you receive a new e-mail from your boss, your brain expects it to say something about a new project deadline. In the same vein, likelihoods also directly affect how much we expect to find a phishing e-mail in our inbox. Since most of us receive mostly legitimate e-mails, chances are high that the next e-mail we see is legitimate too. Our brains' reliance on likelihoods can thus work against us here: because the likelihood of receiving a phishing e-mail is low, our brains are less likely to expect any e-mail to be phishing, until our brains sense something significantly unexpected about an e-mail. Paradoxically, a phishing e-mail detection system with very low false negative rates (i.e., number of missed phishing e-mails) may therefore lead to less e-mail security awareness in users, because it would lead users to have hardly any exposure to phishing.

Reward contingencies relate to the feedback we get on our behaviour that help us learn and unlearn things. Of course, there are external rewards in the sense of receiving money or getting an award that recognises your efforts. They tell your brain you did something well, which makes you more likely to do the same thing again that led you to that reward. We all know how casinos aim to exploit this mechanism. But there also is a sense of internal reward in the sense that it feels good when our brain predicted something correctly and its prediction error is very low.

Let us imagine you just sensed someone took your phone from your pocket. Your brain immediately directs your neck and eye muscles to start looking around for suspects. Then you see someone walking away from you who stood very near to you on the tube. You then run after them and manage to get your phone back from them. The fact your brain predicted that specific person to be the prime suspect and then finding it to be accurate is an incredibly rewarding one. The next time you feel something slid out of your pocket, your brain will activate the same prediction model for finding a thief. On the other hand, if your brain predicted an innocent person who was just walking past you to have taken your phone, the moment you grab them and request them to return your phone to you will generate a big prediction error. They might look frightened and tell you they did not steal your phone. You have to admit you made a mistake. It will feel like a punishment to your brain, after which you need to recalibrate the factors to take as signals of a thief.

Theory of mind relates to understanding others by imagining we were in their situation. Since we do not have direct access to someone else's feelings and thoughts, our best guess for predicting someone else's state of mind is by thinking about what it would be like to be them. If you have known the other person for a long time and are familiar with how they act, your brain has already developed a predictive model about their behaviour that helps you place yourself in their shoes. But when the other person is a stranger and our brain does not have a prediction model for them yet, we may use our own behaviour to guess what they may be feeling and thinking.

We briefly introduced this phenomenon of self-projection in a different context in *Chapter 6: Human fallacies and how to overcome them* – the effect that when we are asked to interpret and judge other people's behaviour, we project our own (moral) values and feelings onto them. In an experiment where participants were asked to rate the emotional expressions in a series of portraits, participants who were made to feel sadder rated the portraits as more negative and, vice versa, participants who felt happy rated the portraits as more positive [16]. Similarly, our own experiments showed that people who lie more themselves also have more suspicions that other people are lying more, and that conversely, honest people believed others were mostly honest too, just like themselves [17]. It is thus conceivable that the thought that someone may be socially engineering one is not considered a possibility as quickly in honest people's minds compared to people who deceive more often themselves. We described how we used this knowledge to create a different phishing detection training in *Chapter 9: Improving organisational cybersecurity.*

These three types of cues – likelihoods, rewards, and theory of mind – interact with one another to form and direct our understanding of the world. Likelihoods become associated with rewards and theory of mind (e.g. when we correctly predicted someone's feelings), and likelihoods about the general human behaviours we observe over time become intertwined with theory of mind predictions. We generally seek rewarding and avoid unrewarding things in the world. We may accordingly anticipate the likelihood of a reward by avoiding something bad from happening. For instance, when an e-mail tells us to reset our password to avoid getting hacked. Together, these factors shape how we perceive the world, and judge what is true, honest, and "real", as opposed to fake or ingenuous. In other words, what we can believe and what not. Let us consider how these factors play out as someone falls for a social engineering attack.

References

1   FBI, "FBI, DC3, and NPA identification of North Korean cyber actors, tracked as TraderTraitor, responsible for theft of $308 million USD from Bitcoin.DMM.com," Washington, D.C., 2024.

2 A. Adams and M. A. Sasse, "Users are not the enemy," *Communications of the ACM*, vol. 42, no. 12, pp. 40–46, 1999, doi: 10.1145/322796.322806.

3 A. Whitten and J. D. Tygar, "Why Johnny can't encrypt: A usability evaluation of PGP 5.0," in *Proceedings of the 8th Conference on USENIX Security Symposium - Volume 8*, USENIX Association, Washington DC, USA, vol. 348, 1999; Z. Benenson, G. Lenzini, D. Oliveira, S. Parkin, and S. Uebelacker, "Maybe poor johnny really cannot encrypt - The case for a complexity theory for usable security," *ACM International Conference Proceeding Series*, vol. 8–11-Sept, pp. 85–99, 2015, doi: 10.1145/2841113.2841120.

4 C. Shen, T. Yu, H. Xu, G. Yang, and X. Guan, "User practice in password security: An empirical study of real-life passwords in the wild," *Computers & Security*, vol. 61, pp. 130–141, 2016, doi: 10.1016/j.cose.2016.05.007.

5 S. Das, J. Abbott, S. Gopavaram, J. Blythe, and L. J. Camp, "User-centered risk communication for safer browsing," Springer, Feb. 2020. doi: 10.1007/978-3-030-54455-3_2; S. Burns and L. Roberts, "Applying the Theory of Planned Behaviour to predicting online safety behaviour," *Crime Prevention and Community Safety*, vol. 15, no. 1, pp. 48–64, Feb. 2013, doi: 10.1057/cpcs.2012.13.

6 T. Singh, *Cybersecurity, Psychology and People Hacking*. Cham: Springer International Publishing Imprint, Palgrave Macmillan, 2025.

7 G. A. Miller, "The magical number seven, plus or minus two: Some limits on our capacity for processing information," *Psychological Review*, vol. 63, pp. 81–97, 1956.

8 E. M. Redmiles, S. Kross, and M. L. Mazurek, "How well do my results generalize? Comparing security and privacy survey results from MTurk, web, and telephone samples," *IEEE Symposium on Security and Privacy*, vol. 2019-May, pp. 1326–1343, 2019, doi: 10.1109/SP.2019.00014.

9 S. Ghorbani Lyastani, M. Schilling, M. Neumayr, M. Backes, and S. Bugiel, "Is FIDO2 the kingslayer of user authentication? A comparative usability study of FIDO2 passwordless authentication," *IEEE Symposium on Security and Privacy*, vol. 2020-May, pp. 268–285, 2020, doi: 10.1109/SP40000.2020.00047.

10 Y. Chen, Z. Yang, R. Abbou, P. Lopes, B. Y. Zhao, and H. Zheng, "User authentication via electrical muscle stimulation," in *Proceedings of the 2021 CHI Conference on Human Factors in Computing Systems*, Yokohama, Japan, pp. 1–15, May 2021, doi: 10.1145/3411764.3445441.

11 D. C. a. P. A. Knill, "The Bayesian brain: The role of uncertainty in neural coding and computation," *TRENDS in Neurosciences*, vol. 27, no. 12, pp. 712–719, 2004; M. C. a. P. Seriès, "Bayes in the brain—On Bayesian modelling in neuroscience," *The British Journal for the Philosophy of Science*, vol. 63, no. 3, pp. 697–723, 2012.

12 M. Koskinen, M. Kurimo, J. Gross, A. Hyvärinen, and R. Hari, "Brain activity reflects the predictability of word sequences in listened continuous speech," *Neuroimage*, vol. 219, p. 116936, Oct. 2020, doi: 10.1016/J.NEUROIMAGE.2020.116936; F. Huettig, "Four central questions about prediction in language processing," *Brain Research*, vol. 1626, pp. 118–135, Nov. 2015, doi: 10.1016/J.BRAINRES.2015.02.014.

13 A. Clark, "Whatever next? Predictive brains, situated agents, and the future of cognitive science," *Behavioral and Brain Sciences*, vol. 36, no. 3, pp. 181–204, 2013, doi: 10.1017/S0140525X12000477.

14 And then even our eyes do not always agree with what others see, as was demonstrated by a viral social media post in 2015 that included a picture of a black and dark blue striped dress, which some people perceive as white and gold (source: Wikipedia "The dress"): https://en.wikipedia.org/wiki/The_dress

15   The brain learns to predict for these event likelihoods over time.

16   P. C. Schmid and M. Schmid Mast, "Mood effects on emotion recognition," *Motivation and Emotion,* vol. 34, pp. 288–292, 2010, doi: 10.1007/s11031-010-9170-0.

17   S. Y. Zheng, L. Rozenkrantz, and T. Sharot, "Poor lie detection related to an under-reliance on statistical cues and overreliance on own behaviour," *Communications Psychology*, vol. 2, no. 1, p. 21, 2024, doi: 10.1038/s44271-024-00068-7.

11 How we take the bait

At the start of the previous chapter, we mentioned the cyber-attack that led to a $300m worth Bitcoin harvest for North Korean hackers. Let us use our imagination to explain how the employee in question, whom we shall call Bob Hiddleston for the moment, may have fallen for the social engineering campaign that preceded the incident. Bob is a technically skilled employee of a Japanese company that creates cryptocurrency wallet software. He had been with the organisation for a while and built up a wealth of technical experience in the crypto industry. Since people with this profile are in high demand, they may often receive random job offers through LinkedIn. One day, Bob receives a LinkedIn message from someone, let us call them Anne Wilson, who presents herself as a head hunter for an American tech company. So far, the message is within the normal range of events that can be expected in a legitimate scenario. The thought that Anne may not be a real head hunter and checking whether the company she claims to work for is registered anywhere do not even occur to him.

Although Bob was not actively looking for a new job, he wanted to test the waters and see how much he is currently worth on the labour market. He responds to Anne that he would like to receive further details and is impressed by the salary range that would come with the job. He is imagining the potential reward of doubling his salary if he would land the role and decides to apply. Anne mentioned that she needs his e-mail address to send him a programming challenge to test his technical skills. Even though she knows from his LinkedIn profile that he has many years of experience, she mentions to him it is standard company policy to let technical staff complete these types of assessments. He has 48 hours to complete the test, which is set to a maximum of two hours. Anne confirms with Bob whether he received the assessment e-mail and wishes him good luck.

Since Bob does not have much time to do the assessment, he schedules it during his lunch break the following working day. The evening before, he practices a few similar challenges on LeetCode [1] and after a good night's sleep feels ready to slay. Next day around noon, he retrieves Anne's e-mail in his personal inbox that contains a link to a custom programming assessment. The website looks similar to other browser-based coding platforms he has seen before. The only difference is that he is required to install a plug-in that allows the platform to monitor his performance to ensure he is not cheating. Without thinking too much about it, he

DOI: 10.4324/9781003610533-14

provides the system admin password to approve installing the plug-in and finishes all programming tasks within the two allotted hours. Bob feels confident about his performance and lets Anne know he completed the assessment, after which he has to rush back to his main job tasks. Anne replies swiftly by thanking him for the quick turnaround and that she will be in touch with him soon about the next steps.

What Bob did not realise is that the plug-in monitored all of his keystrokes, which allowed the hackers to obtain Bob's login credentials to critical work applications. Through this, the criminals accessed the company's master trading account and set up a large Bitcoin transfer with it that same day. Bob had no idea of all this, until the next morning, the chief financial officer calls for an urgent meeting with the tech team to understand who made the transfer.

Although we are just filling in the blanks here on how the social engineering attack could have been carried out, this is a common and effective social engineering scenario, because people on LinkedIn are used to receiving job offers from strangers and can easily be tempted by offers that entail significant improvements in pay, status, and flexibility. In other words, there was a high likelihood for Bob to receive a job offer like the one from Anne with a high potential reward. Theory of mind here was used in the language Anne used in her messages to Bob. They sounded professional, had no spelling or grammar mistakes, and made Bob believe Anne knew what she was talking about. Bob thus mostly experienced a state of "cognitive fluency". Only the plug-in installation prompt gave Bob's brain a prediction error, but he wanted to get the assessment done quickly before he had to go back to his actual work. Moreover, he thought it was a reasonable request from the programming platform to prevent people from using artificial intelligence (AI) to complete the assessment. This is a perfect example of when someone experiences conflicting beliefs (i.e., cognitive dissonance) and puts more weight to the belief that leads to choosing the riskier option. In this case, that finishing the assessment with a plausible requirement of downloading a plug-in is deemed more important than the likelihood of being proctored by a nefarious party.

The phenomenon of cognitive fluency is powerful in how people form beliefs. If beliefs are what people predict to be true, honest, real, and plausible, cognitive fluency is when we find ourselves in a situation with very few prediction errors [2]. We can experience it when we go to our favourite web shop and the user experience is exactly as we expect from a great website: fast, without glitches, easy to navigate, and aesthetically pleasing. On the contrary, if a website takes more than seven seconds to load, has an ill-functioning menu, and does not present all the product details we need when shopping online, we experience many prediction errors and therefore low cognitive fluency. This, in turn, makes us doubt the legitimacy of the website.

Indeed, marketing studies have associated bad user experiences with lower conversion rates and, importantly, lower trust ratings [3]. Similarly, the myriad of studies on how people detect lies in "offline" verbal communication has shown that people attend to behaviours they associate with "dishonest demeanour", such as stuttering, longer-than-average pauses, and gaze avoidance [4]. Put differently, we start doubting the trustworthiness of something or someone when they give

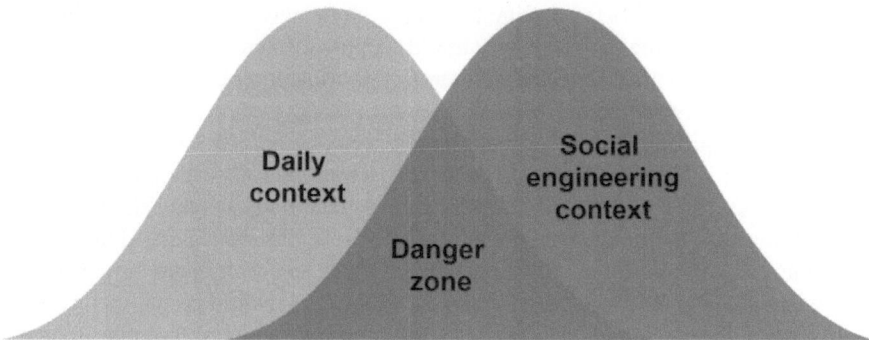

Figure 11.1 Social engineering attacks become harder to detect, as the likelihood of their ostensible context increasingly overlaps with the distribution of events in a target's default, daily context.

us the opposite feeling of being "fluent". They let us experience "cognitive dissonance" – when our brains have a difficulty creating a predictive model for something or have multiple conflicting predictions.

To further illustrate this, think of a time you had a conversation with someone new who used words you do not tend to use. Because of that, you felt there was little "chemistry" between you two. Now think of when you met someone for the first time who seemed to speak your kind of language, had similar interests, and even grew up in the same area as you. Whom would you trust more? Most likely the latter person that seemed more similar to you. Your brain will find it easier to predict what this person is saying. As a result, you feel more understood and experience cognitive fluency, as opposed to cognitive dissonance with the former person. This is precisely the effect that cybercriminals typically seek to create with their social engineering attacks: to have the targeted individual believe nothing considerably out of the ordinary is going on that would make them decide the message cannot be trusted, as detailed in *Chapter 3: How an attack is devised*. Essentially, they try to craft a message with a malicious request that fits well within a target's daily life context that keeps neural prediction errors to a minimum, as we saw with Bob's job offer. This is depicted in Figure 11.1 by the overlapping distributions of events in people's daily context and the context of a social engineering attack (i.e., the "danger zone"):

A psychological phenomenon worth mentioning here that is closely related to cognitive fluency is that people rate information as "truer" if they had seen it before, regardless of the actual veracity of said information [5]. In numerous studies, even when researchers explicitly tell participants about this "illusory truth effect", participants rate statements as more truthful after they had previously been exposed to those statements compared to statements they had never seen before. When we think about the way (social) media platforms work, the algorithms that determine what people see in their "news feed" are set up to show information that is similar to what people previously have interacted with. For instance, if you regularly comment on political posts on climate change, your news feed will soon be filled with content on whether and how we should address climate change. If this content happens to be inaccurate, or even deliberately fabricated political "fake news" by adversarial nation-state actors, you will be more likely to believe these falsehoods due to your frequent exposure to that same content.

We tested this idea in two experiments with a total of 260 participants whom we presented with true and false health-related and general knowledge statements [6]. After seeing 60 statements, we showed half of these to them again, along with an equal number of new statements, and asked participants to indicate how true they thought each statement was, as well as how much they would be inclined to share each statement with others. Through this study, we discovered that people would share the repeated statements more compared to the non-repeated statements, even when the statements were false [6]. It is not difficult then to see how political actors, such as hacktivist groups, can successfully misuse social media platforms to manipulate public discourse on critical topics. They know you will take the bait, as long as they show you enough of the same misleading content through armies of fake accounts and further amplify the illusory truth effect.

The illusory truth effect tells us something very fundamental about how we form beliefs about what is true and real. It may suggest that when we have previously seen or read something with our own eyes, this experience in itself tells us that *that* something exists, and therefore is truer than something our brains have never registered before. Of course, it would be short-sighted to conclude that something's mere existence would equate to truth and honesty. But in our fast-paced modern world, our brains may be under continuous pressure to make judgements on how to interpret a wealth of online information, that we naturally resort to shortcuts commonly referred to as cognitive biases [7]. What we perceive as true then becomes a function of our brains' ability to process complexity (i.e., the number of possibilities it can predict for) and tolerance for its own limits (i.e., to what extent it has to rely on shortcuts).

Technical people have human brains too

When we speak about targets or victims of social engineering attacks, we may often think about vulnerable groups, for example, the elderly and people with cognitive impairments. Yet, as discussed in *Chapter 9: Improving organisational cybersecurity*, anyone could be targeted and victimised by a social engineering attack – including people with a technical background. Their brains are not immune to the psychological phenomena we elaborated on in the last two chapters.

In one of our qualitative studies, we closely observed how people process e-mails to understand how they detect phishing attacks [8]. We asked 27 participants, of whom 19 had a technical background, to roleplay a professor who came back from holidays and started checking their inbox, and to reason out loud about what they were looking at. The inbox was made to look just like the Outlook web interface to make the participants feel as if they are actually checking their e-mails. Most of the e-mails were legitimate and directly adapted from our own academic inboxes, but some were actual phishing campaigns. We wondered what thoughts went through people's minds when they encountered these phishing e-mails, as well as what made them suspect a legitimate e-mail of being a phishing attack.

Overall, people considered the same types of information in every e-mail: whom it was sent by and what the e-mail was about. It did not matter how they went through the inbox – whether they started by skimming over the list of e-mail thumbnails on the left to triage for any urgent e-mails or messages from more important people, or if they read each e-mail in full and in chronological order – nor whether they had a technical study background.

What did matter was that people had widely varying ways of inferring who sent the e-mail. Some people only looked at the sender's display name, some only at the name in the bottom of the e-mail, and others also checked the sender's e-mail address. When it came to the "what" part, people mentioned things like "it depends on whether I deal with…" or said straight away "this is phishing". In other words, they inferred how *likely* it would be for them to receive a certain message and had a strong learned response to e-mails urging them for a "password reset" to retain their account. Overall, people did not tend to use the word "phishing", but just distinguished between relevant and irrelevant e-mails – phishing obviously being irrelevant.

Seeing first-hand how experienced professionals and technically schooled individuals perform a mundane computer task like processing e-mails was truly eye-opening. It showed how even tech-savvy people can arrive at vastly different conclusions, despite having access to the very same information. Not necessarily because of differences in people's technical prowess, but because of the cues they (learned to) pay attention to. Some people put more weight to the meaning of a message, others to the importance of the sender's relationship toward them, and still others only looked at whatever was urgent and left any non-urgent e-mails for later.

These different ways of weighting information likely affect what types of phishing attacks people are more susceptible to. This exemplified how important the daily context of a potential target is in determining whether their brains will flag a message as suspicious. What's more, this study showed that in practice, security behaviours such as checking links and sender e-mail domains only "kick in" after our brains detect something unexpected – an odd request, the promise of an unusual reward or aberrant behaviour from someone that it would not imagine engaging in oneself. Unless someone or a message does not "make sense", we tend to take them at face value. This secondary nature of security behaviour has been noted before by other researchers too [9] and is an important reason for why many conventional approaches to improve people's cybersecurity behaviour are not as effective as hoped for. Said differently, they do not align with how our brains work.

Know yourself to protect yourself

By describing how our brains give rise to what we believe is real or true, we explained how individuals could become victims of social engineering attacks. People need to experience a large enough prediction error, something unexpected, for them to consider the possibility that something or someone may be disingenuous. Only then we may start to apply the security checks typically taught in cybersecurity training and education programmes – and still, we may be tempted to deliberately take a chance anyway and see what happens.

Now, what is unexpected to your neighbour or colleague, may not be unexpected to you. Since each of our brains has been exposed to different environments, it is natural for us to have differing interpretations of what is true or false, honest or dishonest, and real or fake. Our judgements and decisions are only a complex function of how we weight the likelihoods, rewards, and theory of mind-related factors in our proximal world. We think about all the possible scenarios our brains can predict and estimate how we would feel in each case. We consider the potential rewards and punishments we believe each scenario would bring. We worry about how doing something would make us look, and whether and how someone else would do it. You may be particularly sensitive to the potential rewards. Others may be more preoccupied with theory of mind. As a result, you may fall for a particular social engineering attack, whereas someone else would not.

If you want to reduce your susceptibility to social engineering attacks, you thus need to start with understanding yourself. What are you easily tempted by? What triggers you? What people do you typically surround yourself with? Do you believe people are mostly honest and would not try to take advantage of you? How do stress and negative moods affect your judgements? What values do you hold and project onto others?

As we have seen with the self-projection phenomenon, our moods and general attitudes affect how we judge others. If we often feel stressed and in a low mood, this may lead us to pay more attention to unhelpful information and put less weight on helpful information, perhaps because the latter would take more effort to understand. Furthermore, people who have repeatedly fallen for social engineering attacks such as online scams and fraud, may hold onto certain unhelpful beliefs and behavioural patterns. If you are naturally gullible and expect online interactions to be mostly honest, cybercriminals may notice and target you more, as they will learn how to talk you into another scam.

By being aware of your pitfalls and sensitivities, you can train yourself to be more vigilant when you are presented with certain triggers. Business opportunities, sales and discounts, investment schemes, unsolicited requests, urgent matters, lending money, personal questions, job offers – these are all triggering situations often used in social engineering attacks. Whenever you encounter such situations, no matter who allegedly contacts you about them, you should always do your due diligence and prevent giving in to a need for instant gratification.

We thus have three rules of thumb to prevent you from falling for a social engineering attack:

1. **Maintain your digital household by practising basic cyber hygiene**: Take proactive measures to secure your personal and financial information. This includes staying informed about new and common scam scenarios, using strong passwords (e.g. "pass phrases") and multi-factor authentication, regularly

monitoring your bank accounts and credit reports, being careful with what personal information you share online and on social media, keeping your software up to date, configuring who can access essential/sensitive personal documents and backing them up, and not blindly clicking on links and buttons.

2. **Do not rush in responding to requests**: Take your time and do not rush into sharing sensitive information or transferring money until you have done your due diligence, even if the requestor claims to be a person of authority or someone familiar. On the phone, for instance, ask questions to verify whether the other party is indeed who they claim to be or possibly just an AI bot [10]. On social media, do not automatically trust and connect with profiles from people you have not met in real life. If anyone asks you for money, or sensitive work-related or personal information, try to contact them via a different communication channel. If the initial message was sent via e-mail, see if you can use an officially registered phone number or internal company chat application to validate the request. Alternatively, just wait and see if after one or more days you are still being chased by the same or even other people for the same information. Because if anything is truly urgent, absolutely necessary and/or important to sort out, someone will try to formally get a hold of you through various means, not just through one communication channel.

3. **Ask people in real life to help verify unsolicited offers and other unexpected messages**: Whether you receive a "special discount", notification about a product you did not order or shop you do not visit, job offer, investment or organisation opportunity, or *any* other unexpected message really, you have to double check whom it came from, consult a third party to know whether they are from an officially registered organisation or ask the actual person you know in real life who purportedly made the offer about it. Of course, if it concerns a financial investment, you may want to take a risk sometimes, but then be aware of the risk appetite you can permit yourself. There are victims out there unfortunately who bet all of their pension funds on a fraudulent scheme and lost a lifetime of savings in one go. If you are unsure, ask your spouse, your best friend, or a colleague from a different department to look at the offer or message too. It can be easy to slip into a habit of figuring out things on your own when you are browsing the internet in your private time. Do not forget that we can always ask someone else in the physical world who has an independent pair of eyes to help check something you received.

References

1 LeetCode is a popular online platform with computer programming challenges at all different levels. People seeking to test their programming skills and prepare for coding assessments may spend hours, if not days and weeks, practising these challenges to eventually get offered a top-tier tech job.

2 R. Reber and C. Unkelbach, "The epistemic status of processing fluency as source for judgments of truth," *Review of Philosophy and Psychology*, vol. 1, no. 4, pp. 563–581, Sep. 2010, doi: 10.1007/S13164-010-0039-7/FIGURES/1.

3 E. Costante, J. Den Hartog, and M. Petkovic, "On-line trust perception: What really matters," in *2011 1st Workshop on Socio-Technical Aspects in Security and Trust (STAST)*, Milan, Italy, pp. 52–59, 2011, doi: 10.1109/STAST.2011.6059256.

4 M. Zuckerman, B. M. DePaulo, and R. Rosenthal, "Verbal and nonverbal communication of deception," *Advances in Experimental Social Psychology*, vol. 14, pp. 1–59, 1981, doi: 10.1016/S0065–2601(08)60369-X.

   T.R. Levine, K.B. Serota, H. Shulman, D.D. Clare, H.S. Park, A.S. Shaw, J.C. Shim, and J.H. Lee, "Sender demeanor: Individual differences in sender believability have a powerful impact on deception detection judgments," *Human Communication Research*, vol. 37, no. 3, pp. 377–403, 2011.

5 A. Dechêne, C. Stahl, J. Hansen, and M. Wänke, "The truth about the truth: A meta-analytic review of the truth effect," *Personality and Social Psychology Review*, vol. 14, no. 2, pp. 238–257, May 2010, doi: 10.1177/1088868309352251.

6 V. Vellani, S. Zheng, D. Ercelik, and T. Sharot, "The illusory truth effect leads to the spread of misinformation," *Cognition*, vol. 236, p. 105421, 2023, doi: 10.1016/j.cognition.2023.105421.

7 This is not to say that the cognitive fluency phenomenon is a bias, but that taking fluency as a sign of truth or honesty is.

8 S. Y. Zheng and I. Becker, "Checking, nudging or scoring? Evaluating e-mail user security tools," in *Nineteenth Symposium on Usable Privacy and Security (SOUPS 2023)*, Anaheim, CA: USENIX Association, Aug. 2023, pp. 57–76.

9 S. L. Pfleeger, M. A. Sasse, and A. Furnham, "From weakest link to security hero: Transforming staff security behavior," *Journal of Homeland Security and Emergency Management*, vol. 11, no. 4, pp. 489–510, 2014, doi: 10.1515/jhsem-2014–0035.

10 T. Singh, *Artificial Intelligence and Ethics: A Field Guide for Stakeholders*. CRC Press, Abingdon, Oxon, UK, 2024.

Part IV

The psychology of a Chief Information Security Officer (CISO)

12 Responsibilities of a CISO

Finally, we want to give you an insight into the world of the chief information security officer (CISO). The "final boss" in the cybersecurity chain has to cover many grounds. We, therefore, dedicate this last part of this book to the specific context in which CISOs operate (discussed in this chapter), and provide practical recommendations on risk management and maintaining psychological wellbeing in *Chapter 13: The psychological toll on CISOs*.

We see the role of a CISO as more than just protecting an organisation's technology infrastructure. It involves leadership for a team of security professionals, building relationships with stakeholders, and making tough decisions that can impact the entire organisation. As a result, being a CISO can also take a toll on one's mental health. It is, therefore, essential to have a resilient mind to manage the challenges that come with the job. In this chapter, we will explore the unique psychological powers affecting CISOs and how understanding this can help build a successful and long-lasting career.

At its core, the CISO is a senior-level executive responsible for overseeing an organisation's information security strategy, ensuring that systems and data are protected against cyber threats and vulnerabilities, ensuring compliance with regulatory requirements and managing security incidents. The CISO typically reports to the chief information officer or another senior executive, and works closely with other departments, such as legal and risk and compliance. In today's digital age, the role of a CISO is becoming increasingly critical, as cyber-attacks can lead to reputational damage, financial loss, and legal consequences for organisations – as outlined throughout this book. Effective CISOs must be able to balance the need for security with the organisation's goals and objectives, while also staying up to date with emerging threats and technologies.

The specific obligations and duties of a CISO will differ, depending on the organisation. A small organisation adopting software as a service and cloud computing will have different security concerns than a large enterprise with innumerable old on-premises systems and enormous volumes of sensitive data. Yet, when examining the CISO position across a number of organisations and sectors, certain common tasks frequently show up. Typical duties and responsibilities one should be familiar with when embarking on the journey to become a CISO include implementing the organisation's Information Security Management System (ISMS).

DOI: 10.4324/9781003610533-16

This system aims to increase the security of the organisation's information technology systems, networks, resources, and data, through a comprehensive programme that includes detailed policies, procedures, and standards.

Naturally, securing information and assets is core to the role. To avoid a cybersecurity incident, CISOs must stop bad actors from getting unauthorised access to information and assets. We are responsible for ensuring that security controls like data loss prevention are implemented and that they are regularly reassessed and improved upon. Compliance management is another fundamental responsibility. CISOs are responsible for ensuring that their organisations adhere to all applicable laws, regulations, and industry standards related to security, for example, the EU's General Data Protection Regulation and other data protection regulations. An often-overlooked responsibility is stakeholder management. For instance, CISOs are responsible for managing relationships with executive team members and the board of directors. Furthermore, incident response planning is crucial to ensuring the organisation is prepared for a cyber-attack. In the event of a security incident, the CISO is in charge of organising the organisation's reaction and making sure the right steps are followed to reduce organisational impact and speed up recovery.

The CISO is also responsible for directly and indirectly managing personnel, which can include people outside their own team. A good CISO will take time to mentor others in the profession and invest in the skills and experience of their team. They recruit apprentices into the profession and educate them on security through to professional standing, as well as setting objectives for the team. CISOs also have significant indirect management responsibilities, such as when they have to govern a third-party Security Operations Centre (SOC) or where they are influencing people across organisational functions to change insecure behaviour.

Information security is a gigantic field to cover and resourcing is often limited. The key areas CISOs must ensure they have a thorough grasp of include, but are not limited to:

- governance, risk and compliance
- information security audit and controls management
- information security programme management and security operations
- information security core capabilities and cybersecurity
- information security strategy, planning, finance, procurement and third-party management

Thus, a CISO is a leader, manager, and technical expert, all rolled into one. They must be able to manage teams, communicate effectively with stakeholders, and stay up to date with the latest security threats and technologies.

The SECCRRT to effective CISOs

Indeed, the CISO role is challenging, as it requires a unique set of skills and attributes to be successful. While technical expertise is an essential component, it is equally important for individuals in this position to have strong psychological skills. Effective CISOs must be able to understand the motivations and behaviours of both attackers and employees, as well as communicate complex technical issues in a way that is easily understood by non-technical stakeholders, to develop effective security strategies that align with the organisation's goals and objectives. CISOs must therefore be resilient, flexible, strategic thinkers with excellent communication skills and technical expertise. They need to be able to make tough decisions, manage stress effectively, maintain a positive outlook, even in challenging situations, and build a support network to maintain their mental health. Indeed, the success of a CISO largely depends on their psychological traits.

As the role of CISOs continues to evolve, it is essential for individuals in this position to hone a diverse set of skills and traits that enable them to effectively manage risks, build trust with stakeholders, and lead their teams with confidence. We believe the following SECCRRT psychological traits will separate highly effective CISOs from their peers and provide insights into the psychology of leadership in the cybersecurity realm.

- **Strategic thinking and risk management** are top priorities. CISOs need to be strategic enablers in the organisation, developing and implementing a long-term security strategy that aligns with the organisation's goals and objectives. Effective CISOs take a risk-based approach to security, prioritising and mitigating the most significant threats, while considering the potential impact of emerging threats.
- **Emotional intelligence** is an important trait for any effective leader, but it is especially important for CISOs who must navigate complex relationships with stakeholders, including executives, employees, and external partners. Effective CISOs are able to manage their emotions and respond to the emotions of others in a way that builds trust and fosters collaboration.
- **Communication skills** with stakeholders are crucial, as CISOs must be able to explain technical concepts to non-technical stakeholders and build trust with both internal and external partners. CISOs must be able to articulate the risks and benefits of different security strategies, as well as communicate the impact of security incidents to stakeholders in a way that enables them to make informed decisions.
- **Curiosity** is an important personality trait that helps CISOs develop through their career. A CISO must be able to quickly come up with potential solutions to issues – be they among people, processes, or technology. Being curious to investigating complex problems from a technology, people, or organisation perspective helps to better understand the motivations of employees, attackers, and other key stakeholders and keeps CISOs motivated in the long run. Continuous learning and professional development are vital in keeping these skills fresh. Effective CISOs are lifelong learners who are committed to staying up to date with the latest trends and technologies in the cybersecurity industry. CISOs must be willing to invest in their own professional development, whether through attending conferences, pursuing certifications, or building relationships with other cybersecurity professionals.

- **Reflexive practice** is vital in cybersecurity. Cristiano et al. (2024) argue that cybersecurity professionals need to be excellent at engaging in reflexivity to understand how they can improve their methods and ensure their professional skills are up to date with best practices [1].
- **Resilience** is the ability to bounce back from setbacks and maintain a positive outlook, even in challenging situations – an integral skill to the CISO role. This needs to go hand in hand with flexibility and adaptability to change, as new threats and technologies are quickly and constantly evolving. A CISO must be able to adjust their strategies and tactics accordingly. CISOs who are open to new ideas and willing to pivot their strategies as needed are better positioned to protect their organisations against emerging threats.
- **Technical expertise and domain knowledge** of cybersecurity play a key role in identifying threats. While psychological skills and strategic thinking are critical for effective CISOs, technical expertise is absolutely essential. CISOs must have a deep understanding of cybersecurity technologies, threats, and vulnerabilities, as well as the ability to stay up to date with emerging trends and technologies. Ideally, a CISO's technical expertise spans more than just information security. They should be inquisitive and develop their knowledge in emerging technologies and their interplay with psychology, supply chain management, risk, and other organisation areas.

In short, the role of a CISO is complex and challenging, and thus requires a diverse set of skills and psychological traits. Effective CISOs must be able to navigate complex relationships with stakeholders, think strategically, and stay up to date with emerging trends and technologies. By honing their psychological skills, technical expertise, and a commitment to continuous learning, highly effective CISOs are able to effectively protect their organisations against cyber threats.

Leading the psychology and cybersecurity integration

Triplett (2022) has argued that senior managers are not taking their responsibility in organisations seriously enough. New systems are rolled out with little training or understanding of user behaviour. Transformational change occurs at significant pace with poor understanding of employees and their interactions. A stressful work environment sets the scene for data breaches and poor security. Complacent and unintentional behaviours arise, enabled by ignorant leaders and employees [2]. In this context, humans *become* the weakest link. This is where CISOs must step in and embody effective leadership as professionals with an understanding of human factors. These human factors comprise data elements, human behaviours, and human performance, with an aim to reduce errors. Here, CISOs have the opportunity to lead by example and encourage education, awareness, and communication.

A human-centred approach is essential in cybersecurity. This approach involves designing systems and policies with the user in mind, taking into account human behaviour and psychology. By understanding how humans interact with technology and the potential for human error, organisations can design systems that are more secure and easier to use. A human-centred approach also involves creating a culture of cybersecurity within the organisation. This includes promoting cybersecurity best practices and encouraging employees to report suspicious activity, as described in Part 2: Inside the line of defence.

CISOs have to realise that prevention of cyber-attacks relies on building trust and providing assurance as core parts of the job. It only takes a single security incident to lose the trust of executive teams, customers, or employees. The consequences of attacks ripple outward, with individuals closer to the epicentre experiencing more severe effects than those farther away. What is guaranteed is that any exposure to acts of violence (i.e., including cyber-attacks) generates a human experience precipitating psychological harm, heightens threat perception, and generates enduring shifts in political attitudes and behaviours. This is the challenging environment CISOs operate in, where a single incident can destroy a career and cause devastation to stakeholder relationships and the organisation they work for. CISOs thus require a combination of strong psychological skills, technical expertise, and a commitment to continuous learning.

Influencing employees across the organisation remains an important factor. Cybersecurity has traditionally mainly revolved around technology, and although there has been some research on cognitive skills, it is not widely acknowledged, let alone incorporated into the field. We hope there will be more focus on human factors in cybersecurity as not all problems can be solved with technology alone. It is important to comprehend how humans think, as well as how attackers operate. Therefore, it is crucial to recognise the significance of people in addition to technology. Rather than relying solely on training courses, it is essential to incorporate learning as a practical part of daily routine. We will describe several tactics to do so.

In cybersecurity, it is essential to maintain one's technical skills, but cognitive readiness is equally crucial. This refers to a mental state of preparedness that enables an individual to respond effectively to changing situations. Organisations must invest in improving cognitive readiness, because the rapidly changing nature of cybersecurity makes it impossible to train for every possible threat scenario. By developing cognitive readiness, individuals can learn to adapt to any situation, making them more agile and effective during incident response. This requires problem-solving skills and situational awareness that traditional cybersecurity training courses do not focus on. Thus, to improve incident response, employees need to know *how to think* and not just what to do. By integrating psychology in cybersecurity, organisations can build more agile, confident, and effective incident responses.

To integrate psychological knowledge into cybersecurity, CISOs should advocate for continuous learning and development for their employees, instead of focusing solely on certifications. This can be achieved by incorporating learning into daily processes to build cognitive readiness. One way is by encouraging reflection or metacognition, which is frequently conducted by the military during after-action reviews. During incident response or post-mortem response reviews, one can reflect by answering questions such as what happened, what was supposed to be done, what was done, what could have been done better, and how to improve in the future. Creating a culture of continuous learning and development is also crucial to establish a psychologically safe space where individuals can make and learn from mistakes.

Although multidisciplinary table top exercises are beneficial in building incident response teams, we tend to find that skill degradation, or skill fade, can occur. To prevent skill fade, it is necessary to practice these skills at least once every two months, which can be both challenging and expensive. Consequently, table top exercises may not be effective in the long run. To avoid this, organisations should promote a culture of continuous learning and development, which involves creating safe spaces that encourage learning. These safe spaces allow us to test ourselves in an environment free from judgement so our human psychology can better adapt during an incident.

When it comes to creating a work environment where people feel comfortable discussing emotional intelligence and psychological pitfalls, there is a significant opportunity for leaders to step up. There have been noticeable advancements in this area, as it is vital for individuals to talk about their good and bad experiences and to take breaks from screens. Moreover, individuals must be aware of their own thinking patterns through cognitive readiness training, as unhelpful biases can thwart security as described in *Chapter 6: Human fallacies and how to overcome them*. In today's world, these aspects are of utmost importance, and although some may have a natural inclination towards them, CISOs and security professionals traditionally do not get encouraged to developed skills in these areas. Thus, it is essential for current and budding CISOs to build emotional intelligence alongside their technical security expertise.

Shaping the organisation's psychological security posture

People are an integral part of cybersecurity processes and understanding their thinking patterns as well as those of attackers can be incredibly beneficial. It is important to recognise that people are just as crucial as technology in our field. Moreover, we need to move away from relying solely on training and education programmes. Instead, making learning a practical and daily habit is key.

Organisations face cyber threats that can be related to both people and technology. Sometimes, security measures may only focus on a specific aspect of the threat, such as protecting digital infrastructure. However, these measures may overlook important factors like mental health, cyber fatigue, and insider threat. This is why it is important to combine different elements of security to ensure that nothing is missed. Despite the challenges posed by limited resources and a dispersed workforce, it is crucial to maintain strong security measures in an uncertain environment.

Influencing an entire organisation, all of its employees and its endemic (security) culture can be difficult. The six persuasion principles as touched on lightly in *Chapter 3: How an attack is devised* when we talked about social engineering can be used here too, but now to influence employees to adopt more secure behaviours [3]:

1 **Principle of reciprocation**: People feel obligated to return a favour.
   Example: When an employee completes a security awareness training or reports a phishing e-mail, reward them with a small incentive, like a gift card or a thank-you note. This creates a sense of obligation, making them more likely to adhere to security protocols.

2. **Principle of scarcity**: When something is scarce, people will value it more.
   Example: Highlight limited-time security resources or training sessions. Emphasise that these exclusive opportunities are crucial for their professional development and the organisation's security, making them more likely to value and participate in them.

3. **Principle of authority**: When a request is made by a legitimate authority, people are inclined to follow/believe the request.
   Example: When implementing new security policies, have them communicated by senior executives or renowned cybersecurity experts. Their authority and expertise will lend credibility to the message, making employees more likely to follow the guidelines.

4. **Principle of commitment and consistency**: People do as they said they would.
   Example: Encourage employees to publicly commit to security practices, such as signing a pledge to help keep the organisation safe on the company intranet. Once they have made a commitment, they are more likely to remain consistent in their actions.

5. **Principle of consensus**: People do as other people do.
   Example: Share success stories and statistics showing that a majority of employees are following security practices, such as using strong passwords or reporting phishing attempts. People are more likely to adopt behaviours that they see their peers engaging in.

6. **Principle of liking**: We say "yes" to people we like.
   Example: Promote cybersecurity initiatives through well-liked and respected colleagues or team leaders – these individuals could be strategically chosen to be security champions. When employees receive messages from people they like and trust, they are more likely to be persuaded to adopt secure behaviours.

Behavioural profiling

Now we want to add a (cautionary) note on using psychological profiling of employees as a preventative security measure. It has become common practice for many organisational recruitment processes to involve psychometric testing. These tests aim to assess various qualities of a person's behavioural tendencies, such as their intelligence, personality traits, memory, and stress tolerance. In certain critical roles in the military, diplomacy, and secret services, for instance, applicants are typically subjected to extensive psychometric testing batteries. It could then be a small step to try to relate these psychometric test scores to people's security behaviour and venture into behavioural risk modelling.

This is a highly contentious topic for two reasons. First, there is no consistent research evidence suggesting that people with certain psychometric traits are more secure or insecure, as described in *Chapter 9: Improving organisational cybersecurity* and *Part 3: The target's perspective*. A highly motivated attacker will continue trying to persuade a target and their ecosystem to perform an insecure action. It is possible, of course, that certain people are stubborn and distrusting enough not to comply with other people's requests, but we would expect this to be a minority in the general population.

Behavioural profiling is also problematic, because it requires collecting an intrusive amount of data on people's behaviours. If they use work devices provided by the organisation, they typically have to agree with use policies that allow organisations to monitor any user interactions with the device. Employers will then know when people are actively working, idle, their whereabouts, what applications they use, their communication patterns, and so on. Using artificial intelligence, it then becomes easy to automatically examine the language people use, detect which employees are not productive or possibly overwhelmed and if they are interacting with people they should not be interacting with. In short, employers could use behavioural analysis to create a digital fingerprint of every single employee and compute a security risk score for them.

Perhaps it is a matter of one's moral and political stance to decide whether the cyber risks are worth using psychological risk profiling techniques. In fact, big tech companies have been doing this for decades by now, but to serve commercial ends and not organisational security per se. But note that employees in the United States have previously sued and publicly complained about their employers over privacy-intrusive surveillance practices that were part of organisational security measures [4]. Such practices may indeed remind us that "big brother is watching us". As a result, most organisations following a western philosophy will typically protect psychometric data and refrain from tracking employees' every step. The exception is when regulators mandate organisations to closely watch over employees in areas such as financial trading and defence. A large American bank, for instance, has recently been fined $348 million over lack of surveillance over its traders [5]. We would advise organisations to be transparent about any such practices from the start and explain why they deem them necessary.

A less intrusive option to influence employees may be through Structured Cognitive Behavioural Trainings, which can be imparted in addition to information security education and awareness training. In our experience, structured interviews with new starters and cybersecurity offenders can also help identify points for improvement in all areas of the security strategy. It can help cybersecurity professionals design training and controls that are more fit for purpose that better influence human behaviour.

Getting security buy-in across the board

During our career, we have witnessed the indomitable spirit of security personnel, as we put up a wall of defence against threat actors before attackers can exploit them. We fight. However, this combative attitude extends to our interactions with colleagues within our organisation, where differing opinions regarding the urgency and best way to address security risks can lead to conflicts. This adversarial cybersecurity-versus-everyone way of operating is detrimental, because it creates a perception of security personnel as detractors and distractors. Adopting an organisation-enabling mindset can break down these barriers and improve collaboration across departments. By empathising with our colleagues' objectives and communicating security benefits in organisation terms, we can integrate security into the overall company strategy [6].

One way to do this is by having open conversations about shared goals and objectives, including defining what success looks like for each team and finding the common thread that ties our organisation together. In addition, security leaders must put extra care and consideration into communication and persuasion with stakeholders to gain buy-in for security initiatives. All teams at an organisation need to engage in open discussions about their shared goals and objectives to increase integration and understanding. Recognising shared objectives while acknowledging each team's unique roles and dependencies allows us to collaborate more smoothly. In addition, cybersecurity leaders must try harder to persuade and communicate their presence and initiatives outside the security team to gain buy-in from other executives.

Al-Hashem and Said (2023) contend that CISOs must increasingly consider psychological factors in their approaches. There is a complex interaction between the human mind and cybersecurity based on a rich tapestry of psychological theories and empirical findings, which we highlighted throughout the first three parts of this book. Especially CISOs, the final bosses of their organisations' cybersecurity, need to understand the effects of psychological factors on the design and implementation of cybersecurity solutions [7].

It is essential to position security in organisation terms during budget discussions to establish the foundation for meetings with CFOs or other relevant parties [8]. Understanding the organisation scenarios the company is considering for the next year, outlining security objectives, and linking them to the organisation's objectives allows us to justify security expenses, while discussing how these objectives may change based on future scenarios. Here, it is crucial to not only clarify how the security expenses benefit the company, but also why it is the right time to invest. It is time to stop fighting and start collaborating. By linking security objectives to an organisation's overall objectives and outlining the potential impact of not investing in security initiatives, security leaders can justify their requests without resorting to fear, uncertainty, and doubt.

Ask members of each team to describe what success means to them. Then consider how it can be accomplished in light of more general organisational goals. Differences are acceptable and to be expected, but the only way to find common ground is to discover the thread that unites stakeholders. It is simpler to comprehend how teams might collaborate to move the organisation closer to these goals when considering broader organisational objectives.

Collaboration will be easier if everyone can agree on common goals while acknowledging the distinctive roles and interdependencies of each team. Communication and a persuasive approach can yield greater security buy-in. Whether we like it or not, cybersecurity leaders frequently have to put in more effort than others to justify our actions. Yet, many of our activities involve many departments and rely on executive-level support.

To gain support, we need to be careful about how we persuade and engage with people outside the security team. There are several factors to take into account while trying to win others' support for a security request or project. First, identify the participants. Recognise the interdependencies of your security endeavour to identify the stakeholders. You need to adjust your messages based on whether they have an accepting or dismissive attitude. Then determine the goals of the stakeholders. The idea is to clarify why security is essential to their goals. What stakeholder needs outside of security does it support? Recognise their priorities, so they will be more likely to back you up. It is crucial to determine what those stakeholders need to know. Some people might not want technical lingo. Other stakeholders place more emphasis on costs than on revenue. Some concentrate on people. To gain the support of the stakeholder, present information that is appropriate for them.

This will help to gain stakeholders' trust. When asking others for money, advice, or time, think about how to show that their assistance will not be in vain. Provide metrics from prior security efforts or mention past successes of your activities to convey trustworthiness. Consider what actions you will take to persuade and communicate with non-security stakeholders to get their support, instead of assuming that others understand what you are trying to accomplish and why the effort is vital.

During budget conversations, it is crucial to frame security in terms of organisation and not in terms of technology. While it is encouraging that spending on cybersecurity has been relatively consistent, any security leader needs to be ready to explain the benefits and negotiate. We need to concentrate on communication and persuasion, given the organisation possibilities that the organisation is thinking about for the upcoming year. Is the organisation anticipating a decline in revenue? Are certain product lines expected to grow? Are there any modifications to the geographical areas that the organisation services? Can you anticipate organisation as usual, or are there going to be severe disruptions to the organisation's operations?

Next, outline your security goals and connect them to the corporate goals for organisation. Be prepared to talk about how your requests might alter, depending on the situation your organisation might find itself in, as the precise future is unpredictable. For instance, you might need to hire a security analyst to assist a new region if the organisation plans to develop an office there. Or, you may have to pay for additional technological training for your application security team if your company is launching a new product.

Be prepared to explain not only how the security expense item benefits the organisation, but also why it is the *right time* to fund that effort, project or individual. Do not base this on instilling fear, confusion or doubt. Instead, explain how the organisation would be affected if that item is not financed.

CISOs cannot simply take a risk-averse approach. CISOs must continually assess and manage risk. This means continuously making risk-based decisions and prioritising threat management. Most of the time, this is in highly pressurised situations with ongoing stresses, as described in *Chapter 5: Operational cyber-security context*. You cannot avoid risks or adopt a blocking mentality. A simple change to orient stakeholders towards a bigger goal could become a game changer. Instead of speaking terms of 'risks to avoid', try using language that orients people towards a desirable future state. For example, tell them how certain security measures will help build long-term trust relationships with suppliers.

CISOs also must acknowledge they cannot do everything themselves. Security functions typically have limited resources and so we must trust our team and think of programmes like security champions to ensure we have a voice across the organisation. Another pitfall is being too technical. Understanding organisation objectives and speaking in their language and on their terms are essential prerequisites to be able to influence other parts of your organisation. Another key CISO skill is being able to sell the need for security in terms of budget and other resources. You have to be able to tell the story and explain the risks of not implementing certain security measures, which is the topic we will turn to in the next chapter.

References

1 F. Cristiano, X. Kurowska, T. Stevens, L. M. Hurel, N. S. Fouad, M. D. Cavelty, et al., "Cybersecurity and the politics of knowledge production: Towards a reflexive practice," *Journal of Cyber Policy*, vol. 8, no. 3, pp. 1–34, 2024, doi: 10.1080/23738871.2023.2287687.

2 W. J. Triplett, "Addressing human factors in cybersecurity leadership," *Journal of Cybersecurity and Privacy*, vol. 2, no. 3, pp. 573–586, 2022.

3 R. B. Cialdini and N. J. Goldstein, "Social influence: Compliance and conformity," *Annual Review of Psychology*, vol. 55, pp. 591–621, 2004, doi: 10.1146/annurev.psych.55.090902.142015.

4 S. Burch, "Apple employee sues over company surveillance policies that 'unlawfully restrain' staff freedoms, suppress speech," 2024 [Online]. Available: https://www.yahoo.com/news/apple-employee-sues-over-company-223932603.html?fr=yhssrp_catchall&guccounter=1&guce_referrer=aHR0cHM6Ly9yLnNlYXJjaaC55YWhvby5jb-20vX3lsdD1Bd3IuUWh5ekpyTm4wcklaSUlCM0J3eC47X3lsdT1ZMjlzYndRWNHOXpBelFFZZG5ScFpBTUVjMlZZqQTNOeS9SVj0yL1; K. Scott, "Apple accused of staff surveillance and censorship in lawsuit," 2024 [Online]. Available: https://tech.co/news/employee-lawsuit-apple-surveillance-censorship; S. Delouya, "JPMorgan Chase staffers complain of being 'watched' all the time as the bank seems to be growing more secretive with its employee-tracking systems," 2022 [Online]. Available: https://finance.yahoo.com/news/jpmorgan-chase-staffers-complain-being-192241949.html?fr=yhssrp_catchall

5 P. Schroeder, "JPMorgan fined nearly $350 million for inadequate trade reporting," 2024 [Online]. Available: https://www.reuters.com/business/finance/jpmorgan-pay-nearly-350-million-penalties-inadequate-trade-reporting-2024-03-14/

6 T. Singh, *Technology Leadership and Strategy*, Cyber Wisdom Ltd., 2023. Available at SSRN: https://ssrn.com/abstract=4896185 or http://doi.org/10.2139/ssrn.4896185

7 N. Al-Hashem and A. Saidi, "The psychological aspect of cybersecurity: Understanding cyber threat perception and decision-making," *International Journal of Applied Machine Learning and Computational Intelligence*, vol. 13, no. 8, pp. 11–22, 2023. Retrieved from https://neuralslate.com/index.php/Machine-Learning-Computational-I/article/view/41

8 A. Varma and T. Singh. *Finance Transformation: Leadership on Digital Transformation and Disruptive Innovation.* CRC Press, Abingdon, Oxon, UK, 2024.

13 Psychological toll on CISOs

The pressure on chief information security officers (CISOs) is greater than ever before. Many of them are at a breaking point. The psychological toll of maintaining constant vigilance against threats within and outside the organisation is hard to fathom. Security teams are being pushed between a rock and a hard place. They are caught between regulators with ever-increasing expectations, and executive boards that simply do not want to invest in control measures or prioritise the need for digital transformation at every turn. Meanwhile, as technologies continue to advance, data breaches have become more prevalent and sophisticated. It is more important than ever to understand the risks associated with data breaches and to take proactive measures to protect sensitive information.

According to a study by the Ponemon Institute, the average cost of a data breach in the United States is $8.19 million [1]. This includes expenses such as legal fees, notification costs, and lost organisation opportunities. Invariably, a CISO and a data protection officer would be accountable for explaining what went wrong and answer questions about the measures they had in place to prevent the incident [2]. As such, data protection and information privacy must be of utmost concern for organisations. CISOs especially grapple with these concerns, as the risks associated with data breaches can have serious consequences for both individuals and organisations. Hence, this last chapter is dedicated to how CISOs can manage cyber risks and the psychological toll they usually face in doing so.

Managing risk

A lack of strategic investment in risk management leads to a poor understanding of cybersecurity threats. CISOs or chief risk officers (CROs) must identify barriers to cybersecurity risk management investment and address these. Small and medium-sized enterprises are particularly at risk, as barriers to cybersecurity risk management often include financial capacity, a lack of awareness, traditional commerce, an absence of risk standards, and overconfidence of decision-makers [3].

Poor risk management can have severe consequences for any organisation, ranging from cybersecurity breaches, a failure to comply with regulatory requirements, and operational disruptions. Many industries, such as healthcare and finance, have strict regulations that organisations must follow to protect sensitive information.

DOI: 10.4324/9781003610533-17

Failure to comply with these regulations can result in fines, legal action, and reputational damage. Cybersecurity breaches can disrupt organisation operations, leading to lost productivity and revenue. In some cases, organisations may be forced to shut down operations temporarily, leading to significant financial losses and reduced customer trust.

Risk assessment is a vital component of cybersecurity planning. It helps identify potential threats and vulnerabilities that could compromise an organisation's cybersecurity. Risk assessment involves the identification, analysis, and evaluation of risks to an organisation's assets, where assets include data, applications, and information technology (IT) systems. The assessment helps determine how likely a cybersecurity incident may occur and assesses the potential impact of such an incident on the organisation. Risk assessment also helps organisations prioritise their cybersecurity efforts, determine the most critical assets that require protection, and allocate resources accordingly. Especially when resources are limited, organisations must focus their efforts on the most significant risks and most critical assets.

Risk assessment follows a structured process that involves several steps. The first step is to identify the assets that need protection. This includes identifying the data, applications, and systems that are critical to the organisation's operations. The second step is to identify potential threats and vulnerabilities. This involves identifying the threats that could exploit the vulnerabilities in the organisation's assets.

Once the risks have been identified, the next step is to analyse and evaluate the risks. This involves assessing the likelihood of a cybersecurity incident occurring and the potential impact of such an incident on the organisation. Based on the risk analysis and evaluation, organisations can develop strategies to mitigate the risks.

Here are a few example data breach types to give you an idea of the typical risks and mitigations:

- **Ransomware attacks**: Potential costs can range from nominal to millions of pounds, depending on the ransom demanded. Preventative measures should include regular backups and anti-malware software. Ensure that data is backed up regularly and stored securely. Advanced anti-malware tools can help detect and prevent ransomware.
- **Phishing and social engineering**: Potential costs can vary wildly and lead to significant breaches of data, resulting in financial losses and reputational damage. Preventative measures include e-mail filtering solutions like Mimecast, Egress, and others to detect and block phishing e-mails. Multi-factor authentication (MFA) adds a layer of security to credential harvest attempts. Educate staff on recognising phishing scams and maintaining strong passwords.
- **(Distributed) Denial-of-service attacks (DDoS)**: Potential costs can be high but short-lived. They can disrupt organisation operations, leading to financial losses and reputational damage. Preventative measures include network traffic monitoring tools to scan organisational networks for unusual patterns. DDoS protection services can help reduce the impact of DDoS attacks. Developing and regularly updating an incident response plan to respond to DoS and DDoS attacks is essential too.

- **Advanced persistent threats (APTs)**: Potential costs can be in the millions. APTs can lead to prolonged data theft and significant financial and reputational damage on a scale that could destroy an organisation. Preventative measures include network segmentation to limit the spread of an attack. Use threat intelligence services to stay informed about potential threats and conduct periodic security assessments to identify and mitigate potential threats.
- **Password guessing**: Potential costs of unauthorised access through weak or stolen passwords can lead to data breaches, identity theft, fraud, and financial losses. Preventative measures include strong password policies, using MFA and a zero-trust approach. Password management tools can help employees with managing and generating strong passwords.

It is crucial to identify and assess the likelihood of these attacks during a risk assessment to develop effective risk management strategies.

Quantifying risk

We can help executive teams better understand the financial implications of cyber risks by quantifying them in terms of cost. This way, cyber risks can be weighed against the cost of investment. Below is an example of how we can determine the potential financial cost of a phishing attack including ransomware, should effective e-mail security *not* be put in place.

Cost = (Loss of revenue in productivity + loss of organisation) × Average days trying to resolve the ransomware attack

Risk management strategies involve taking measures to mitigate the risks identified during the risk assessment. There are four common risk management strategies, namely:

1 **Risk avoidance**: Avoiding the activities or processes that pose a significant risk to the organisation's assets.
2 **Risk reduction**: Taking measures to reduce the likelihood or impact of a cybersecurity incident occurring.
3 **Risk transfer**: Transferring the risk to a third party, such as an insurance company.
4 **Risk acceptance**: Accepting the risk and its potential consequences.

The risk management strategy adopted by an organisation should be based on their risk appetite and the resources available.

To conduct a successful risk assessment, organisations should follow some simple steps:

1 **Define the scope of the assessment**: The scope should be clearly defined to ensure that all critical assets are identified and assessed.
2 **Involve all stakeholders**: All stakeholders, including IT, legal, and organisation units, should be involved in the risk assessment process.

3 **Use a risk assessment framework**: A risk assessment framework provides a structured approach to risk assessment and ensures that all critical aspects are covered.

4 **Update the risk assessment regularly**: Cybersecurity threats and risks are continually evolving. Hence, it is essential to update the risk assessment regularly to ensure that the organisation is adequately protected.

5 **Document the risk assessment**: The risk assessment should be properly documented to ensure that the information is readily available for future reference.

Several tools and technologies are available to assist organisations in conducting risk assessments. Vulnerability scanners can identify vulnerabilities in an organisation's systems and networks. Penetration testing tools simulate cyber-attacks to identify vulnerabilities in an organisation's systems and networks. Security information and event management solutions collect and analyse security-related data from various sources to identify potential security incidents. Risk assessment software provides a structured approach to risk assessment that can make it easier to identify and assess risks.

Conducting a risk assessment for cybersecurity can be challenging, as organisations face several hurdles. One significant and common challenge is a lack of expertise and resources. Conducting a risk assessment requires a specialised skill set and can be a time-consuming process that requires significant investment. Many organisations may not have this expertise in-house and may find it too costly to regularly consult an external party. Another challenge is the constantly evolving cybersecurity landscape, which pushes organisations to keep up to date with the latest trends and technologies to ensure their risk assessment stays relevant. CISOs and CROs must therefore overcome many barriers and win support among senior leadership to embed effective risk assessment. CROs must encourage investment in risk management and explain the benefits, such as the additional insight gained at a strategic level into their technological, organisational, and environmental context [4].

If organisations do not allocate sufficient budget to their cybersecurity programme, cyber risks can quickly grow beyond the understanding of the executive board. There are typically many security wants and needs, and the challenge lays in finding that sweet spot where the limited security budget is applied such that any residual risk aligns with the organisation's risk appetite. When budget and needs are misaligned, there is a *cyber-reality gap*.

The negative relationship between the level of cyber risks and cyber budget is well-established. As a general principle, a more substantial budget enables more risk mitigation, and less budget leads to more cyber risk. Security costs money and excellent security is prohibitive both in terms of financial resources and usability. As a result, trade-offs are the norm. This involves identifying and analysing inherent risk, determining possible risk mitigations with the available resources and being left with a residual risk. Ideally, the residual risk will be within the organisation's risk appetite. However, it is not uncommon to find situations where residual risk exceeds risk appetite. Indeed, in reality, available budgets are typically not commensurate with an organisation's cyber risk exposure. The looming problem then is when this cyber-reality gap exceeds risk appetite and risk tolerance, where risk appetite is the target level of loss exposure and risk tolerance the deviation from the target which could be tolerated (but usually in excess of risk appetite).

Organisations may be accustomed to accepting rewarded risk and the inherent trade-offs between risk and reward. The key then is to get executives to understand that there may be a misalignment of risk profile and approved funding. The cyber-reality gap is a useful tool to communicate residual risk and frame the conversation about the realities of risk appetite and residual risk. We believe the classical reasons for this gap are:

- **Complexity**: Large organisations are incredibly complex, with hundreds of individual technology systems, cloud services, suppliers, and interfaces (e.g. APIs). Some organisations need to radically simplify their IT infrastructure to have anything approaching an affordable cyber posture. The problem here is typically that resource allocation to such bigger, more long-term projects is difficult, given more urgent, short-term matters.
- **Legacy debt:** Organisations often have lots of legacy technology debt and dated supplier arrangements, which lack modern controls and can be expensive to remediate.
- **Known vulnerabilities**: It is common to see known vulnerability lists (e.g. missing patches) in the tens of thousands. Most organisations are improving here, but it is an uphill struggle for technology teams to fully resource vulnerability management and to translate raw vulnerability severity ratings into contextual risk.
- **Lack of asset understanding**: Few organisations have really good asset understanding, which means that discovery is needed, which will in turn reveal further risks and budget challenges in the future.
- **Silent risk acceptance**: In major cyber incidents, a root cause can often be traced back to vulnerabilities on core systems that were already identified and well known by the technology teams for many years, but parked due to a lack of resources or pushback from system owners. However, it is also common in these situations that no "risk acceptance" decision was formalised.
- **Risk appetite**: Many risk appetite statements say the board has zero or "very low" appetite for cyber risk. The truth is that low risk appetite is expensive.
- **Dividends**: The need to sustain or grow dividends is taking precedence over remediating cyber risk (refer to that nasty legacy debt mentioned above).
- **Insecure habits±**: Most cyber incidents have a human factor, and change management is expensive and difficult to achieve, since people have often built up habitual behaviours over time.
- **Suppliers**: A growing portion of the risk is in the supply chain, which is expensive to detect and change, especially if the contract does not mention cyber as a performance outcome.

Boards need to reflect on these dynamics in their own organisations. Can the organisation "tolerate" its own complexity or does it need to simplify first? Is cyber risk being "quietly" accepted without formalised decision-making?

Once you have identified and assessed your cyber risks, you need to develop a comprehensive cybersecurity plan. This plan should outline the organisation's cybersecurity goals, objectives, and strategies for managing cyber risks. Your cybersecurity plan should address all aspects of cybersecurity, including network security, data security, and employee training. It should also include incident response procedures and guidelines for regularly reviewing and updating your cybersecurity measures.

Cybersecurity risk management frameworks

To help structure risk assessment processes, CISOs must choose an appropriate cybersecurity risk management framework. These frameworks are widely used by organisations today and provide a more structured approach to identifying and mitigating cybersecurity risks. Here are some of the most common ones:

- **NIST Cybersecurity Framework**: The NIST Cybersecurity Framework was created by the National Institute of Standards and Technology (NIST) in response to a 2013 executive order from President Obama. The framework provides a set of guidelines for organisations to follow to manage their cybersecurity risks. The framework consists of five core functions: identify, protect, detect, respond, and recover.
- **ISO 27001:2022**: The ISO 27001:2022 standard is a set of guidelines for organisations to follow to establish, implement, maintain, and continually improve their information security management system. The standard provides a comprehensive approach to managing information security risks, and it is widely recognised as the international standard for information security management.
- **CIS Critical Security Controls**: The CIS Critical Security Controls are a set of guidelines for organisations to follow to improve their cybersecurity posture. The controls were developed by the Centre for Internet Security (CIS) and are based on a set of best practices for cybersecurity. The controls are organised into 18 categories and are designed to address the most common cybersecurity risks.
- **HIPAA Security Rule**: The HIPAA Security Rule is a set of guidelines for organisations in the healthcare industry to follow to protect the privacy and security of patient information. The rule requires organisations to implement administrative, physical, and technical safeguards to protect patient information from unauthorised access, use, and disclosure.
- **PCI DSS**: The Payment Card Industry Data Security Standard (PCI DSS) is a set of guidelines for organisations that process credit card payments. The standard provides a comprehensive approach to managing the security of cardholder data. It is widely recognised as the industry standard for payment card security.

Each of these frameworks has its own strengths and weaknesses. The NIST Cybersecurity Framework is a comprehensive framework that covers all aspects of cybersecurity risk management. However, it can be time-consuming to implement. Similarly, the ISO 27001:2022 standard is widely recognised as the international standard for information security management, but can also be complex and resource-intensive to implement. The CIS Critical Security Controls are designed to address the most common cybersecurity risks, but they may not be comprehensive enough for all organisations.

When choosing a cybersecurity risk management framework for your organisation, it is important to consider your specific needs and requirements. Frameworks such as the HIPAA Security Rule and the PCI DSS are specifically designed for certain industries. Other frameworks, such as the NIST Cybersecurity Framework and the ISO 27001:2022 standard, may be more appropriate for larger organisations. Certain frameworks may be more expensive to implement than others, and some require more time and resources to implement than others.

Once you have chosen a cybersecurity risk management framework, the next step is to implement it. Establish a cybersecurity team responsible for implementing and maintaining your cybersecurity risk management framework. Conduct a risk assessment by identifying the risks to your organisation and prioritise them based on their potential impact and likelihood. Develop policies and procedures to address the risks identified in your risk assessment. Implement controls to mitigate the risks identified in your risk assessment. Continuously monitor and evaluate your cybersecurity risk management framework to ensure it remains effective and relevant.

In doing so, beware of common cybersecurity risk management mistakes and how to avoid them. Compliance is important, but it should not be the only goal of your cybersecurity risk management framework. Failing to continuously update your framework would be a mistake, as cybersecurity risks are always evolving. Finally, ensure the human element is addressed adequately. For example, King and colleagues (2018) argue that CISOs need to consider using a human factors risk framework which identifies key characteristics of an attacker, user, or defender, all of whom may be adding to or mitigating cyber risks [5]. Similarly, Hakimi and colleagues (2024) contend that embracing a human-centric paradigm is an imperative for organisations striving to fortify their defences against dynamic and sophisticated cyber threats. CISOs must consider the human element in their cybersecurity strategies. Integrating technology with a profound understanding of human factors is the cornerstone for shaping a resilient and adaptive cybersecurity future [6].

Managing the executive team

Ultimately, the most important task for the CISO is to align cybersecurity with organisational goals. This requires CISOs to speak the language of the wider organisation when they seek support from their organisation's executive team. To do so, CISOs must read and absorb the organisation's long-term plans. They need to frame cybersecurity initiatives in terms of organisational benefits, such as risk reduction, regulatory compliance, and brand protection. That is, CISOs must demonstrate value and highlight how cybersecurity measures can enhance organisational operations, protect assets, and drive competitive advantage. Here, we provide a list of practical advice on how CISOs can best manage their executive team that we learned to implement along the way.

CISOs need to build relationships and trust from the very start. They need to involve executive board members in cybersecurity discussions and decision-making processes early on. During such meetings, CISOs must listen and understand the board's priorities, concerns and expectations, and tailor cybersecurity initiatives to align with their perspectives. Active listening and identifying areas where they can easily build trust and consistently meet expectations will help win over sceptics.

To keep the executive board in the loop about the state of the organisation's cybersecurity, CISOs need to communicate regularly, concisely, and effectively with them on metrics, trends, and progress on key initiatives. Such updates need to avoid jargon and technical details, but instead use clear, non-technical language to explain cybersecurity concepts and their implications. For example, these updates need to report on the organisation's compliance status and address any gaps to ensure the organisation's cybersecurity measures meet regulatory and compliance requirements.

When pitching ideas for cybersecurity improvements that require new investments, frame them in terms of potential return on investment, risk assessments, and cost-benefit analyses to quantify the potential impact of such investments. Sharing examples of successful cybersecurity initiatives and their positive impact on organisations will help. The ideas need to align with a clear, long-term cybersecurity roadmap that outlines goals, milestones, and key initiatives. To build momentum, CISOs need to identify and implement short-term projects that can demonstrate quick wins. They need to be ready to negotiate improvements, as compromise will be needed in some areas to achieve consensus and win support for the cybersecurity roadmap.

To foster a common understanding of cyber risks, CISOs need to educate and raise awareness. Providing tailored cybersecurity training and awareness programmes, table-top exercises and scenario planning sessions for executive board members can help them understand the importance of cybersecurity, potential cyber threats, and the organisation's response capabilities. At the same time, CISOs need to ensure the organisation has a cohesive approach to cybersecurity. This requires collaboration with other departments, such as IT, legal, and finance, to address any cybersecurity challenges and develop comprehensive solutions.

Ultimately, CISOs need to demonstrate a commitment to cybersecurity at the highest levels of the organisation. They must foster accountability by promoting a culture where everyone, from the board to frontline employees, is responsible for cybersecurity. They need to nurture relationships by helping executives to meet their own objectives, without abandoning their own.

By employing these strategies, CISOs can effectively drive cybersecurity improvements, while maintaining strong relationships with the executive board. This collaborative approach can help ensure that cybersecurity is seen as a strategic enabler, instead of a cost centre. As a case in point, we will briefly discuss the 2015 Anthem breach.

Risk management is a collective effort

One of the most significant cybersecurity breaches caused by poor risk management was the Anthem Inc. data breach in 2015. Anthem, one of the largest health insurers in the United States, suffered a data breach that exposed the personal information of over 78 million individuals, including their names, birthdates, social security numbers, addresses, and employment information. It is one of the largest cybersecurity breaches to date that had a significant impact on the affected individuals, the company, and the entire healthcare industry.

The exposed personal information of millions of individuals put them at risk of identity theft and fraud, and resulted in a major financial blow to the company. Reports estimate that Anthem lost $115 million to remediation costs and faced a class-action lawsuit that resulted in a settlement of over $100 million. They had to pay for credit monitoring services for the affected individuals and invest in additional cybersecurity measures to prevent future breaches. The total cost of the breach is estimated to be more than $300 million. But the financial impact was just the tip of the iceberg. The breach had a lasting effect on the company's reputation, and damaged the trust consumers had in the company. The loss of trust could lead to a loss of organisation and has broader implications for the healthcare industry as a whole. It highlighted the need for stronger cybersecurity measures and showed that cyber threats are not limited to financial institutions and that any organisation that handles sensitive data is at risk.

The breach was caused by poor risk management practices, including a failure to encrypt sensitive data and inadequate security controls. The attackers were able to access Anthem's database using stolen credentials from a third-party vendor and install malware that allowed them to exfiltrate data. Anthem had failed to adequately assess the risks associated with its vendors, and it did not have proper controls in place to monitor and detect unauthorised access to its network. Anthem also did not encrypt the personal information of the affected individuals, making it easy for the attackers to steal the data. Encryption is a basic cybersecurity measure that all companies should implement to protect sensitive data, yet Anthem failed to do so.

The Anthem data breach provides several lessons for organisations to learn from. First, companies need to take a proactive approach to risk management. They must identify potential risks and implement measures to prevent them from occurring. Companies must also assess the risks associated with third-party vendors and ensure that they have proper controls in place to monitor and detect unauthorised access. Second, companies must implement basic cybersecurity measures such as encryption to protect sensitive data. Encryption is a simple, yet effective way to protect data and all companies that handle sensitive data should implement it. Third, companies must have an incident response plan in place for data breaches. A response plan should include steps to contain the breach, notify affected individuals, cooperate with law enforcement, and where applicable, implement credit monitoring services to affected individuals and provide transparency about the breach. Finally, organisations must comply with regulatory requirements. Regulatory requirements are there to protect sensitive information and must be followed to avoid fines and legal action. Underlying all these (basic) cybersecurity measures is the ability of CISOs and other security leaders within an organisation to convince other parties of implementing said measures. Although it is not public knowledge what precisely went on internally at Anthem that allowed for such basic security flaws to persist, it would be shortsighted to only blame the CISO's (in)competencies. Other (executive) leaders who had not taken cybersecurity measures seriously enough to invest in had just as much responsibility in ensuring their business could run and withstand adversity.

Indeed, as discussed in *Chapter 9: Improving organisational cybersecurity*, leadership plays a crucial role in risk management. All too often, the CISO is left to face the wrath, when in reality the organisational culture and wider executive boards should take collective responsibility. Organisations whose employees participate in risky cybersecurity behaviours will likely suffer disastrous consequences either directly or indirectly from actions linked to such behaviours [7]. Leaders must, therefore, create a culture of risk management within the organisation and ensure that everyone understands the importance of managing risks. They must also allocate resources to implement cybersecurity measures and ensure that the organisation has adequate response plans in place. They must lead by example and prioritise cybersecurity, ensure that the organisation complies with all cybersecurity regulations and that employees are trained on cybersecurity best practices. Finally, leaders must be transparent about breaches and take collective responsibility for any failures in risk management. To encourage these practices, we recommend executive boards to tie cybersecurity risks to executive bonuses and salaries, and that regulators impose fines on executives instead of focusing on CISOs – who often do their best in the midst of huge uncertainty and risk, while facing opposition from a more senior level.

Overcoming stress and building resilience

We have mentioned throughout this book how the operational cybersecurity profession has a high turnover rate due to the high levels of stress and burnout (e.g. see *Chapter 5: Operational cybersecurity context*). The constantly changing adversarial threat landscape and ever-changing industry mandates can make the cybersecurity work environment feel like a war zone [8]. Especially CISOs often have to work long hours and their job does not end when the workday is over. CISOs must be available at all times to manage security incidents and respond to emergencies. It is no wonder we are seeing short tenures in senior roles for security executives. The lack of professionals with a social-behavioural background further adds to the poor understanding of risk and appreciation of the role of cybersecurity [9]. Indeed, the constant need for cognitive readiness takes a toll on security leaders' mental health.

A major challenge for CISOs, apart from the general cybersecurity context, is that they must strike a balance between securing the organisation's information assets and enabling the organisation to operate effectively. This requires effective resource management [10]. In doing so, a primary cause of frustration for CISOs and security leaders is the need to convince people of the importance of security and need for funding for (additional) resources, including budgets, staff, and technology. Many stakeholders outside the security field may not see security as a priority integral to their organisation. CISOs and security leaders therefore need soft skills and training to overcome organisational biases and become more adaptable. The combination of a psychological safe space, and the right communication and leadership training can reduce stress and burnout, and improve overall mental wellbeing.

Throughout our career, we have often seen a lack of soft skills in cybersecurity teams. This is not because cybersecurity professionals are unable to develop them, but because of an extreme emphasis on technical skills and getting certifications. Although technical expertise is key to working in cybersecurity, learning "soft" people skills is at least as important for security leaders to be successful. People in cybersecurity would benefit from training in social competences, starting with attribution reasoning – examining the reasons behind our actions. We need to learn about the social drivers of incidents and how different people handle them. Moreover, understanding the differences between the technical, strategic, and organisation sides of the industry, and being able to communicate effectively across them, is essential.

Another challenge is when stakeholders believe that if something cannot be measured, it has no value. This perspective can be limiting when it comes to training people in psychological abilities important to security and organisational culture, such as cognitive readiness and attribution reasoning. Learning does not always directly lead to behavioural change. Some people who only want hard evidence with measurable outcomes find this difficult to grasp or accept. But when it comes to people's psychological states, there is no thermometer we can stick into people's brains to compare one's cognitive readiness to that of others. It does not mean evaluating people's cognitive preparedness is impossible, but it may require a more indirect long-term approach, as opposed to quarterly key performance indicators related to tangible, material things. CISOs and professionals in the cybersecurity awareness branch specifically may therefore have a difficult time pitching for more resources for soft skills training.

The impact of these challenges on a CISO can be significant and even lead to mental health issues. Managing stress and maintaining mental health is thus absolutely critical. Some simple strategies can help:

- **Create a work-life balance by taking time off, delegating tasks, and setting boundaries**. It is essential to have hobbies and interests outside of work to maintain a healthy work-life balance.
- **Seek support from family, friends, and colleagues**. They should also consider seeking professional help if they are experiencing stress, burnout, or mental health issues. We have seen up close how people in our field sometimes need counseling or psychotherapy to fully recover from cyber-attacks.
- **Practicing mindfulness, meditation, or deep breathing exercises** can help reduce stress and improve mental health.
- **Take breaks regularly throughout the day** to recharge and avoid burnout. They need to be able to go for a walk, listen to music, or do something else that they enjoy.

- **Improve self-awareness and emotional intelligence**. Self-awareness helps CISOs understand their strengths and weaknesses, and how their actions impact others, to lead more effectively. Emotional intelligence helps CISOs manage their emotions and communicate effectively with stakeholders, including executives, technical and non-technical staff.
- **Be open to learn from setbacks** to become more resilient. CISOs should view setbacks as opportunities to learn and grow. They must understand why employees may not follow security policies and procedures and develop long-term strategies to address these issues. They must also understand the motivations and tactics of attackers to develop effective security strategies.

References

1 https://www.ponemon.org/research/ponemon-library/
2 T. Singh, *Cybersecurity, Psychology and People Hacking*. Cham: Springer International Publishing Imprint, Palgrave Macmillan, 2025.
3 A. A. Alahmari and R. A. Duncan, "Investigating potential barriers to cybersecurity risk management investment in SMEs," in *2021 13th International Conference on Electronics, Computers and Artificial Intelligence (ECAI)*, Pitesti, Romania, 2021, pp. 1–6, doi: 10.1109/ECAI52376.2021.9515166.
4 A. A. Alahmari and R. A. Duncan, "Towards cybersecurity risk management investment: A proposed encouragement factors framework for SMEs," in *2021 IEEE International Conference on Computing (ICOCO)*, Kuala Lumpur, Malaysia, 2021, pp. 115–121, doi: 10.1109/ICOCO53166.2021.9673554.
5 Z. M. King, D. S. Henshel, L. Flora, M. G. Cains, B. Hoffman and C. Sample, "Characterizing and measuring maliciousness for cybersecurity risk assessment," *Frontiers in Psychology*, vol. 9, no. 39, pp. 1–19, 2018, doi: 10.3389/fpsyg.2018.00039.
6 M. Hakimi, M. M. Quchi, and A. W. Fazil, "Human factors in cybersecurity: An in depth analysis of user centric studies," *Jurnal Ilmiah Multidisiplin Indonesia (JIM-ID)*, vol. 3, no. 01, pp. 20–33, 2024, doi: 10.58471/esaprom.v3i01.3832.
7 P. Ifinedo, "Effects of security knowledge, self-control, and countermeasures on cybersecurity behaviors," *Journal of Computer Information Systems*, vol. 63, no. 2, pp. 380–396, 2023, doi: 10.1080/08874417.2022.2065553.
8 T. Singh, A.C. Johnston, J. D'Arcy, and P.D. Harms, "Stress in the cybersecurity profession: A systematic review of related literature and opportunities for future research," *Organizational Cybersecurity Journal: Practice, Process and People*, vol. 3, no. 2, pp. 100–126, 2023.
9 C. Nobles, "Stress, burnout, and security fatigue in cybersecurity: A human factors problem," *HOLISTICA – Journal of Business and Public Administration*, vol. 13, no. 1, 2022, pp. 49–72, doi: 10.2478/hjbpa-2022-0003.
10 T. Singh, *Digital Resilience, Cybersecurity and Supply Chains*, 1st ed. Routledge, Abingdon, Oxon, UK, 2025, doi: 10.4324/9781003604969.

14   Concluding remarks

We live in a world where peace has become inextricably linked to cybersecurity. Highly motivated actors are conducting increasingly sophisticated cyber-attacks every minute. As a result, cybersecurity professionals are under unprecedented pressure and anyone could be targeted.

Most people instinctively know and agree with the importance of adequate cybersecurity measures. Awareness is not the main problem. The real issue is that cybersecurity has historically focused disproportionately on the technical aspects of securing information and communication systems. Although there is academic research into the human factors in cybersecurity, such findings are not yet widely incorporated into the field. The numerous security breaches highlighted throughout this book indeed exemplify that operating on a blind spot for people's psychology does not work. Given that we already rely heavily on digital communication and information systems, it is high time for cybersecurity to centre around the people it aims to protect.

In this book, we honed in on the psychological and situational factors that make the key personas in the cybersecurity field. We used crime science theories to understand under what circumstances hackers and other people behind cyber incidents arise. It takes a viable target and attack opportunity, as well as the psychological desire and ability to seize that opportunity for cyber threats to materialise. We described the lives of three notorious hackers and got a glimpse of real-world cybercriminals, along with how they operate common attack vectors. On the defence side, we got a taste of the pressurised cybersecurity context that explains the high turnover rate of security professionals at all levels.

Here, it was striking how both cybercriminals and cybersecurity professionals are facing similar psychological burdens from working in this domain. Perhaps, it is not within all of our nature to collectively choose a more peaceful way of living next to each other. We have seen what points both sides of the coin are trying to prove – being skilled, having valuable knowledge, being a revered smartass, and all the collateral effects this can have in terms of enforcing cognitive fallacies, biases, and perpetuating toxic behaviour. Some of the cybercriminals we interviewed even mentioned themselves how important it is to care for their mental health. In the same vein, we described practical tactics for cybersecurity professionals to cope with the pressures of the field. In particular, how cyber risk management should be a shared responsibility among the senior leadership of an organisation.

DOI: 10.4324/9781003610533-18

We also elaborated on blind spots in the cybersecurity profession, such as operational resilience, the need to stop the unhelpful shaming of people after cyber incidents, the underappreciated contributions and value of women and other underrepresented groups in tech, and making usability a key performance indicator for any user-facing security feature. We then described the latest research on how human-centred security measures can be improved already and how focusing on the systemic facilitators of secure behaviour in an organisation is a more effective strategy than seeking out groups of "risky individuals". Furthermore, we included the five situational crime prevention principles to encourage generating new ideas for human-centred security measures. We then dove into the world of fundamental neuropsychology to explain how anyone could fall for social engineering attacks and described various phenomenological properties of how each of us constructs a unique worldview.

Especially given the recent technological advances in artificial intelligence (AI) and increasingly individualistic culture, we need to incorporate this psychological understanding of what leads people to judge something to be true and whom to trust into the way we communicate about cyber risks. Even though many people now spend a great amount of time attending to their own screens, we should not neglect our deeply social nature. When we receive any unsolicited request or otherwise surprising digital message, we should always consult with someone else in the physical world, preferably in a different role from us, to look at it with a fresh pair of eyes. In this vein, an organisation with a strong social cohesion will always be a stronger defence force than a remote, loosely connected group of individuals. Lastly, we put ourselves in the shoes of a chief information security officer to understand what is required for adequate cyber risk management and how to manage the psychological impacts of this role. We thus provided a comprehensive view on the psychological aspects of cybersecurity – from the attackers and defenders, to victims and chief information security officers, and how to manage their associated psychological vulnerabilities.

It is worth emphasising the importance of context and situational awareness in this field. Understanding the contexts people find themselves in explains why some people become hackers, why people choose to work in cybersecurity, why people make mistakes, why people fall for social engineering attacks, why security policies may work for one job role but not another, and how misunderstandings arise.

Everything we do, including cybercrime, is the result of how our brains interpret our environment. If that environment facilitates cybercrime, we are sure to see more cybercrime. If that environment encourages secure behaviour, we can be certain organisations will be more resilient to cyber-attacks. Less tangible measures, such as organisational culture, nudges and implementing security-by-design are essential, precisely because they help bolster a secure environment. Accordingly, security measures should aim to both reduce the prevalence of cybercrime by curbing opportunities for carrying out cyber-attacks, as well as making targets better equipped at detecting such attacks.

Now, in an ideal world, we would have found ways to live with one another agreeably, regardless of our differences, and rid ourselves from incentives to create cyber-attacks in the first place. Or, on the other extreme, we become capable of predicting and capturing cyber threats before they can materialise – which would also reduce the incentive to conduct cyber-attacks. Whereas the former requires excellent soft skills to unwrap and align the cocktail of emotions that fuel our beliefs and desires, the latter relies on technological advances that are likely to happen anyway.

The psychological sciences have certainly pointed out many idiosyncrasies in human behaviour over the past two centuries, notably the myriad cognitive biases that affect us all. Slowly, we are even uncovering the mysteries around the hard problem of what consciousness is. It may in fact arise from our brainstem, instead of higher-order parts of our brains, that forms an affective dimension to the very things we see, hear, smell, taste, and touch – just like we can both hear *and* see a thunderstorm [1]. In other words, to be conscious is to feel what we perceive.

Feelings, from hunger and lust to despair and happiness, indeed are at the heart of everything we do. They underpin people's desires, and how they perceive their abilities and opportunities. Without them, we simply would not have any motivation or sense of direction. We attach them to the people we meet, the words they say, the thoughts we think, and the objects we cherish. But their intangible nature makes them a less obvious basis for cybersecurity strategy – even though teaching people emotional regulation and communication skills from a young age could possibly have a tremendous impact on reducing people's desire to commit offences. In fact, the cybersecurity profession as a whole could benefit from learning these skills to reduce turnover rates, and improve stress management and organisational culture as described throughout this book.

The historic trend that wealth grows with technological innovation, in contrast, is unlikely to falter, especially given the ongoing geopolitical tensions and ageing societies across the world. We are already living in symbiosis with technology, to the extent we go on "digital detox" retreats to take a break from our smartphones and other devices. This will be exacerbated over the next few decades, as we will witness an ever-increasing dependency on technologies in all parts of life – including healthcare, childrearing, education, the workplace, and the military.

Think of humanoid social robots to care for when we become elderly, expanding domestic and public Internet of Things (IoT) networks, as well as brain–computer interfaces and other technologies to augment our physical capabilities, with AI as the main catalyst. Furthermore, nations with offensive inclinations are investing more and more in defence and intelligence innovation, underscoring the looming threat of hybrid and cyberwarfare. This suggests an overt weaponisation of technological innovation, the same way financial markets, for instance, have become weaponised. These developments will pose new risks both in terms of inherently new attack vectors, as well as new targets of cyber-attacks with potentially more invasive damage.

What this means for cybersecurity is two things. First, that it needs to be recognised as an absolutely indispensable part of progress, for organisations and societies at large. Technology misuse cases should be addressed earlier on than is the case now. But because risk and security can be understood as synonymous with stifling innovation, it is an underused practice in especially young tech companies. Cybersecurity professionals or even cybersecurity champions can help improve this.

The unstoppable infusion of technologies in our lives also means that the only constant factor cybersecurity can build on amidst all the political, economic, social, and technological changes, is, in fact, people. Hence, we talked extensively about the importance of cyber risk management processes, implementing systematic reviews, providing regular cybersecurity training and education programmes, deploying usable authentication methods, deliberating and choosing an acceptable risk level, incident response and business continuity plans, and so on. These measures will remain relevant with every technological advance, as they rely on (collaboration between) people. Improvements in the quality of their implementation and effectiveness then can only be achieved by better understanding and managing people's behaviour. In short, the need for organisations to address the human factor in cybersecurity is only going to intensify, and it is our shared responsibility to protect ourselves better.

That said, there are some clear cross-disciplinary developments that try to incorporate psychological knowledge into cybersecurity software. For example, in the context of the Snowden effect and organisations' psychological security posture, we described how machine learning algorithms could be used to create individual risk profiles of potential attackers and employees. Although automated individual profiling is possible, we need to ask what ethical factors need to be considered before implementing such intrusive cybersecurity measures. Here, cyberpsychologists and legislators have important roles to play in researching and raising awareness on the implications of such practices, as they need to be weighed against privacy values, for instance, as found in General Data Protection Regulation's principles of purpose limitation and data minimisation.

Other open questions that deserve further attention are what makes cybersecurity solutions usable and adopted by human users, what reasonable expectations we can have for people's security behaviour (e.g. to establish benchmarks for to be expected phishing victimisation rates), what (other) psychological principles to follow to design more effective cybersecurity training programmes, and what strategies, tools, or technologies can be used to prevent cognitive biases from impacting cybersecurity practices and decisions.

We are seeing a switch to more tailored cybersecurity training and use of questionnaires to better understand employees, but this is just the beginning. Psychologists now have the excellent opportunity of improving our understanding of the root causes of poor security behaviour and the psychology of cyber-attackers, as well as testing the effectiveness of alternative methods such as reflexive practice to prevent human error. Indeed, the future of cybersecurity is exciting, with psychology playing a growing role in shaping it.

Meanwhile, we can expect hackers to leverage emerging technologies to continue wreaking havoc. They, too, will improve their understanding of human psychology to better manipulate their targets, using highly realistic impersonation tactics with AI. Nefarious actors have already mined social media platforms for data to train behavioural analytics models to direct disinformation campaigns. With AI, such highly targeted, mass manipulation tactics can be automated and scaled up even further – for instance, for extortion and blackmailing, as well as recruiting employees to encourage insider threat. They could also use compromised virtual assistants to gather information or execute malicious commands without the user's knowledge. Furthermore, we can expect hackers to exploit devices connected to IoT systems, including robots, to launch attacks, and exploit the isolation of remote workers to gain access to corporate networks. It is thus crucial for individuals and organisations to stay vigilant, invest in continuous education, and adopt human-centred security measures to protect against increasingly sophisticated cyber-attacks.

On the defence side, we can expect a similar increase in use of AI systems, as well as a need for securing larger networks of different types of autonomous, invasive, and even symbiotic devices. Machine learning will play a crucial role in automating threat detection and response, analysing vast amounts of data to identify anomalous patterns. Albeit quantum computing is not a mature technology yet, research into quantum-safe cryptography is needed to protect current computing systems from quantum attacks. The use of cloud services will continue to grow, necessitating stronger security measures to protect data stored and processed in the cloud. Cloud providers will accordingly implement more robust security features. Authentication methods will also evolve, as wearable technologies for human augmentation (e.g. brain-computer interfaces) and virtual or augmented reality become more commonplace. Organisations will increasingly be pressured to adopt a zero-trust model, as it will likely become the standard for securing complex, distributed networks, especially in cloud and hybrid environments. We might even see more widespread use of blockchain technology to create more secure, decentralised networks that are less vulnerable to certain types of attacks.

In addition, we need better methods to detect deepfake content to prevent fraud and impersonation, and may consider obliging cybersecurity education from the age people start using digital technologies. Governments will continue introducing new regulations and standards to address new cyber threats and ensure compliance with best practices. International cooperation will be crucial in combatting cyber-crime and protecting critical infrastructure. Cybersecurity will shift from merely defending against attacks, to building resilience and capacity for recovery. Accordingly, organisations will (have to) invest in robust incident response plans and recovery strategies to minimise the impact of cyber-attacks. These trends highlight the dynamic nature of cybersecurity and that continuous adaptation and innovation are key to stay ahead of threats. By embracing these changes, organisations can better protect their assets and ensure a secure digital future.

We hope this book helped you see that cybersecurity is not just about technology, but also very much about human behaviour. Cyber-attacks are successful, because they exploit vulnerabilities in human behaviour. So, as human behaviour drives the need for cybersecurity, our future world depends on the beliefs, desires, and cognitive fallacies of all stakeholders involved, especially of those in power who can move the needle on the geopolitical compass. In the end, it only takes someone smart to know how to assemble a (cyber) bomb, but someone wise to know whether to do so...

Reference

1   M. Solms. *The Hidden Spring: A Journey to the Source of Consciousness*. New York: W.W. Norton & Company, 2021.

Glossary

Attribution error A cognitive bias that occurs when people overemphasise a person's character or personality traits, and underemphasise the situation or environment that led to their actions. This error can affect how people judge others and can lead to arguments, misinterpretations, and other unhelpful outcomes.

Cognitive bias A systematic thought process caused by the tendency of the human brain to simplify information processing through a filter of personal experience and preferences. This filtering process is a coping mechanism that enables the brain to prioritise and process large amounts of information quickly.

Cognitive dissonance Cognitive dissonance is a feeling of mental discomfort that occurs when a person's beliefs, attitudes, and/or actions are inconsistent. It can also be described as a state of mental tension.

Cognitive fluency Cognitive fluency, or processing fluency, is how easily and quickly the brain can process and understand information.

Data breach An incident where sensitive, confidential, or protected information is accessed, stolen, or distributed without authorisation. This information can include personal information, financial information, or intellectual property. Data breaches can occur through a variety of methods, including hacking, phishing, malware, physical theft, and human error.

Distributed Denial of Service (DDoS) A type of cyber-attack where an offender floods a target website or network with traffic, causing it to crash or become unavailable.

Hackathon Combination of marathon and hacking. An event where people gather to try to hack into a system for a set amount of time.

Hacking The process of exploiting vulnerabilities in a system to gain unauthorised access to data or information, that is, without permission. Someone who performs hacking activities is named a hacker.

Hacktivism Derived from combining the words "hack" and "activism", hacktivism is the act of hacking, or breaking into a computer system, for politically or socially motivated purposes. Someone who performs an act of hacktivism is named a hacktivist.

Illusory truth effect   The tendency to believe something is true after repeated exposure. It can occur even when people know the information is false.

Malware attack   Installing malicious software on a computer system, which can lead to data theft or system damage.

Nudge programme   A nudge programme is a strategy designed to subtly influence people's behaviour by making certain choices more appealing or accessible through small changes in the way options are presented, often based on behavioural economics principles. That is, "nudging" people towards a desired outcome without forcing them to do so, like a gentle prompt to make a specific decision.

Open-source intelligence (OSINT)   The process of collecting and analysing publicly available data to examine cyber threats and gather intelligence.

Penetration testing   Penetration testing, also known as pen testing, is a simulated attack on a computer system to assess its security. It is a security exercise that helps identify vulnerabilities that attackers could exploit.

Post-mortem analysis   Process to analyse and discuss a recent cyber incident, aimed at resolving any inadequate or ineffective cybersecurity measure for the future.

Prediction error   A prediction error is the difference between what is expected (i.e., what the brain predicts will happen) and what was observed (i.e., what actually happened). Prediction errors are a key part of learning and are evident in brain activity.

Ransomware attack   Attack in which an adversary encrypts an organisation's data and demands a ransom in exchange for the decryption key.

Red teaming   Red teaming is a cybersecurity process that involves simulating a cyber-attack to identify and fix vulnerabilities in an organisation's systems.

Security patching   The process of updating software to fix security vulnerabilities. When a system vulnerability is not addressed, we call it an "unpatched" security issue.

Self-projection   The (involuntary) act of attributing one's own feelings, beliefs, and/or values to others. In other words, interpreting and judging other people by projecting our own behaviour onto them.

Static analysis tools   Programming tools that automatically analyse and detect security vulnerabilities in programming code.

Theory of mind   The ability to understand what other people may be thinking and feeling by imagining we were in their situation.

Zero-day attacks   A cyber-attack that exploits a previously unknown vulnerability in hardware, firmware, or software. A zero-day attack is a type of cyber-attack that takes advantage of a security gap before it can be patched. It happens where an attacker finds a software vulnerability before it is known to the software or antivirus vendor, creates an exploit, and uses it to attack.

Zero-trust approach   An architectural approach where inherent trust in a network is removed, the network is assumed to be hostile and each request is verified based on an access policy. It is based on the idea that no one should be able to access an organisation's IT systems, unless it is absolutely necessary.

Index

Note: **Bold** page numbers refer to tables and *italic* page numbers refer to figures.